# Marlene

## ALSO BY CHARLOTTE CHANDLER

*I Know Where I'm Going: Katharine Hepburn, A Personal Biography*

*She Always Knew How: Mae West, A Personal Biography*

*Not the Girl Next Door: Joan Crawford, A Personal Biography*

*Ingrid: Ingrid Bergman, A Personal Biography*

*The Girl Who Walked Home Alone: Bette Davis, A Personal Biography*

*It's Only a Movie: Alfred Hitchcock, A Personal Biography*

*Nobody's Perfect: Billy Wilder, A Personal Biography*

*I, Fellini*

*The Ultimate Seduction*

*Hello, I Must Be Going: Groucho and His Friends*

# *Marlene*

**MARLENE DIETRICH, A PERSONAL BIOGRAPHY**

## Charlotte Chandler

**APPLAUSE**
**THEATRE & CINEMA BOOKS**
An Imprint of Hal Leonard Corporation

Applause Theatre & Cinema Books
An Imprint of Hal Leonard Corporation
7777 West Bluemound Road
Milwaukee, WI 53213

Trade Book Division Editorial Offices
33 Plymouth St., Montclair, NJ 07042

Published by Applause Theatre & Cinema Books in 2012

Originally published in hardcover in 2011 by Simon & Schuster, Inc.

Printed in the United States of America

Book design by Joy O'Meara

The Library of Congress has cataloged the Simon & Schuster edition as follows:
Chandler, Charlotte.
    Marlene: Marlene Dietrich, a personal biography / Charlotte Chandler.—1st Simon
& Schuster hardcover ed.
        p.        cm.
    Includes index.
    1. Dietrich, Marlene.   2. Entertainers—Germany—Biography.   3. Motion
picture actors and actresses—Germany—Biography.   I. Title.
    PN2658.D5C53 2011
    791.4302'8092—dc22
    [B]                2010036893

ISBN 978-1-55783-838-4

www.applausebooks.com

# *Acknowledgments*

## With Special Appreciation

Bob Bender, Burt Bacharach, Douglas Fairbanks, Jr., Leatrice Gilbert Fountain, Mary Meerson, Paul Morrissey, David Rosenthal, and Joshua Sinclair.

## With Appreciation

Michael Accordino, Marcella Berger, Charles William Bush, Jack Cardiff, Fred Chase, René Clair, Wilkie Cooper, Tony Curtis, Gypsy da Silva, Bette Davis, Mitch Douglas, Jean-Louis Dumas, James Ehrhard, Mark Ekman, Vera Fairbanks, Marie Florio, Joe Franklin, Bob Gazzale, Cary Grant, Dolly Haas, Alfred Hitchcock, Patricia Hitchcock, Peter Johnson, Daniel Kaplan, Edward Kennedy, Alexander Kordonsky, Karen Kramer, Ted Landry, Fritz Lang, Robert Lantz, Johanna Li, Joshua Logan, Jamie MacMurray, Sue Main, Tim Malachosky, Ray Milland, Sheridan Morley, Dieter Mueller, Jeremiah Newton, Arthur Novell, Dale Olson, Joy O'Meara, Marvin Paige, Tom Pierson, Otto Preminger, Felipe Propper, Leni Riefenstahl, Robert Rosen, Isabella Rossellini, Roberto Rossellini, Maximilian Schell, John Springer, June Springer, Jeff Stafford, James Stewart, Richard Todd, Brian Ulicky, Herman G. Weinberg, Mae West, Audrey Wilder, Billy Wilder, Will Willoughby, Jelko Yuresha, and Fred Zinnemann.

The American Film Institute, the British Film Institute, the Film Society of Lincoln Center, the Cinémathèque Française, the Mitch Douglas Archives, the Hermès Museum, the Tim Malachosky Archives, the Paley Center for Media, the Potsdam Film Museum, the New York Public Library for the Performing Arts, and the UCLA Department of Theater, Film, and Television.

**TO MARLENE**

# Contents

# Marlene

# Prologue

"Marlene Dietrich was on her farewell tour and she was going to be at the Ahmanson Theatre in Los Angeles for two weeks, in 1968," publicist Dale Olson told me. "I received a call from the Ahmanson, and they were worried. They had heard that she would be a terror, that she would be unreasonably demanding, and they wouldn't be able to work with her. They said they wanted to hire me for the two weeks because they knew I had a good relationship with her, and they wanted me to look after her. I think what they really meant was they wanted me to look after *them*.

"I said yes.

"When she arrived, I told her what they had said, that they were afraid of her.

"She laughed. 'They are right,' she said. 'They are right to be afraid of me.' She was laughing as she spoke.

"She said there was one thing she wanted. She had to have an extremely large refrigerator for her dressing room. I said they had one which was large enough for champagne bottles, smoked salmon, and caviar, which doesn't take up much room, the usual for the dressing room of a star.

"She said, 'No. That isn't what I want. I want the largest refrigerator.'

"So I went back with her request. They didn't understand and weren't pleased. They wanted to know why she wanted such a large refrigerator. I certainly didn't know. I wondered if she was going to cook her famous goulash for everyone. She loved to cook for people, and her goulash was delicious, but I didn't think that was likely. Anyway, she got her huge refrigerator.

"On opening night, I was in the dressing room. When she went out, I couldn't resist. I was curious about what she had in the refrigerator. I opened the door and looked in.

"She had removed the shelves. It was completely empty.

"She was wonderfully received. After her opening night performance, there was tremendous applause, a standing ovation, and people in the aisles with bouquets of flowers, and single flowers, rushing up to throw their flowers on the stage.

"After absolutely everyone had left the theater, she went out on the stage, all by herself. She had changed from stiletto-heeled shoes to perfectly flat ballerina-type slippers. She began picking up the bouquets. She brought them back to her dressing room. She didn't stop until she had picked up the last single rose and carried it back to her dressing room. Then, she began carefully arranging them in the refrigerator.

"We hadn't seen the last of those flowers. The next night, the ushers had them ready for the end of her performance. The flowers were all thrown on the stage. The next night the same. And so on.

"At the end of the two weeks, on the night of the last performance, there they were. The flowers were performing for the last time. They were pretty wilted, but the audience didn't know. From where they were sitting, the flowers looked fine.

"She was quite a showman."

# I. *Berlin*

don't mind meeting you because you didn't know me before, when I was young and very beautiful." These were Marlene Dietrich's first words to me when I saw her in Paris in 1977.

She had agreed to speak with me for that very reason, because I would not be comparing her to her younger self, and even more important, because my introduction was from Mary Meerson of the Cinémathèque Française in Paris.

I knew Mme Meerson, the widow of Lazare Meerson, the French opera scenic designer and artist, in her later life at the Cinémathèque Française. She worked there with its legendary founder, Henri Langlois, to preserve as many of the significant films of our time as possible. He and Mme Meerson risked their lives many times during World War II to save films condemned by the Nazis.

It meant more to Marlene that Mary had called her than if Langlois had called. She had the greatest respect for him, but she knew that Mary totally understood how she, Marlene, felt. Mme Meerson had chosen a life without the constant battle of preserving her beauty against the passage of time.

"Mary was a truly great Russian beauty," Marlene explained to me when we met. "She was a model for famous artists. But since she has become so fat, she doesn't want anyone who knew her when she was so slim and beautiful to see her now. Mostly, she speaks with people on the phone, and sometimes she sees very young people who didn't know her before.

"Can you believe that when she was a girl, she was as thin, thinner, than I am? But she gave up. It was too hard for her to be thin like that, so if she couldn't be beautiful, she didn't care about being somewhere in between. She decided she preferred to eat and leave that other life behind her. After a certain point, there was no going back, even if she had wanted to.

"She only wears those huge caftans, and they fit her like a sheath dress, so you don't know where the dress ends and she begins. But no matter how fat she gets, you can always see how beautiful she was. It was no ordinary beauty. Even now, it shines through. Luminous.

"So, she understands how I feel. It can be a curse being beautiful, after a certain point, as it slips away, as age steals it.

"From the first I can remember when I was a little child, people said to my mother, 'What a beautiful child you have,' meaning me. I didn't think much of it then, and just accepted it as my due. It was part of our daily routine.

"As I grew older, it was very convenient and pleasurable, and fun. It provided wonderful opportunities, but it was not the driving force of my life.

"Then Jo [Josef von Sternberg] came along. After Mr. von Sternberg took charge of my looks, sometimes I thought they belonged more to him than to me. The emphasis on the way I looked became a burden to bear, almost too great to enjoy."

BEFORE GOING TO VISIT Marlene Dietrich, I asked Mme Meerson if Miss Dietrich ate chocolate. I wanted to bring her a box, only I wasn't certain if anyone as slim as she ever indulged in chocolates. The response was that Marlene might eat the entire box at once.

"We used to eat chocolates together. I had two and she had twenty. I love chocolate, too, but every chocolate I ever ate is visible as a part of me, now and forever.

"I'm six of her now, as you can see, but when I was young and an artist's model, I was as slim as she. Can you imagine that? I almost can't believe it myself.

"Ask her about her secret of eating so much, whatever she wants, and staying so slim. If you find that out, you *will* have a best-seller."

Along with the Swiss chocolates, I brought some French marmalade. It was in a set of jars from Fouquet, the shop around the corner from her Avenue Montaigne Paris apartment.

"That's very good," Marlene said. "Marmalade, not jam, with pieces of the whole fruit.

"There are many things about me that aren't quite as good as they were, but one thing that is as good as it ever was is my taste buds.

"There are some wonderful restaurants in my neighborhood which send over delicious food. I've eaten in great restaurants all over the world. Now, I don't need so much food as when I was very active. I cook on my hot plate. I can always make do with a nice liverwurst sandwich.

"I'm a wonderful cook. I have a great butcher shop, and the Plaza Athénée is just across from my apartment. If I don't want to cook, they give me room service.

"Let me know if you get hungry. I have delicious things around here, and I can always call one of the neighborhood restaurants, and they will deliver faster than you can believe.

"Now I prefer to eat at home. I can make do with a nice bacon, lettuce, and tomato sandwich on toast from the Plaza Athénée. In fact, it's one of my favorite luxuries."

She asked me if I wished to smoke. I said that I didn't smoke.

"Did you give it up?"

"No, fortunately, I didn't have to, because I never began."

"Well, you missed something wonderful. It was so pleasurable. I gave it up, but I'm not altogether happy that I did. You might ask why I did it.

"Well, there was all that talk about how it wasn't healthy, and my friend Noel Coward told me he was giving it up, and he said to me, 'I know *you* won't be able to give it up.'

"Well, that was all he needed to say to me. A red flag before a bull. He had dared me.

"I accepted the dare, and I gave up smoking. Whenever I saw Noel, he would say, 'Are you not smoking?'

"'No, I don't smoke anymore,' I would say. 'I've given it up *permanently.*' And so I had.

"Noel was always astounded that I had done it so easily. Well, it wasn't easy at all. It was unceasing pure torture. The desire took years to wear off totally, that longing. I'm not certain that it ever went away completely. Before I gave up smoking, I scarcely drank. Afterwards, well, I had to replace the lost delight with something, so I increased my alcohol intake.

"Noel believed me because that was what I conveyed to him. Little did he know what I was going through at the very moment when, in an offhand way, I assured him it had not been a problem. I never considered going back to smoking, because it had been so difficult giving it up that I knew if I started, I would never be able to stop again.

"People probably say to you, you're lucky you never started. Well, I can't say that, because I know what you've missed."

There was a small partially open carton on the floor in the living room. "That's my treasure," she said. "I'll show you."

She reached in and took out a jar of cold cream. "This is my beauty secret. I get it from London, from Boots, the pharmacy drugstore chain. It's not one of those expensive cleansing creams, unless you count the shipping cost."

She encouraged me to take the jar. I told her I would be stopping in London, so I didn't want to take hers.

MARLENE SHOWED ME A lovely picture in an art nouveau silver frame of herself as a golden-haired little girl with long curls. In the old photograph were Josephine and Otto Dietrich, her parents. Marlene was about three years old in the picture, which dated from 1904.

"These are my parents. I always say 'are,' not 'were,' because though they are long gone, my mother *some* years ago, and my father many, *many* years ago, they are always a part of me. To tell the truth, I don't remember very well *how* my father looked. My memory of him is this faded photograph. No matter. My parents live as long as I live."

One side of the picture had been trimmed by someone who appeared to have used cuticle scissors to cut off an unwanted person, but who hadn't been totally removed. Part of a dress and part of her arm remained.

"I suppose you wonder who was cut off and why," Marlene said. "I cut off my older sister, Liesel, who was only a year older than I, in this photograph of us as little girls. I could show you the piece I cut off with my sister's picture, but I can't find it. I know it's here somewhere, because I saved it carefully.

"It appears I cut off the person because it was someone I didn't like. It looks like I did it because I hated the person. Exactly the opposite. I did it because I loved her dearly.

"The reason I cut her off was because I wanted to protect her. For years I have told everyone, *everyone*, that I never had a sister. I insisted, but now I feel that I can tell you the truth, because now I'm permitted to have my sister again.

"We were not so much the same, though I think we looked quite a lot alike, but we loved each other very much when we were little girls. I told Liesel all my secrets. She didn't tell me any. I think it was because she didn't have any to tell.

"Losing our father was so terrible, and then losing our step-father, we didn't really know well, but our mother did, and so it was upsetting for us. It made us huddle even closer together.

"When my mother chose to stay in Berlin during World War II, of course having no idea what such a decision meant, Liesel also chose to stay in Germany, or I should say her husband chose, and Liesel, who was always the dutiful wife our mother had taught her to be, would only remain at his side. Usually, she was more likely to be a few steps behind him and, after her only child was born, she would be holding the small hand of her young son, Hans, who was very dear to her.

"After I made it clear to the Nazis that I would not return to Germany, and I became a U.S. citizen, denouncing the Nazis and working toward their defeat, I feared for the safety of my sister. I could not be in contact with my mother and sister, so I tore Liesel out of my picture frame and tried to tear out her very existence. I was afraid the Nazis could punish her—retribution, revenge, you know.

"I began insisting because of the war, but I had lied so insistently, it became a habit and easier to go on with the lie. My mother and I never liked her husband, but she was so in love.

"I remember when my mother said to me, 'There's nothing to do about it. She would follow him to hell.' I remembered my mother's all-too-prophetic words over the next years."

"YOU KNOW, I DIDN'T *have* to become a film actress," Marlene told me. "There were other things I could have done just as successfully.

"I'm a great seamstress. I really can sew, and I value seamstresses, especially the best ones. I would bring the ones at the studio cakes I had baked. I had stitch-respect.

"It was more important to me that I could repair my clothes than that I could make them. I was taught by my mother to make perfect stitches and the art of stitch placement to create different effects. The stitches were close to embroidery. This was invaluable to me when I was on the road and my costumes and dresses and pants needed repairs. Usually there was no one to turn to who could sew nearly as well as I could, and I enjoyed doing it. Sometimes I did it for others in the cast. Thank you, Mama.

"I could have been a milliner, too. I make wonderful hats."

"But do you think you would have been happy through a long lifetime of making hats?" I asked her.

"Why not? But I don't know because that wasn't the life I lived. I remember wishing when I was very busy that I could stop and make a hat, but maybe if I knew that was all I had to do and what I had to do for the rest of my life, I might have hated hats. You don't know till you try a thing out. Nothing is ever quite the way you imagine it.

"But I can tell you this much. I don't have to act on the stage or in films to be happy. There are many who don't feel that way, who pin all their hopes and dreams on a career which can be ephemeral or even nonexistent. My greatest happiness has always been in my dear child, and in my family. I might have stopped working at some point, but I am too poor. Taxes, you know. And what would I do? Stay home knitting?

"I think I could have been a wonderful nurse. I love to help people who need care, to make them feel better. I like to feel that I am a useful person, making a contribution. Seeing them get well gives me a wonderful feeling, and I know I had a special talent for helping people get better."

"I HAVE BEAUTIFUL JEWELRY, which I wish I could show you. I don't have so much, but what I have is the best. I'd show you some, but I keep it in the bank. I don't wear it these days because I'm living a different life, and the truth is I can't afford insurance. I'm not destitute, but insurance is very high if you live in a flat and do not have a lot of watch-people to protect your possessions, especially your jewelry. Even if you do, it is expensive to have your jewelry at home where you can play with it and enjoy looking at it, even if you don't take it out of your home. I admit I would like to try some of it on, just alone here in my flat. I'd like to look at it and to touch it. I love the sensation of feeling it against my skin. I remember how it looked, but sometimes I can't remember how it felt. I enjoyed using some of it in films and in the theater. Theater people are wonderful, and nothing was ever taken.

"I hope to stay in this apartment the rest of my days, not to mention my nights. This apartment suits me. The moment I saw it, I knew it was just right for me. Not too big, not too small. Not a burden to take care of. And I could rent it without having to buy it.

"I always have too many boxes, and I can't hide them anymore, even from myself. I have grown used to them, but it is jarring when I allow someone to come into my apartment, which isn't very often. I see the expressions on their faces. I see my clutter through their eyes. Then they avoid looking in that direction again, and so do I.

"Personally, I love knowing that all of my things are here, safe and secure, my memories. All I have to do is go through them, which is never the way I want to spend my time. It means making decisions about what to throw away, what is just junk. I'm always afraid of throwing away something I later want and won't be able to find. But I must do something so I don't leave it all for Maria to go through. She won't like doing that. She is my daughter. It's impossible for her. She doesn't live in Paris, and she has her own family. She stays at the lovely Plaza Athénée, but it's so expensive. I have more time now than I did, but less energy. The only thing to do about a problem like going through my things is to shut it out.

"Life is a constant struggle, a fight to protect your illusions. People are very keen on making you aware of the truth, but it's *their* truth, not yours. Certainly not mine. Illusion is fragile and has to be protected. The reality which people acclaim is usually something negative, and often a way to make you feel as badly as *they* do. But I don't want to be so serious.

"When I was a child, so young I can't remember my exact age—I just know it was a long time ago, probably when I was about five or six—I had a premonition. It was before I knew what the word 'premonition' meant.

"I don't know how it came to me or why, but suddenly I knew I was going to die young.

"After that, no one could convince me it wasn't true. No one tried because I never told anyone my secret. I never wanted pity. It was too tragic to share, even though I felt it was very romantic, like poetry. It made me feel sad because I loved life.

"I think it shaped the way I lived. It was a reason to spend my money and not save for the future.

"After my little girl was born, I hoped, most of all, that I would have the chance to see her grow up. It may have been a reason in the back of my mind that I was happy to marry early and to have my baby early.

"It seems I have outgrown my premonition. It's too late for me to die young." Marlene was in her seventies when she told me this.


"I'M NOT SURPRISED YOU want to hear about my life. I've had an interesting life. *I* found it interesting. That's the important thing. Wouldn't it be terrible if you didn't find your own life interesting?

"When I was a child, I wanted to have an exciting life. And I did. But what I learned was it's important *not* to have *too* exciting a life.

"The wonderful thing about youth is it seems endless when you possess it. Nothing to think about, it's wonderful not to think about money. More wonderful than not thinking about money is not having to think about time."

Marie Magdalene Dietrich was born on December 27, 1901. Her sister, Elisabeth ("Liesel"), was born the year before. The family lived in the prosperous Schöneberg district of Berlin.

Marlene's mother, Wilhelmine Elisabeth Josephine Felsing, was born in 1871. She was the youngest daughter of Conrad Felsing, head of Felsing's. Their fashionable retail shop at 20 Unter den Linden was highly regarded throughout Europe, especially for its watches and clocks. In 1898, Josephine married Louis Erich Otto Dietrich, a lieutenant in the Royal Prussian Police. As a major in the German army during the Franco-Prussian War of 1870–71, Dietrich had been awarded an Iron Cross for bravery in action.

Berlin at that time was not only the capital of Germany, but one of the most important manufacturing, commercial, financial, and cultural centers in the world. When Germany became a nation in 1871, the population of its capital was 826,000 people. By 1910, the city grew to 2,076,200. German rivaled French and English as an international language. Students from all over the world were just as likely to choose Berlin as Paris as a place to study. German culture, science, and products were held in high esteem all over the world. This was the proud Germany into which Marie Magdalene Dietrich was born. "I had a very privileged childhood," she told me.

It was not quite the aristocracy, and it was a life of spartan values. Although Marlene's family was never short of the necessities of life and routinely enjoyed the luxuries that money could buy, she remembered her mother admonishing her when she didn't eat everything on her plate. Her mother sometimes added, "and remember there are starving children in the world who would be happy to eat what you have left." It made a very young Marlene, who was still Marie Magdalene, feel a little guilty, because she would gladly have shared her delicious meal with a hungry child, but she didn't know how to do that and her mother didn't explain.

Marie Magdalene rarely questioned her mother. "My mother seemed to know everything," Marlene said, but she didn't believe information was meant to be shared with children, who were taught only obedience. "When I went out in the afternoon with my mother to call on someone for tea, I was never told which of her friends we were going to visit. It was not considered appropriate for a child to ask."

Strict Prussian military values of duty and obedience shaped the Dietrich household. "My mother constantly tried to instill obedience in us. Children were always taught to obey their parents, without question. Unquestioned obedience was also the role of a woman with her husband. The man was the superior person and he was always right. It was his will which was to be followed. My mother would never have questioned anything my father said, nor spoken out loud any disagreement with him, or criticism of him, and I don't believe she ever even had such a thought.

"For her that was what marriage meant, obedience. In her mind, marriage was like the military, the husband was always the general, and the wife, if she was a good wife, was always a lower-ranking officer, there to take commands, even unspoken ones.

"My older sister loved school. I remember her telling me when we were little children—she was about nine—that she never wanted to leave school. She studied to be a teacher, got her certificate, and became a teacher, so she didn't have to leave the world of school at all. She just moved from being a student to being a teacher.

"She was a very conscientious and dutiful child. When she came home from school, immediately she performed all of her duties around the house, and then she rushed to do her homework. I would see her smiling to herself as she did it. She was in another world, transported by learning and perhaps pleasing all of our teachers. I didn't feel that way about doing my homework. I did it only because I knew I had to do it, except, of course, the French lessons.

"A sad thing for Elisabeth, whom we called Liesel, was when she had a cold or a childhood illness, and she had to stay home from school. She had all the colds and childhood illnesses, and I had none. If it was for any prolonged period, my mother instructed her, and she also paid tutors, so my sister would not fall behind at school. If anything, it put her ahead.

"I didn't feel at all the way my sister felt about school. I loved learning, but I didn't feel the school we went to offered a good opportunity to learn what was useful. The teachers wanted to teach us what they believed we should learn, not what we wanted to learn. Maybe it was because that was what they knew how to teach. Latin, for instance. I only wanted to learn French. I didn't have anywhere I wanted to go where I could speak Latin.

"I was my mother's girl and my sister was my father's girl. My mother told me I resembled my father rather than her, and she said that it was lucky for me because my father was such a handsome man. I always thought my sister and I looked alike.

"My sister liked walking with my father. He was tall and straight, with Prussian military posture and an air of authority that made him an ideal escort for a promenade. Even when he was out of uniform, he seemed to be in uniform.

"My sister would look up at him worshipfully and loved to be seen in his company, knowing if she met any of the girls from school, they would envy her. She always hoped to meet at least one of those girls, and often did.

"Looking back, I'm afraid I see my father as rather empty, like a book with a beautiful cover but nothing printed on the pages inside.

"I preferred my mother's company. She knew the secret of making the best apricot marmalade in Berlin, in Germany, perhaps in the world, and she shared her secret recipe with me.

"I thought, even back then, my sister's walk would come to an end, right after she returned home with my father on a Sunday afternoon, while the buttermilk soup I had learned to make that day, working at my mother's side, would be valuable for the rest of my life."

In Marlene's Paris apartment, she had a lovely antique mirror, and she saw me looking at it, actually looking *into* it. "There will come a time in your life," she said, "when old, smoky mirrors are the best. They are much more romantic. To put it plainly, a woman looks younger in them. I don't know why anyone would want to see every pore.

"I remember when I was very young, my mother scolded me when she saw me standing in front of our big full-length mirror. I was standing so close, I was almost going into it. I seemed to her to be too pleased by my reflection, and to like what I saw, excessively. I was not hiding my pleasure. 'Very bad,' my mother thought, 'revealing your feelings, even to yourself.'

"My mother valued modesty. Along with obedience, it was one of her prime values, and she thought I ought to revere it, too. I respected my mother, and I wanted her to be happy, so I tried to appear modest, but it was false on my part.

"My mantra has always been, 'Be noticed.'

"But I was taught by my mother that the most important rule for a lady to observe is *not* to be noticed! Above all, she must never deliberately *try* to attract attention. In fact, it was even wrong to attract attention that was *not* deliberate." Her mother never explained specifically how a beautiful young woman could *avoid* attracting attention.

"Once, when my mother was admonishing me again about how I shouldn't attract attention, I asked her how I accomplished that. I suppose I was about four at the time. She said something like, 'Make yourself part of the wallpaper.' That wasn't much help. She didn't explain how I could do that, especially when the walls were painted and there wasn't any wallpaper.

"From the first moments I can remember, people were always saying to my mother, 'What a beautiful daughter you have!' My mother was very pleased by that, no matter how oblivious to it she acted. I was pleased by the compliments, too.

"Even when I was with my sister, *in front of my sister,* they would glow over me and say, 'What a beautiful child.' It was always clear which of us children people were extolling. It was strange, because I thought my sister was the more beautiful one.

"I wondered if my sister minded all of the compliments I received. Well, of course, she *had* to mind. Liesel's eyes usually were cast down, as we had been taught to do, because of our girlish modesty. Liesel did not show any expression. Our mother would have been proud of her. I could not suppress a smile. I suppose my mother would have been ashamed of me for that show of vanity in recognition of the compliment.

"Liesel never said anything about it. She was more in-going and I was more outgoing. Partly, it was her nature, and partly I think it was because of me. She didn't get her share of praise or appreciation, but she never showed any sign of resentment, any sign of being jealous of me.

"Well, I *was* pleased with the way I had turned out. And truth be told, so was my mother.

"My mother was very conservative about the way I was dressed. She only wore black herself after the death of her two husbands. I think she grieved especially for my father.

"Mother was old before her time, before she was thirty, I think. She knew she had begun losing my father's attention even before his sudden death. I can remember her dutifully caring for little me and my sister, in her stiff, dour way.

"While my mother's dress philosophy was never to be noticed, I had a flamboyant inclination. Her own mother, my grandmother, told me, 'You should be noticed for your good taste.' My grandmother gave me advice I could understand.

"She taught me how to dress correctly for different occasions, so that I would attract only favorable attention. She taught me what colors to wear at different times of day, how to mix and match subtle tones, how to select accessories, especially purses and scarves, and when I was older, to consider perfume an accessory to be well chosen, and more than anything, which jewelry to wear for which occasion. Jewelry was my heritage, the heritage of my mother's family, after all. My grandmother's advice was a lot of fun, and she gave me lovely little pieces of jewelry, too, which helped me to pay attention and remember it all.

"I've always loved jewelry. My grandmother would take me to our family's jewelry store near the Adlon Hotel. She gave me small pieces from her own collection as gifts, and she let me try on hers, as well as pieces at our family store. I loved standing among the well-dressed ladies as they tried on jewelry, and I did the same as they did."

The Adlon Hotel was at 1 Unter den Linden, an elegant boulevard, perhaps the grandest in Berlin, and guests at the hotel often visited the Felsing's shop at 20 Unter den Linden to purchase jewelry or clocks. The visitors included royalty, celebrities, and the richest people from all over the world. Kaiser Wilhelm himself enjoyed the hotel. Its decor boasted enormous chandeliers, wonderful marble, huge porcelain vases, oriental hangings, velvet drapes. It was bedecked with every symbol of elegance. Wondrous food was routine—pheasant, caviar, smoked salmon, and of greatest interest to Marie Magdalene, the dazzling pastry cart.

"It was the most expensive place in Berlin," Marlene said. "Tea and the tea cart with sweet delicacies were affordable, however, if one chose to spend one's money that way. What better choice? And the waiters were always especially generous to me. Napoleons, petit fours . . . I stuffed myself, but I never got sick. Eating, no matter how great the quantity, especially of cream cakes, the richer the better, never made me feel anything but happy.

"When I went to Felsing's, I felt like it belonged to me. I loved every piece of jewelry in the shop, some more than others. My grandmother was very pleased. She said I had a good eye. I wondered why she said that, because I had two eyes. Was only one of them good? They both seemed very good to me.

"I remembered what she said, and only years later did I recall her words and understand what she meant. Afterwards, she said it was 'in the blood.' Generations of my family had been involved with jewelry, as well as clocks.

"My grandmother wore wonderful jewelry from the shop. She was an elegant lady who carried herself proudly. She always wore several pieces of jewelry which looked wonderful, but never too much. She would instruct me about how to wear my jewelry some-day when I would have more important pieces.

"I'll tell you one funny thing, though. She taught me a trick for wearing wonderful brooches. Every time she wore one which was valuable, or which she liked very much, she would sew it onto her dress so it couldn't be lost, and she didn't have to worry about it. She would sew it on lightly, so it wouldn't mark the dress, but firmly enough so that it added to the protection of the lock, and she felt secure.

"One of my favorite childhood memories was, and still is, the very high cream cakes that were made in Berlin and probably throughout Germany, though my world at that time was very limited, and I was only familiar with Berlin and its environs. But that was more than enough cake for me. Sunday afternoon was our family day at a favorite café, which had wonderful cakes. The displays were dazzling. One also eats with one's eyes. I do.

"With my grandmother, any day could be a cake day. Cream cake was always at the end of our afternoon excursion, when my grand-mother and I had good conversation to share about the day's activi-ties. We talked like birds chirping at the end of the day.

"I remember my grandmother's lavender eyes very clearly, or I think I do. Sometimes what we think are our memories are really other people's memories which they have impressed on us from *their* memories. For example, even though I can see the unusual color of her eyes very clearly in my mind, it may be something I was told rather than something I really saw.

"And her perfect sense of fashion, which she taught me, became a part of me, not because I followed everything she said, but because I had the perfect basis and could choose the variations I wanted for myself. I have kept as many of my clothes and accessories as I could. They are reminders of happy times.

"It's not to say I am unhappy now. I am not. But there is an absence of the highs of happiness that I knew in the past, and there is the recognition that I probably will not experience those again."

On occasion, young Marie Magdalene was so tempted by the fat éclairs that she gave up a cream layer cake in favor of one of the éclairs, which she believed was a French pastry. Only when she arrived in Paris years later did she learn the difference between a German éclair and French éclair, "two totally different things," she discovered.

"At first, the French éclairs seemed to me to be ridiculously small, and the outside pastry was so thin, you could barely taste it. At first bite, I was disappointed, but I quickly accustomed myself to the éclairs in the country of their origin. I came to like the *raffiné* French ones best, but in my mind, I always have the picture of those big, fat, obscene éclairs. I can't quite remember how they tasted, but the way they looked was unforgettable. It's no wonder Jo von Sternberg told me I had to go on a diet. He only had to say it once because I saw myself on the screen, and I knew he was right. I began the diet as soon as the words left his mouth. I closed mine. I didn't reduce the quality of what I ate, only the quantity."

"SOMETHING I ENJOYED DOING as a child was cooking with my mother," Marlene told me. "I remember being in the kitchen with her before I was tall enough to reach the table. I was drawn there by the wonderful smells. There is no perfume equal to goulash. It's essential to know how to do a perfect schnitzel. Strawberry Jam Number Five, Raspberry Jam Number Seven. . . .

"I was an indoors girl when my mother was in the kitchen, and I could join her. I always got as close to my mother as I could without being in her way. That gave me a great sense of security. I liked feeling her skirt brushing me. Sharing the activity with my mother made it especially wonderful for me. In the winter, when there was ice, I loved to skate, but I never skated away from cooking opportunities at home.

"I loved ice-skating when I was a child. It came naturally and easily to me. I just put on a pair of ice skates. The first pair fit perfectly and off I went. It didn't occur to me to be afraid of falling, and I never did. I just skated off.

"On the other hand—or maybe I should say on the other foot— my sister, Liesel, even though she was a year older, didn't start skating till after I did. She wasn't really tempted, which I couldn't understand, because the skating rink in Berlin, when we were small children, twinkled like a fairy-tale land.

"Liesel was always afraid of falling, and she always fell. She would have had more than two skinned knees if she'd had more than two knees. She said it was because she had weak ankles. I couldn't imagine what she was talking about, what it would be like to have weak ankles. But later, I understood what she meant. I maybe had weak ankles, too. Better not to know those things.

"My mother had such wonderful bowls and dishes. There was a beautiful Dresden cookie plate and a hand-painted Austrian pitcher for milk with tiny painted snow scenes encircling it.

"When my mother saw the careful way I handled all of the dishes and bowls even when my tiny hands could barely hold them, she said, 'I'm leaving them to you, Marie Magdalene, because you appreciate them.'

"At that time we didn't know what the future held. As it turned out, it held a lot of broken dishes.

"From the first, I truly loved to cook. I consider cooking much more of an art than a science. If you love to cook, you cannot help but be good at it, or you *can* become good at it. If you don't like to cook, determination won't be enough. Look around for some good restaurants.

"All my life, I've been going into the kitchens of restaurants not only to collect their recipes, but to join in the cooking. I know everyone doesn't have celebrity privilege, but you can try, and someone will appreciate your enthusiasm and let you stay.

"I've never been someone who believes in following recipes exactly. A recipe is a guide, and it's more useful the first time you try to prepare something. Once I've done it, the recipe is mine. But more important than measuring spoons and a good scale is to have tasted what you're making as prepared by someone who made it at its best. That is how you know you have achieved what you want when you taste it. You have to have a standard."


IN 1907, SHORTLY AFTER the Dietrich family moved to Weimar, Marie Magdalene's father, regarded as an excellent rider, was thrown by a horse and died. Whether he died from the fall, perhaps striking his head, or from a heart attack brought on by the accident, or whether he had a heart attack and then fell, his daughter never knew.

"My mother never discussed any of the details with me. When it happened, I was six years old, too young to understand much of anything except my father had disappeared from my life, leaving behind only a silver-framed picture of him in the drawing room and his boots in his bedroom, which my mother kept highly polished, as if my father might be returning at any moment. They were like a shrine, those two empty boots, standing at attention.

"Once in a while in my childhood, my mother would look at me and, unsmiling but glowing slightly, say, 'My little soldier.' I was too young to completely understand, but I recognized it as a wonderful term of endearment. I understood she was linking me to my father, the great love of her life. I reminded her of him. It made me very happy.

"But as I've grown older and I've been alone so much, a strange thing has happened in my relationship with my father. We have grown closer, so that now, some of the time, he is sharing my flat with me.

"During the few short years of my early childhood, he was my shadow father. He was the person my mother was always cleaning the house for, living for his praise. I think she would rather have had him praise her beauty, but there was nothing she could do about that, so she kept her house the best it could possibly be kept. My father never admired the floors, even when she redid them after the maid had done them. Her standard for my father was almost unattainable. He took it for granted, and he just assumed his home would be perfectly kept by my mother and the servants. She made the best meals for my father, even when he didn't arrive home to eat them. It was simply a Prussian household of its day.

"I think my mother was a very passionate woman, but she didn't know it until the marital bed, with my father. The most romantic part of the marriage, I believe, was before I knew my parents, before my sister was born and before I was born.

"I came to understand another factor in the marriage, my mother's ample dowry. She had fears of being an old maid, and she had never dared to hope that her Felsing dowry would be sufficient for such a match with a dashingly handsome military hero who had become an officer in the Imperial Police Force, a highly respected career in the Prussia of that time. Mother was from a successful merchant family which was able to offer a better dowry than could many aristocratic families.

"For at least two years, the life of my mother revolved around babies. If we had been two boys, it might have been different. As it was, I remember my mother waiting longingly to hear his key in the keyhole of our front door. For me, Father was a hat with a plume, a mustache, and a pair of the shiniest boots I ever saw.

"Not long ago, I woke up, and I thought I saw my father in my bedroom on his horse. The room was too small for a horse, so I wanted to warn him because I'd been told he had fallen from his horse and died. I wanted to save him, but it was only a dream, or an apparition, or something like that.

"I'd never spent much time with my father, because he was always doing his duty and didn't have so much time to spend with a little girl. There were times when he was gone, I wished I'd taken some of those walks with him. It wasn't because I missed him so much. I can't honestly say I deeply missed him, because you can't deeply miss someone you didn't know. I missed knowing him better, so I could miss him more. I missed missing him.

"I was especially conscious of his absence on Sundays. We no longer bought bags of chocolate creams and went to the café and had hot chocolate with patisserie. Birthdays, which had always been luxurious events, were not so important. It might be one or the other with Mother, but life became a matter of choices, one or the other. Luxury was the casualty in our household. Mother conveyed that the absence of little pleasures was character-building. I wasn't persuaded. When a choice was offered, I always chose luxuries over necessities.

"My mother never complained, but I felt she missed those joys in life that had disappeared. She was a consolation to my sister and me, but I don't know if we were a consolation to her. We certainly were a responsibility. That may be of use because, in my life, I cannot imagine not being needed. For me, being needed is what makes life worthwhile.

"I know my mother missed my father terribly. She never cried, at least not in front of us, but she was terribly lonely, I think. It had been such a triumph for her when my father had asked for her hand in marriage. She devoted herself to her duty and satisfying the needs of my sister and me, but the light had gone from her eyes. The bloom was gone from her cheeks. Her black outfits did not flatter her, and she seemed to age rapidly.

"When I was older, I asked my mother to tell me more about what had happened to my father, but this always upset her very much. Because she wouldn't tell me any more details, I grew up thinking the secrecy meant there was some mystery about my father's death.

"But now I don't think that anymore. Now I think my mother didn't tell me any more details because she didn't know any more herself.

"Do you want to know what my mother called me when I was very little? It was only a few times, but I remember it very well. The first time I heard her say it, I didn't understand it was me she was speaking to. 'I'm speaking with you, Paul,' she said, looking directly at me. I looked around, but I was the only one there. She only did this when I was very, very little. One time she called me 'Little Paul.' I asked her why she called me Paul.

"Usually she didn't answer my questions. She didn't believe that parents were required to answer their children's questions. Parents always knew best. This time, she answered me, softly, 'It was the name your father chose for you. It was what we were going to call you if you had been a boy. We were expecting a boy.'

"My mother didn't say that they *wanted* a boy, but there was that implication.

"I felt my father must have been disappointed that I was a girl. He didn't mind that their first child was a girl, but then to have a second girl . . .

"Mother had let him down. *I* had let him down.

"Maybe if I'd been Paul, my father would have been around the house more, and my mother would have been happier."

• • •

" 'MARLENE' WAS NOT the name I was given when I was born. I was called Marie Magdalene, which I did not like because at that time so many girl babies were being given that name. I wanted a name that was all mine, only mine. There was no one else named Marlene."

Shortly before World War I, Marie Magdalene Dietrich started calling herself Marlene Dietrich, a name she had created for herself when she was eleven. "I thought Marlene was a much more glamorous name," she said.

"When I created my name, the first person I told was my sister. I told her that I didn't like my name because it was too common a name in Germany.

"I told Liesel I had decided to combine Marie and Magdalene to make a new name for myself, Marlene.

"My sister said I would have a very peculiar name. No one else in school would have a name like Marlene. That's just what I wanted to hear. My sister was called Liesel, and there were many Liesels. She disliked anything that was out of order.

"I was very happy with my new name. It had a kind of French aura.

"I fell in love with France, with Paris, before I ever saw it. My ears fell in love before my eyes did. I knew it was a beautiful language, the most beautiful I'd ever heard, even when I'd only heard it spoken with a German accent.

"I loved the sound of French from the first moment I heard it. At home I was encouraged to learn French. I didn't need encouragement, because it was just what I wanted to do. My mother began teaching it to me, and then I had some German teachers of French. I knew even with their German accents, it must belong to wonderful people in a beautiful place.

"My mother told me she didn't want to speak French with me because she had a German accent and she didn't want me to speak French the way she did. Her mother, my grandmother, sometimes spoke French with me, and it sounded very nice. I pretended we were in Paris, though I couldn't really imagine what Paris was like. She had studied with French teachers from France, and she loved the language. She talked with me about fashion, clothes, accessories, purses, shoes, and jewelry in French. She said I should think of clothes and accessories as friends to accompany me through life.

"When I started school, my family chose a school where I would have classes in French. There was a real French teacher from France. I adored her. She was chic in a proper way, wearing ladylike clothes. Her suits always had feminine touches, ruffled ecru blouses, and a jabot with a brooch strategically placed. She wore gloves, fine white linen in the summer, fine leather with little pearl buttons for the rest of the year, in colors that matched her outfit. I'd never seen pastel kid gloves before, only dark colors, and my mother had white for Sundays."

The teacher, Marguerite Breguand, recognized her student's interest in French, and Marie Magdalene felt they had a bond. Sometimes they would sit on a bench outside the school and speak in French. It made the little girl feel very special. She studied hard and wanted to grow up quickly.

Mlle Breguand taught classes in advanced French for the older girls. Marie Magdalene could scarcely wait for the time she would be old enough to attend the advanced classes taught by Mlle Breguand. She dreamed of the day she would see Paris. She knew it wouldn't let her down when she did, and it didn't.

Every day she could scarcely wait to go to school because she was so eager for French class. Then, one day, she went to school, and it was all different. All of the French classes had been canceled. She couldn't find her French teacher, who was not German. Mlle Breguand apparently had disappeared. When Marie Magdalene asked about her, she sensed a distinct chill. She was told that Mlle Breguand had left the school and would not be returning. "Where has she gone? Why isn't she coming back?"

She was shocked and sad. She couldn't believe that Mlle Breguand would have left without saying anything to her.

Marie Magdalene missed her friend. She waited months, looking each day in the post for a note, in French, from the teacher, saying goodbye, perhaps saying something about the future. The note never came.

When she told her mother what had happened, her mother explained that Germany and France were at war. Her teacher, as an enemy alien, would have had to leave Germany immediately, or she might have been imprisoned. For Marie Magdalene, the concept that France was an enemy was not something she could understand or accept. She could not imagine Mlle Breguand as an enemy.

"I'VE NEVER BEEN ABLE to enjoy knitting because of the circumstances of my childhood contribution to the German war effort at the beginning of World War I. We children, the girls, were assigned the task at school of knitting mittens and scarves. The yarn was provided for us. I think some of our work must have surprised the recipients. There were some six-fingered gloves and no six-fingered soldiers. Most of us only did mittens.

"At the beginning, people in Germany were happy about the approaching war. Can you imagine that? Especially the very young soldiers who were so pleased with themselves, proudly marching off in their uniforms, a brief excursion to fulfill dreams of glory. It would turn out to be neither brief nor glorious.

"Many of those young men were never coming back to live out their lives. They didn't seem to understand that possibility and each one appeared to be convinced of his own immortality."

By 1915, food was strictly rationed. Milk was rare. Marlene felt that her lifelong weak bones were the result of being deprived of calcium when she was growing. She was happy that her teeth were good.

Potatoes were the regular diet, until even potatoes became scarce. Marlene said she never minded potatoes every meal, and she missed them as the war went on.

"In 1916 there was only pretend coffee. You had to be a very good actress to pretend that it was coffee. It didn't taste good. For a time, I didn't think I liked coffee.

"There was luxury food available for those who had money, the very rich. The very rich could enjoy *real* chocolate cake."

Her uncle Max and two cousins were killed in battle. "I had met my uncle," she said, "but they were not a real part of my life. Death, however, was coming into everyone's life. Innocence was lost."

In the third year of the war, Josephine was forced to take a job as a housekeeper to support her family. Working in that capacity for the von Losch family, she met her second husband, Eduard von Losch, a colonel in the Grenadiers.

In 1916, she and von Losch were married. She wore a black dress, not a good omen. She was still in mourning, in dress and in her heart, for Marlene's father, who had died so young and so unexpectedly.

Marlene did not recall her stepfather very clearly. "He was like a ghost," she told me. She never found him interesting but didn't mind her mother marrying him, because she understood that Josephine was worried, burdened, and lonely. She was still young and needed a man on whom she could lean, and another pair of boots, if a smaller size, that she could polish.

Marlene's new stepfather did not replace her father. Von Losch was scarcely present because he was a career military officer, stationed at the front and not often home. He was able to offer them tinned luxuries, which were available to an officer on active duty. With the extra money he gave the family, Josephine was able to provide everyone with a better-balanced and more interesting diet.

In the summer of 1917, Colonel von Losch died on the Eastern Front.

His military career had taken him away most of the time. When he was at home he was reserved, even shy. He did not establish any more than a polite relationship with the adolescent Marie Magdalene or her sister, and they did not develop any real feeling for him. Marlene, however, was grateful that he made things better for her mother. She remembered the yellow dress he gave her mother with a small bouquet of matching yellow flowers. She saw her mother smile and rush to the bedroom to try on the dress. The door was open a crack. "She looked lovely, and she was smiling at herself in the mirror. Then she rushed to the door and closed it all the way.

"My stepfather was like a shadow for me then. Of course, he is much more of a shadow after all these years. If I were walking in the street now and he approached me, looking exactly as he did then, I would not be able to recognize him.

"When my stepfather died in the war, we were poorer, having only his pension, and not his salary, but we still had a good home, music and books, and the right values. When we had to move again, my mother always held everything together. She was sad, but for her, it was worse to have your emotions showing than to have your slip showing. I think my mother's outer garb of stoicism was a cloak for her truly emotional soul."

"ONE OF MY EARLIEST memories is of a very tall vase in our reception hall. It was much taller than I or it was at least when I began remembering it, which was when I was about three. It made a tremendous impression on me. I knew it was very valuable, because of the gentle way my mother dusted it.

"Usually, my mother cleaned and polished with unbelievable vigor. She was a very energetic lady, so my sister, Liesel, and I did not need to be told that the vase was of great value. We always stepped around it, never touching it, making certain our clothes never brushed it. I remember the wonderful colors and all of the gold trim on it. It was real gold, I think.

"By the time I was five, the vase was no longer taller than I was. In my memory, I would say by then the vase and I were about the same height.

"After the death of my father, and then of my stepfather, we moved several times. It seemed we were always moving. It wasn't too hard on me. I didn't have many friends and changing schools didn't bother me. I found it kind of an adventure, because I was pretty bored with school, except, of course, French class. It was more difficult for my sister because she loved school, the teachers, and her girlfriends.

"I knew my mother didn't like being questioned about anything, but I couldn't resist. One day, I took a deep breath and asked her where the tall vase from the reception hall was. She said, 'We don't have a reception hall anymore.'

"That was all she ever said, and I never asked again."


MARLENE WANTED TO BE a violinist, but not just *any* violinist. She wanted to be a *great* violinist.

"I've always loved music, and I was fortunate in having a mother who recognized my feeling for music and developed it, even if she had to make sacrifices. As a child, I loved to hear my mother play piano. That was wonderful. My mother played beautifully, and she was partly responsible for my love of music."

Her mother was strongly supportive of a career as a violinist for Marlene. Josephine believed a woman should have a proper way to remain a lady while being able to support herself. In case Marlene's beauty and Felsing dowry didn't produce a husband of means, she wanted her daughter to be independent.

When Marlene graduated from the Viktoria-Louise School for Girls in 1918, Josephine enrolled her in the Berlin Hochschule für

Musik, and Grandmother Felsing paid the tuition, even though she had misgivings. She didn't think the violin would enhance her granddaughter's social life, and playing the guitar would do more for her marital prospects.

"It was exceedingly difficult to support my violin lessons at the level I had hoped for. My mother gave up a great deal to buy me a very expensive violin and bow, the price of a small suburban house.

"I practiced for six hours a day or for as long as I could lift the bow. Then, one day, I had muscle spasms in the fingers of my left hand, and they didn't go away. A doctor told me I had injured the bones of the hand. I believe it probably had something to do with the low-calcium diet that caused all of my bone problems. If I did not play demanding pieces, my hand would probably recover; otherwise it could get worse. My heart was broken, but at least I knew I wanted to be a performer. Being a film actress never crossed my mind. It was a life-defining moment for me. The violin is a symbol of my broken dreams."

In retrospect, she may have been guilty of a bit of poetic hyperbole. She dearly loved poetry all of her life. There is no doubt, however, that Marlene's injury and its subsequent effect on her ability to play the violin represented a broken dream for her mother.

From the moment that Josephine recognized the gravity of her daughter's injury, she was faced with the reality that Marlene could never have the musical career she had envisioned for her. Josephine knew her daughter was not afraid of hard work and she had diligence and perseverance, but from the moment the doctors informed Marlene about her injury, she lost her drive to practice.

If Marlene could never have the concert career she had dreamed of, she could at least play in theater orchestras or be the accompanist for silent films when times were hard and the family needed money. "As it turned out," she said, "it probably was a lucky thing I hurt my hand.

"I dropped out of the music high school and told my mother I knew what I wanted to do with my life. I wanted to be a model or an actress. Not only did my mother not have much hope that I would have a very successful career and be able to support myself, but it seemed she would be even unhappier if I were successful in a career she considered rather demeaning, not befitting the Dietrichs or the Felsings. The tragedy of 'the Great War,' however, was changing such conventional thinking.

"When I was a girl in Berlin, my favorite actress was Henny Porten," Marlene told me. "I know you've never heard of her. I adored her. I worshipped her back then. She was a great movie star in a time before there were many movie stars. She was a child star and then a grown-up movie star in silent films like *The Princess's Kiss*. She wasn't beautiful, but she had a lot of appeal for audiences, something like Hollywood's Mary Pickford. She made more than a film a month, but she could never make enough for me. I still keep a picture of her which I take out and look at sometimes. That picture has been with me since I was a child."

Marlene collected picture postcards of Henny Porten. She said she would like to show them to me, but it would take too long to find them. "I always concentrate on preserving my things, not on organizing them. I may have to search for days, but I can be certain if I look long enough, I will find it. The most frustrating thing is when you look for something that has been thrown away in a moment it wasn't valued.

"My most memorable moment with Miss Porten was when I found where she was living. I sneaked away and went there. I took my violin with me and serenaded her in front of what I guessed was her window. I'd guessed right, because Henny Porten herself came to the window. She was wearing the most elegant negligee I had ever seen. It took away my breath so I was afraid I wouldn't be able to play my violin. But I did. Always the performer at heart. I did my best serenade.

"She waved and smiled at me, and closed the window.

"Looking back, I always have the picture in my mind of how gracious she was to a little girl. I know how hurt I would have been if it had turned out differently, and I try to think about it when fans approach me. I know I'm not always as nice as she was. She gave me a happy memory that lasted the rest of my life."


"As a girl in World War I," Marlene told me, "I was guilty of treason—in my heart. I didn't do anything subversive, but I felt it. I did not feel like a German child was supposed to feel.

"I didn't believe in war. I saw it hurting people, who paid a terrible price. In school, they treated the war as something glorious and said it wouldn't take long for our side to be victorious.

"I didn't believe them, especially when they said God was on our side, on the side of Germany. I wondered if girls my age in France were hearing the same words in French in their schools, the only difference being that God was on the side of France.

"I remember walking in the country one spring and passing a prisoner-of-war camp for French soldiers. One of them put his hand through the barbed wire and I impulsively picked up some wildflowers and put them into his hand. He clutched them like a gift from God. I said a few words to him in French.

"Some girls from my class saw this and reported me, and I had to miss some school. It was considered a disgrace, but I didn't feel disgraced.

"One thing I knew for certain was that God is not on anyone's side in war. I couldn't believe that Mlle Breguand and I were enemies. I suppose in my heart, I was a traitor or there were many who would have considered me one. I didn't want Germany to win. I didn't want France to win. I wanted peace and for the violence to end.

"My thoughts were of the very young men who didn't return at all and others who left important parts of themselves behind. In Germany, the young soldiers did not return enthusiastically, even if they came back in one piece. They were too tired. Most of them were too poor, as the German money's value dropped. Then, they were not received as heroes, because they had lost the war."

"IF ANYONE ASKS ME, I always say I had a wonderful childhood," Marlene said. "I say it even if they don't ask. Those who knew about my childhood wondered how I could say that. I was half an orphan at six. We had problems about money and we had to move to less expensive places after the death of my father.

"We were hungry and malnourished during what they stupidly called 'the Great War.' I lived on potatoes until they were replaced by turnips. Ugh! Turnips even for dessert. Turnip Napoleon, turnip éclairs."

After the armistice in 1918, life didn't get better. Conditions worsened. As a result of the continuing Allied blockade, malnutrition and starvation were common, claiming nearly a million lives, while the influenza epidemic claimed thousands more. The winters were unusually severe with no heating. Unemployment was the norm and political extremism widespread. Near anarchy prevailed. The final blow was the Treaty of Versailles, which was harsher than Germany had expected. The armistice seemed to have turned into an unconditional surrender, even revenge. As Germans came to accept the conditions of a humiliating defeat, they were thrust into the uncertainties of the Weimar Republic with its unfamiliar federal government.

In 1921, just before her twentieth birthday, Marlene got her first job modeling. Most of the photographs reproduced in magazines or on posters showed her legs. "In those days," she said, "it was my legs that were most appreciated, no matter what the product was. There was always a lot of emphasis on my legs." The emphasis on her legs held true for jobs in chorus lines.

"My mother still hoped that maybe I would follow my career as a violinist. Not to be. My love for the violin never diminished, but the time I spent playing it did. I knew my bow would never provide enough financial support."

As Marlene became better acquainted with the theater, she realized that she wanted to become an actress, but this ambition required training. She applied to the world-famous Max Reinhardt drama school.

Although she was initially rejected, she did catch the eye of an assistant director who offered to help her. Eventually, she appeared unnoticeably in two Reinhardt theatrical productions, and she was allowed to take some classes, but not with Reinhardt.

At the beginning of the 1920s, the film industry was one of the few commercial enterprises that was thriving in Germany. Thanks largely to UFA, Universal's European affiliate, films made in Germany were welcomed all over the world, and there was no language barrier because there was no spoken dialogue. The German film industry, centered in Berlin, was bringing in badly needed foreign exchange, while at the same time providing employment for a large number of trades and professions. Marlene decided that she wanted to become a film actress.

IT WAS A TROUBLED time in Germany. The Weimar Republic was not functioning effectively and the stringent terms of the Versailles Treaty, which, among other things, burdened Germany with a $33 billion reparations debt, were contributing to a growing psychological malaise and a burgeoning inflation.

"In 1923," Marlene recalled, "some Germans were pushing wheelbarrows full of marks to the baker for a loaf of bread and coming home with a slice. Others were wallpapering their houses with marks and burning them to keep warm. Some were using it for toilet paper."

The troops and workers who had revolted against the war in 1918 had been replaced by extreme nationalists such as Adolf Hitler, who staged a mini-revolt in Munich that was quickly put down, but which signaled trouble ahead. Little of this turmoil was reflected in the films being produced by UFA, which, like Hollywood, tried to create a dream world in which one could escape from the problems of postwar Germany.

"Marlene prefers not to discuss her early German films," Mary Meerson had warned me. "She says they were small parts in films she doesn't think would enhance her reputation. But the real reason is she feels they make her seem older. She likes to begin her film career with *The Blue Angel*."

Many agreed with Meerson that the reason Marlene didn't want to talk about her German films was that they represented the work of almost a decade and made her seem older. Marlene, however, pointed out that she never tried to hide her age. How could she, with her young daughter growing up in plain view?

When Marlene was asked by the press to talk about the films she is known to have appeared in before *The Blue Angel*, she would reply coolly, "I made none."

She explained to me, "What I meant was, I didn't make any that counted." She described them in German for Maximilian Schell in the film he made about her as *Quatsch*, literally *squash*, figuratively *nonsense*.

"I don't like to talk about my early German films, because I don't like them, and I don't like them because they weren't very good."

Marlene's first film was shot at UFA in 1922 just after she appeared on stage as a last-minute walk-on replacement in *Der grosse Bariton* (*The Great Baritone*), which starred the renowned Albert Bassermann.

At the time, Berlin offered the dual advantage of being the German language theatrical center and film center. Marlene, a movie fan, wanted to enter the film world, too. She importuned an uncle to get her a screen test through his show business friends until he finally acquiesced. He asked a friend at a small film production company to make the arrangements.

After a long day of shooting, a tired cameraman named Stefan Lorant was approached by Marlene, pleading for a screen test. She was determined, and the test was made. After Marlene became a Hollywood superstar, Lorant spoke about the incident with Billy Wilder, who described it to me.

"The test was a fiasco. Marlene, in her fervent desire to succeed in her first effort before the cameras, tried too hard. She jumped around and made faces. Her performance was appalling to everyone except Wilhelm Dieterle, who was a star at the Reinhardt theater about to start his directing career. In the film he hoped to make when he got the financial backing, he needed an impish character like Marlene."

Not in the least deterred by the apparent failure of her camera debut, Marlene continued to ask her uncle to use his influence to arrange another screen test for her, under more favorable conditions. Uncle Willi had a friend named Georg Jacoby, who was planning to produce and direct a Napoleonic comedy for a new production company called the European Film Alliance, or EFA. Such a film would surely have a lot of small parts for pretty young women.

Originally titled *So sind die Männer* (*Men Are Like That*), the film was first released in Vienna in the fall of 1922 as *Napoleons kleiner Bruder* (*Napoleon's Little Brother*). When it was later released in Berlin early the next year, the original title was changed to *Der kleine Napoleon* (*The Little Napoleon*). Marlene played a lady's maid and was twelfth in the credits.

### Der kleine Napoleon (The Little Napoleon, 1923)

With the help of her maid (Marlene Dietrich), a young noble-woman (Antonia Dietrich) resists the lecherous advances of Napoleon's younger brother, the newly appointed king of Westphalia (Paul Heidemann), until the emperor himself arrives and intervenes on her behalf.

Marlene said that she found no visual poetry or emotional power in films that could not speak. She preferred to think of herself as an unsentimental person who always lived in the present. Only when reminiscing about the Berlin that she once knew did she reveal her strong emotional ties with the past.

After she appeared in *Der kleine Napoleon*, Marlene was seen at Max Reinhardt's Deutscher Theaterschule by Rudolf "Rudi" Sieber, a handsome young man who was producer Joe May's assistant. May, sometimes called the Cecil B. DeMille of UFA, was casting for a new film starring Emil Jannings, one of Germany's leading actors. Sieber told Marlene that he would like to talk with her about trying out for a part in this film. Though it was a small part, he explained that it was very noticeable, and he thought she would be the perfect actress for it. From his accent, Marlene recognized the man as a Sudeten Czech. She learned that he came from a town near Prague. He was only a little older than she.

Thinking Marlene was on her way to a class, Sieber returned the next day only to be told she didn't have any classes that day. He was given her mother's home address. Marlene was still living with her mother.

From the first moment after Josephine opened the door and Rudi entered the apartment, Marlene remembered a chill that permeated the atmosphere. She knew that a sensitive person like Rudi must have felt it, though he showed no sign of feeling unwelcome. He had an easy charm, never trying too hard. His refined manner should have pleased Josephine and undoubtedly would have if she hadn't been wary and overly suspicious of any man who called on her daughter, especially if he had any connection with films or the theater. She did not trust the moral code of show people when it came to her carefully brought-up, beautiful child. Marlene's mother was ever-watchful.

Marlene offered her guest some coffee. She was proud of the coffee she made, and she had some *kuchen* she herself had baked that morning. Rudi had a better idea. He told her that he would like to take her out to lunch. Marlene was as happy as he to leave the awkward and stiff, though outwardly cordial, atmosphere that her mother offered. At the nearby café, which Rudi knew, they were free to be themselves and to get to know each other.

"And we did," Marlene remembered. "I'll never forget our first meeting. First meetings are often difficult, but this was not like that. It can be difficult to make conversation. For us, it was as if we had always known each other, only more exciting. It was clear even before we ordered that both of us loved the theater. The goulash seemed delicious, if not as outstanding as the one I could make, but I don't know anymore if the goulash was so exceptional or it was because of the company. We both had so much to tell."

Marlene appeared at the UFA studios the next morning. "Rudi and I had been so engrossed at our first meeting, he forgot to tell me how to dress in order to make the best impression on Mr. May. I borrowed one of my mother's best dresses and fixed up my hair in what I thought was the latest Parisian style. Rudi was pleased, but when Mr. May saw how I was dressed, he was not pleased. I was instructed to go to the costume department and put on something better suited to the part of the judge's mistress, the part I was trying out for.

"I found a sexy peignoir with feathers, but that didn't seem sufficient. Then, I found a monocle in the costume department, which I believed added just the right touch for a judge's mistress. Joe May thought so, too, and I got the part. It was my favorite role until I did *The Blue Angel*. Everyone remembered me wearing the monocle and then using the opera glasses in the courtroom scene. Using the opera glasses was my idea. I'd always loved opera glasses, and it showed how far back a mistress had to sit.

"The monocle which I actually wore in the film was my father's. It had been saved by my mother. She couldn't bring herself to throw it away because, she said, it would have been like throwing away a piece of my father.

"I couldn't see anything through it. Nothing. And I had to keep my other eye partly closed to hold it in. When I wore it, I was always insecure, fearing that the monocle might fall out on stage, especially if I moved with any exuberance. It never happened, so as time passed and after a number of performances, I grew more secure, though the monocle was no more secure. The fear was only in my mind. So it was foolish, because nothing happened. I stopped worrying. Maybe that was more foolish. Well, that's where fear is, in the mind, isn't it?"


"I DON'T LIKE TO wear panties. They are so confining. And when they show through and make a line, it looks so terrible. I've never understood why this absence of panties was so shocking and was considered a mark of not being a decent woman. My sister would never have considered going out without her panties. It was un-thinkable. Unspeakable.

"Elisabeth never spoke of my transgressions, even to me. I think she was too shocked and too modest herself to say anything, but I saw the disapproving look on her face. I suppose when she saw what I was doing, or not doing, she was embarrassed on my behalf.

"In school, I couldn't have any of the other girls, even my best friends, know my secret. I had to be especially careful on gym days.

"If she had caught me, my mother would have punished me for my guilty secret. She would probably have slapped me because she believed it was her duty to get her message through, unforgettable when discipline was concerned. She believed in a moderate dose of corporal punishment, a slap, if that was required. She never slapped very hard. Fortunately, the revelation that I was not a lady, even when I was only a little girl, didn't happen and it was not exposed that I was exposed. Then, finally the day came when I didn't have to answer to anyone.

"When Rudi made the discovery, he didn't say anything. I don't think he minded. Rudi never seemed to mind anything I did. I suppose for me, that was one of his most lovable of qualities.

"Rudi and I were tremendously attracted to each other. No doubt about that. He asked me if there was anyone else in my life I cared about. I told him truthfully, no. There wasn't. I cared only about him. Rudi said there was no one else for him, either.

"Rudi was a very handsome man, and his job made him even more attractive to women. He was in the position of being *more* than a casting director, and every pretty young thing with film aspirations, which was just about every pretty young girl around, offered temptation.

"One who was clearly enraptured by Rudi was Joe May's daughter. She was young and beautiful, and he thought she would get over it. She did. She killed herself.

"Suicide usually has more than one reason. Often the real reason isn't the one that *seems* to be the reason. I've always believed that most suicides would regret it if they had a second chance, but usually they don't get a second chance.

"I don't have to tell you that Rudi no longer had his privileged position with Joe May. He no longer had *any* position with May, who probably never wanted to see him again after his daughter's tragedy, of which Rudi was apparently the cause, even if unintentionally so.

"He swore he had not encouraged her, though he did admit he hadn't *dis*couraged her, either.

"Joe May and his wife were heartbroken. It really was something too horrible to bear. I don't know how people can go on. After Rudi and I had our little girl, I understood even more about possible pain. My pleasure was so great, it was almost painful. I cannot even imagine a pain so great as the loss of a child. I could not have gone on."

"NOBODY GETS ANYWHERE IN show business without help from someone, and maybe some-two, or even some-three. I was especially lucky in being given the chance I needed, the help to do better and learn, and encouragement, early, when I most needed it—and perhaps didn't always deserve it.

"When I found the career I wanted, what I wanted to do in life, and began going to try out for parts, I saw right away that I wouldn't have a chance to show what I could do unless someone was looking.

"Even if I didn't get reviewed favorably, I was mentioned. I got noticed. For an aspiring actress getting noticed is the most important thing.

"Rudi told me what he saw first, what attracted his attention to me, were my bright green gloves. He always talked about those green gloves I was wearing. After he saw such atrocious gloves, he had to take a good look to see who was wearing them.

"So, what my mother had said was the right thing for a girl to do, not to be noticed, wasn't right for me. I did what came naturally to me, the exact opposite of what she had said, and that was what turned out to be right.

"I never told Rudi, but the funny thing was, I don't remember ever having any green gloves."

## Tragödie der Liebe (Tragedy of Love, 1923)

Musette (Erika Glässner), a chambermaid, is discovered by her lover, Ombrade (Emil Jannings), making love with the butler. The professional wrestler kills the man and then accepts Musette's excuse that he was taking advantage of her.

When Ombrade is arrested, the trial becomes a sensation. Everyone wants to attend, including the judge's mistress, Lucy (Marlene Dietrich). The judge (Kurt Vespermann) refuses her request, but Lucy attends anyway, viewing the proceedings from the spectators' gallery through opera glasses.

The trial seems to be going in Ombrade's favor until Musette breaks down and reveals everything. Ombrade is found guilty and guillotined.

With her striking appearance in *Tragödie der Liebe*, Marlene became a presence, if a small one, on the German screen, and thus, in world cinema. Any film starring Emil Jannings produced and directed by Joe May was certain to be noticed.

Some idea of the film's ambitious scope can be surmised from its length. *Tragödie der Liebe* was shot in four parts that were released at two different dates. Parts one and two were released in March 1923, and parts three and four that May.

Marlene was never impressed with Jannings. "He was a dreadful ham," she said, "but it was more appropriate in the silents than later, when he got to talk on the screen. He overdid that, too."

WILHELM DIETERLE WAS A well-known leading man in the German cinema, but he wanted to direct his own films. He finally got the backing he was looking for to launch his directorial debut, with the help of some friends from the Reinhardt theater. A script was fashioned from a folktale written down by Leo Tolstoy.

### *Der Mensch am Wege (The Man by the Wayside,* 1923)

Schuster (Alexander Granach), regarded as the village idiot, offers a lost, wandering stranger (Wilhelm Dieterle) food and shelter for the night. The stranger leaves without thanking him.

Schuster's luck changes. He is no longer an object of ridicule. Problems in his life that seemed insurmountable are suddenly solved. His hopeless infatuation with a beautiful peasant girl (Marlene Dietrich) becomes a romance.

The stranger was a lost guardian angel looking for a soul worth protecting. Schuster's generosity helped him to find that soul.

The film went unnoticed, which surprised nobody but which did not disappoint Dieterle. He had carried through a film project of his own, and it had been distributed. That was all the satisfaction he expected. For Marlene, it was another film credit with hopes for more.

Dieterle, changing his first name to William, went to Hollywood in the early 1930s, where he had a distinguished thirty-five-year directorial career. Among his many films were *A Midsummer Night's Dream, The Hunchback of Notre Dame, The Devil and Daniel Webster,* and *Portrait of Jennie.* He directed Marlene once again in *Kismet* (1944).

MARLENE'S PERFORMANCES AT MAX Reinhardt's intimate Kammerspiele Theater in plays by Maugham, Molière, Bjørnson, and Wedekind began to receive favorable critical mention, and it appeared she was on her way to a successful Berlin stage career. She continued, however, to accept whatever film jobs came along, no matter how small. In 1924 she had a role in a film called *Der Sprung ins Leben*.

### Der Sprung ins Leben (The Leap into Life, 1924)

A wealthy young intellectual (Paul Heidemann) offers to transform a female acrobat (Xenia Desni) into a lady so he can marry her. She makes good progress but cannot get her ex-lover, a high-wire artist (Walter Rilla), out of her mind. Realizing that her place is on the high-wires with him, she leaves the rich young man.

While they are performing, the intellectual rushes onto the ring and implores her to return to him. After a tense moment, she bids him farewell forever.

The rejected lover unhappily returns to his former girlfriend (Marlene Dietrich).

ON MAY 17, 1923, Marlene and Rudolf Sieber were married. She signed her name Marie Magdalene Dietrich. Marlene was just twenty-one years old. She was Lutheran and he, Catholic.

"I was totally in love," Marlene told me. "Every girl should have that experience—once. Then you know what it is, what it feels like, the real thing. You can never be fooled once you have known true romance, true passion, true love!

"When I was a girl, I dreamed of lasting love, romance, and passion in my marriage. When I married Rudi, it was wonderful. I'm glad we had that joy.

"We might not have known where our next job was coming from, but that was part of a performer's life. Even in the best of times, we knew it would always be that way, but we were committed to working at what we loved. If we had been rich, we would have worked for free, but we weren't rich. And like everyone in Germany, we found ourselves getting poorer by the minute.

"Rudi was the love of my life, my soul mate. Until that moment, it was the happiest day of my life. Even now, looking back, I have had few days that were that happy. One not long after was when I held my perfect baby, our little miracle.

"Mutual sexual attraction was an important part of what Rudi and I had together. We had it until I found out that I was having a baby. I decided I should give up sex until after the baby was born. I was afraid that we might do some damage. Rudi accepted that."

On December 13, 1924, Marie Elizabeth Sieber was born. Marlene was just two weeks short of turning twenty-three. She called the baby Heidede. Later she would change her name, as she had changed her own name, to Maria.

"It had been instilled in me—largely indirectly, but to some extent directly—that a home isn't a home without children and that a woman's role is to complete the home with children," Marlene said. "Rudi was thrilled when we learned I was having a child.

"I wanted a girl. I asked Rudi what he wanted. I thought he would say a boy. Men all do seem to want a son. But Rudi was Rudi. He said he wanted whatever I wanted. And it was true. It was the way he was. He wanted my happiness more than he wanted his own. But what was so wonderful was almost always we wanted the same thing. Rudi was never disappointed that she was a girl.

"He was so worried about me. Poor Rudi. I think he would have had the baby for me if he could have.

"When he heard me scream during childbirth, I think that was when, if not consciously, at least unconsciously, he felt that one child would make a very tidy family.

"Her birth was so difficult for me that it was recommended I take several months at home to recuperate. I was not ready to think about sex. Then, after months, I knew I didn't want another baby.

"When my baby was born, I was so dedicated to motherhood that it was an all-consuming passion. There were people who said I was obsessed. I didn't hear those comments. I was too busy nursing my baby.

"During Maria's infancy, I was the complete mother, cradle-obsessed. I had put everything I had into Maria. I nursed her for eight or nine months, and I would have gone on for at least a year if my breasts had cooperated. They ran out of milk, so then I couldn't starve my baby.

"My baby was working so hard and getting so little nourishment for her efforts that I worried she would be emotionally damaged by the frustration. My little girl loved to eat. She was a big, healthy baby. I couldn't go on starving her, so I had to turn to commercial meals. I didn't know if she would accept it. I knew she would be disappointed not to have her regular feast, but I was wrong. She adjusted immediately to the bottle and seemed to enjoy the variety and new taste treats, but I had a more difficult time letting go of my little girl. I felt we could never get that close again.

"I was told the experience would spoil my breasts. They were right, but it was worth it.

"I cannot put into words what being a mother meant to me. My career hadn't really taken off, and it didn't require the investment of time and energy that it would later require. I was desperate not to miss anything. Her first smile. The first time she turned over. How happy she was with her father was thrilling for me. From the first, she knew *he* was her father.

"I had only the one child, but my baby consumed my feelings in a way I could never have imagined until I first held her in my arms.

"From the first moment, without hesitation, I would have given my life for her. And that was strange for me, because I had always thought of myself as a selfish person, a very selfish person. It had always been my belief that you have to love yourself before you can love anyone else.

"I was sometimes asked by interviewers what feature of mine I didn't like. I answered them, 'I like everything about me.'

"'Oh, there must be *something*,' they would say. 'Everyone has something they don't like about themselves.'

"'All right,' I said. 'You got it out of me. My legs!'

"They always looked at me for a moment in shock, and then they laughed. Someone would say, 'You're kidding.' And I said, 'Yes, I am.' Foolish questions deserve foolish answers. Everyone knew my legs are perfect.

"But I am going to tell you about my one defect. Since they first developed, I always had beautiful breasts. Perfect. They weren't big, but they were perfect. They were pale porcelain with light pink. My mother never mentioned them. My mother would have considered it inappropriately familiar for her to say anything. My grandmother thought they were lovely. They pointed up, and they were sensitive and responsive, as I grew up, to the right touch by the right man. My husband, Rudi, was enthralled by my beautiful breasts.

"Then, after I nursed my precious baby, both breasts pointed permanently down.

"But I was never sorry. I believe that mother's milk is the best diet for a baby, and Maria always had good health, and I think it produces a marvelous bonding between mother and baby."


G. W. PABST'S *Die freudlose Gasse* (*Joyless Street*, 1925) is a post–World War I Viennese predecessor of *EastEnders*, the long-running BBC television series. The people of a big-city neighborhood live out the joys and hardships of their daily lives in the context of postwar Vienna. Many international stars of the time were in the cast, including Greta Garbo, Asta Nielsen, and Werner Krauss. Marlene's brief uncredited appearance was cut from the film, but she appears in publicity stills of a breadline and a crowd.

### Die freudlose Gasse (Joyless Street, 1925)

In postwar Vienna, housewives barter sex for food and shop girls are forced into prostitution.

Greta Rumfort (Greta Garbo), takes in lodgers to survive, but when she falls in love with an American (Einar Hanson), her father takes away her livelihood. Greta is saved from prostitution by the American.

In other stories, a young banking official (Henry Stuart) is cleared of a murder he didn't commit, while a butcher (Werner Krauss), who traded meat for sex, is murdered, and his shop is raided by hungry housewives.

*Manon Lescaut* was Marlene's first substantial role in a major motion picture, though she dismissed it as "pure rubbish," adding, "and I was lucky to get the work." The film was critically acclaimed and successful with an international audience. This adaptation of the famous opera was Marlene's first appearance on film in America.

### Manon Lescaut (1926)

Manon Lescaut (Lya de Putti) flees a convent with young Chevalier des Grieux (Vladmir Gajdarov), who delays entering the priesthood to live with her in Paris.

While des Grieux is away trying to raise money, the Marquis de Bli (Fritz Greiner) saves Manon from debtors' prison. Leaving de Bli, Manon is arrested on false charges filed by her angry wealthy benefactor.

De Bli's confidante, Micheline (Marlene Dietrich), delivers a letter to des Grieux implying Manon's unfaithfulness. Escaping, Manon convinces des Grieux of her love.

He decides the only way to curb her extravagant nature is to marry her. While des Grieux looks for a priest, de Bli has Manon jailed again.

Manon escapes but is recaptured and deported. Des Grieux arrives at the port too late to save her.

*Eine Dubarry von Heute* was the first of two silent films Marlene made for director Alexander Korda. In it, she plays a character who is billed simply as a "coquette." During the 1920s, this was a popular term for describing a frivolous young woman. The film was released in America as *A Modern Dubarry*, and offered U.S. audiences their second view of Marlene, billed as "Marlaine" Dietrich.

### Eine Dubarry von heute (A Modern Dubarry, 1926)

With the help of sympathetic male admirers, Toinette (Maria Corda) rises from shopgirl to model in a stylish dress salon. When she borrows a dress that is being altered, it is recognized in a nightclub by its owner (Marlene Dietrich), who makes such a public fuss, loudly threatening never to patronize the dress salon and to tell all her friends about what has transpired, that Toinette loses her job.

Toinette becomes a successful entertainer and the lover of Sandro (Jean Bradin), the young king of a small country. When he is overthrown, the couple escapes aboard the yacht of an American banker (Friedrich Kayssler) who had inadvertently financed the revolution.

Marlene appears in *Madame wünscht keine Kinder* (*Madame Wishes No Children*) only briefly, as an *edel-comparse*, or "noble extra," in formal party scenes. One of her fellow background extras was British actor John Loder, who, in Hollywood, would become Hedy Lamarr's third husband.

The film is based on a Belgian novel that later became a play, and was remade as a sound film in 1933 with a Billy Wilder script. The theme of the sexual equality of men and women closely followed that of political equality.

### Madame wünscht keine Kinder (1926)

Playboy Paul Le Barroy (Harry Liedke), weds Elyane Parizot (Maria Corda) because he is ready for children, and his mistress, Louise Bonvin (Maria Paudler), is not. After the honeymoon, Elyane informs Paul that she doesn't want children, either. "Children are a luxury of the poor," she says.

When Paul leaves her, Elyane blames Louise and confronts the ex-mistress with a gun. Louise advises Elyane to have the children Paul wants. Then she will have everything *she* wants, too. Soon, Paul and Elyane are happily back together again, and she is pregnant.

Having had three scenes as an important minor character in her previous Korda film, Marlene was disappointed at being only an *edel-comparse* in this one. At this point in her career, however, Marlene had less ambition than Rudi. She was happier at home caring for her child, though later, with her growing success, Rudi took on the responsibility so Marlene might devote herself to pursuing her career.

Marlene may or may not have worked as a "dance extra" when Rudi was assigned as a production assistant to Korda, on *Der Tänzer meiner Frau* (*My Wife's Dance Partner*, 1926). As a production assistant, Rudi made certain that his wife was placed in positions of prominence in order to attract attention to her highly individual beauty. He was convinced that she had a wonderful career ahead of her.

It was on the set of this film that Rudi met a Russian chorus girl named Tamara Matul. Her real name was Tamara Nikolaeyevna, and she was a young Russian dancer. She later became his longtime mistress, with Marlene's approval.

"I didn't select Tamara for Rudi," Marlene said. "He selected her. But if I hadn't liked her, Rudi never would have chosen her as a companion. They would have had a few dates, nothing more. And Maria liked her, too. Tamara cared about our little Heidede even before she became Maria.

"I always knew I was number one in Rudi's heart. But I understood he needed a sexual companion who was on the same continent.

"It was convenient that Tamara wore the same size dress I did, everything the same size. She was just a little smaller and thinner. I thought she should have had my things taken in, but she left them loose. Rudi never had to buy her anything. Sometimes I gave her a dress I had never even worn, but never one I was sentimental about."

In *Kopf hoch, Charly!* Marlene plays a French coquette, a minor character. It was her first for Ellen Richter Films, an independent company formed by the actress with her director-writer husband, Willi Wolff, to produce pictures starring her. The film's theme of sophisticated infidelity was popular in 1920s Berlin.

### *Kopf hoch, Charly!* (Head High, Charly, 1927)

After Charlotte Ditmar (Ellen Richter) ends an affair with steamship owner John Jacob Bunjes (Michael Bohnen), her husband leaves her, and Charlotte is rescued from a life of despair and dissipation by Bunjes.

The star of Marlene's next film, *Der Juxbaron* (*The Phony Baron*), Reinhold Schünzel, later became a preeminent writer-director of the German cinema. His *Amphitryon* and *Viktor und Viktoria* are considered classic German films.

Schünzel was said to have been Hitler's favorite director until Hitler found out he was a quarter-Jewish. In 1937, Schünzel migrated to Hollywood, where he found occasional work as a director but was mainly a character actor. In the 1947 *Golden Earrings*, Marlene was the star and Schunzel (without his umlaut) a supporting player.

### Der Juxbaron (*The Phony Baron*, 1927)

A socially ambitious mother (Julia Serda), learning that a baron is visiting her daughter (Colette Brettel) and son-in-law (Teddy Bill), hopes her youngest daughter, Sophie (Marlene Dietrich), can meet and, hopefully, marry the nobleman.

The baron unexpectedly departs and the couple hires a street musician (Reinhold Schünzel) to replace him for the visiting family. The phony baron is exposed, however, after he proposes to Sophie.

Following his departure, they learn that he is a real baron who gave up a life of privilege to be a carefree strolling player.

Harry Piel, who directed and starred in Marlene's next film, *Sein grösster Bluff*, was considered a combination of Douglas Fairbanks and Harold Lloyd, specializing in physical comedy and melodramatic farce. Marlene plays an ex-prostitute who is trying to improve her status in society by becoming a jewel thief.

### *Sein grösster Bluff (His Biggest Bluff, 1927)*

Jewel thief Yvette (Marlene Dietrich) steals a valuable gem from a shop in Paris. Since the piece had already been sold to the Maharaja of Jahore (Kurt Gerron), Henry Devall (Harry Piel), the shop's manager, enlists the aid of his smarter twin brother, Harry (Harry Piel), to recover the gem before the shop's owner, Madame Andersson (Toni Tetzlaff), discovers the theft.

The trail of the stolen merchandise leads them to Nice where, after some dangerous encounters with criminal gangs and a false maharaja, they recover the jewelry and Harry falls in love with Madame Andersson's daughter, Tilly (Lotte Lorring). Yvette proclaims her intention to be honest.

At one of Betty Stern's Sunday salons, Marlene met Willi Forst. Stern was the wife of a wealthy man, and she loved being with show business people. Rudi knew her, and when he was invited, he brought Marlene. Forst, a famous Viennese actor, a star of German-language films, was among the other guests.

Forst was making pictures in Austria for Sascha-Filmindustrie, owned by an eccentric Hungarian millionaire nobleman Count Alexander Joseph Kolowrat-Krakowsky. Sascha was Austria's most important production company. It had just made the phenomenally successful *Sodom und Gomorrah*, directed by Mihály Kertész, who in Hollywood would become Michael Curtiz, the director of *Casablanca*. Forst was certain Kolowrat would love Marlene, who would soon be appearing on stage in Vienna in a revue called *Three's Company*.

Kolowrat saw the show and, influenced by Forst's suggestion and enthusiasm, approved her for the part of a flapper in the upcoming *Wenn ein Weib den Weg verliert (When a Woman Loses Her Way)*. But director Gustav Ucicki did not like Marlene. Since the part was small and undemanding, though essential to the plot, the director was overruled by Forst, backed up by Kolowrat. Marlene had left Rudi and Heidede to wait for him in Berlin, and it was rumored that she and Forst were having an affair.

The movie was based on *Die Liebesbörse* (The Love Market), a play by Felix Fischer. The film's working title was considered too long and unsuitable for international distribution, so it was shortened to *Café Electric*.

### Café Electric (1927)

Erni (Marlene Dietrich), daughter of wealthy builder Göttlinger (Fritz Alberti), loves Fredl (Willi Forst), a criminal, but Fredl prefers Hansi (Nina Vanna), a prostitute at the Café Electric. Max (Igo Sym), a Göttlinger architect, loves Erni until he discovers her relationship with Fredl.

Recuperating at the Café Electric, Max falls in love with Hansi. Göttlinger also likes Hansi, so Max is fired.

Max, now living with a reformed Hansi, leaves her when he suspects she has returned to prostitution.

At the Café Electric, Fredl stabs her. Max, now a reporter, covers the story. Since Hansi is innocent, they reunite.

Count Kolowrat died just as the picture was being released. He had become quite enthusiastic about Marlene's work. Perhaps in homage to him, Marlene's character in von Sternberg's 1931 *Dishonored* is named Widow Kolverer.

Igo Sym, who appeared in *Café Electric*, taught Marlene to play the musical saw. This skill came naturally to her since the saw was played with a violin bow. She later used the skill to entertain American servicemen during World War II.

While *Café Electric* was shooting, Forst suggested to Marlene that she try out for the Viennese production of the New York and London success *Broadway*, by Philip Dunning and George Abbott. It would be the perfect role for someone with Marlene's legs. She played Ruby, one of the six featured chorus girls.

I spoke with George Abbott just before his 100th birthday at his Monticello, New York, home. When our conversation got around to *Broadway*, I mentioned that Marlene Dietrich had played one of the chorus girls in a European production of the play.

He smiled and said, "It figures. Good choice." Abbott was famous for his directness and simplicity. When I asked him the greatest change in the theater during his long lifetime, he answered, "Electricity."

Following good reviews for *Broadway*, Marlene stayed on in Vienna for another play, this time, *The School of Uznach; or the New Objectivity*, by Carl Sternheim. The performances of the play alternated at the theater with the successful Broadway play *Abie's Irish Rose*, directed by the young Otto Preminger, whom Marlene came to know. They always wished they could make a picture together, but never did. "She's very hard to cast, you know," he told me. "She's such a strong personality, you cannot just stick her into a picture. The picture has to be built around her."

Preminger spoke about her with me in the backyard of his Manhattan townhouse, where he kept his large Henry Moore statue of a woman. It was a disappointment to him not to have been able to direct or produce a Marlene Dietrich film. "Or it could even have been something for the stage," he said.

"You cannot imagine how the young, *really* young, Marlene looked and was. *No* man could have resisted *her*. Most would have been too intimidated to try to know her. I wasn't one of those. I don't know which I missed most, working with her professionally or knowing her intimately. At that moment, I would have liked both.

"She was a free spirit which some women, jealous, interpreted as loose. She was never loose. She always knew just what she wanted to do and what she was going to do. I recognized in her a tremendous discipline. She was just a girl, but she had that extraordinary sense of strength of will. I recognized it because I was brought up to always be conscious of duty and to prepare myself for a respectable and successful career, preferably in jurisprudence, the field in which my father was a leader.

"I tried everything, but I wasn't successful in persuading her to stay in Vienna. Then I had the brilliant idea of taking her home to my family at Christmas holiday there in Vienna in 1927. I had a wonderful family, very impressive, and we lived beautifully. The food and festivities for the holiday were very special. We lived very happily, thinking it would always be that way, not knowing what our being Jewish was going to mean in just a short time. Marlene was very impressed by my family. They liked her, too. It was all wonderful, but then she went back to Berlin, to her husband and her little girl, and then on to Hollywood. It had all been written before I met her."


IN BERLIN, MARLENE CONTINUED playing Ruby in the run of *Broadway* there, though she said she would have preferred to play the ingenue, Billie. While training for the part, she fractured her arm, but went on without reporting the injury.

One of the assistant directors of the Berlin production was a young playwright named Felix Joachimssohn. He and Marlene became good friends, and they talked about their hopes and dreams. In Hollywood, as Felix Jackson, he would be reunited with Marlene when she played in *Destry Rides Again*, which he co-wrote. He married Deanna Durbin, and when her career ended, they went to live in Paris.

In 1928, Marlene played the title character in *Prinzessin Olala*.

### Prinzessin Olala (*Princess O-la-la* or *The Art of Love,* 1928)

In a mix-up of identities, Prince Boris (Walter Rilla), falls in love with a woman he believes to be Princess O-la-la (Marlene Dietrich), an infamous teacher of the art of seduction, only to discover at the altar, after a series of mishaps, that she is really his intended bride-to-be, the Princess Xenia (Carmen Boni).

Marlene summed up the film as "more foolishness."

Fred Zinnemann, who would later direct such famous films as *High Noon, From Here to Eternity, The Nun's Story,* and *The Day of the Jackal,* was the assistant cameraman on the film, and he clearly remembered Marlene. When I spoke with him in London many years later, he began by saying she was "a good-times girl."

"That's how I remember her, but please understand. I mean that in the best possible way. She was fun and not tense. She made everything a good time. There was nothing stiff or frozen about her. The crew loved her. Everyone loved her. She was beautiful when you met her, but she became more beautiful as she smiled at you. There was nothing snobbish about her. It was obvious she had greater rapport with men than with women. She told some off-color jokes, always to men, not women.

"She was very relaxed and easy, and that put everyone on the set at their ease. The crew would have done anything they could for her. I'm sure many of them dreamed about her at night.

"At the time, I remember she was always nice with me, but I didn't get to know her very well.

"She was very intelligent, but she didn't flaunt her intelligence. In fact, I think she tried a bit to hide it. She came from a time, especially in the German-speaking world, when mothers encouraged daughters to hide their intelligence because a little intelligence could go a long way, and too much could turn off a suitor.

"Marlene was a master of lighting, a mistress of lighting. She was always attuned to it. She noticed and studied it with every film she was in, even from the days when she only had small parts. She learned what to do, but more importantly, she learned what *not* to do.

"She studied her own face and combined makeup with the right lighting. The greatest directors would listen to her lighting ideas. Some of the great cinematographers paid tribute to her feeling for light. I add my voice. It was her feeling for it that astounded me. There is only so much you can learn. What she had was within her. She had the eye."

### *Ich küsse Ihre Hand, Madame* (*I Kiss Your Hand, Madame*, 1929)

Recently divorced, Laurence Gerard (Marlene Dietrich) is currently being wooed by Count Leisky (Harry Liedtke), a Russian nobleman who regularly takes her dining at the Café Grillon. When she finds out he is an impostor and really the headwaiter of the Café Grillon, she is at first furious, and then sorry when she causes him to be fired. It turns out that he really *is* a Russian nobleman, and she has fallen in love with him. The couple is reunited in a frenetic elevator chase.

*I Kiss Your Hand, Madame* had a soundtrack and some synchronized sound sequences, chiefly of songs. Also in 1929, director Kurt Bernhardt chose Marlene to be "the woman one longs for," based on her performance on stage as Hypatia in George Bernard Shaw's *Misalliance*.

### *Die Frau, nach der man sich sehnt* (*The Woman One Longs For*, 1929)

To save his family's business, Henry Leblanc (Uno Henning) marries wealthy Angela Poitrier (Edith Edwards). During their honeymoon, he meets Stascha (Marlene Dietrich), "the woman one longs for," who is with Dr. Karoff (Fritz Kortner).

Henry and Stascha plan to run off together, but Karoff threatens to reveal her involvement in her husband's murder if she leaves him.

In a fight, Karoff knocks Henry out. As the police arrive, Stascha is shot by Karoff. She dies in Henry's arms, lamenting that she has lost love three times: her husband's, Karoff's, and now, Henry's.

Henry returns to his bride, who forgives him.

Though a silent feature, *The Woman One Longs For* was released in the United States in 1931 with synchronized music and soundtrack. Its American title, *Three Loves*, referred to Marlene's last words in the film. Director Kurt Bernhardt later relocated in Hollywood as Curtis Bernhardt.

Marlene's next picture, *Das Schiff der verlorenen Menschen* (The Ship of Lost Men) was directed by Maurice Tourneur, a French director who specialized in films that emphasized character, mood, and suspense. His son, Jacques, the assistant director, took this style to Hollywood, where he directed such classics as *Cat People, I Walked with a Zombie*, and *Out of the Past*.

### Das Schiff der verlorenen Menschen (The Ship of Lost Men, 1929)

American aviatrix Miss Ethel (Marlene Dietrich) crashes while trying to break the solo speed record across the Atlantic. She is picked up by a ship carrying dangerous fugitives, all male. The captain (Fritz Kortner) entrusts her to sympathetic young Dr. Cheyne (Robin Irvine).

With the help of the cook, Grischa (Vladimir Sokoloff),

Cheyne is able to hold off the men until a mutiny is threatened. Then another ship, summoned by an SOS sent out by Grischa, arrives in time to save Miss Ethel.

At the same time Marlene was making her next film, *Gefahren der Brautzeit* (*Dangers of the Engagement Period*), she was appearing onstage in the musical comedy *Zwei Krawatten* (*Two Neckties*), with Hans Albers, the matinee idol of that era. In this musical comedy, she played an American girl and spoke a few lines in English. Hollywood director Josef von Sternberg saw the show and was impressed not only by the way she looked and by her performance, but by her ability to speak English. He was casting for *Der blaue Engel* (*The Blue Angel*) and hoped to find actors who could speak English for the American version of the film.

Marlene was now not only a popular stage and screen personality, but also a recording star. Her recordings of the songs "Peter" and "Jonny" were hits.

What was important to her and Rudi was that they were happy and working. Marlene's last German film before *The Blue Angel* provided the critics who wanted her to give up screen for stage with proof that she should stop making films. Looking back a half-century later, Marlene agreed about the quality of "my long-forgotten films which even I have forgotten." Marlene said what she enjoyed most about *Gefahren der Brautzeit* was working with Willi Forst, "a dear friend."

### *Gefahren der Brautzeit* (*Dangers of the Engagement Period*, 1929)

Baron van Geldern (Willi Forst), a Dutch Don Juan, is saved from the homicidal intentions of a jealous husband by an American (Ernst Stahl-Nachbaur), and they become best friends. The baron boasts of recently seducing a beautiful, innocent young woman. The American recognizes her as his fiancée, Evelyne (Marlene Dietrich).

In a rage, the American shoots the baron, then is sorry. The baron assures him that he is only slightly wounded and that it was not Evelyne he seduced. After the American has left, the baron writes a suicide note and dies.

It was generally assumed that the decision had already been made concerning who was going to play Lola Lola in *The Blue Angel*. Lucie Mannheim was not only a popular and highly regarded actress of the time, but, equally important, she was a friend and favorite performer of Emil Jannings, the star of the film. The famous actor made it clear that she was *his* choice, and that he would frown on anyone else. Jannings had just won an Oscar in a Hollywood film and was an international star.

UFA producer Erich Pommer conceded that Dietrich was not without promise, but he felt she was too plump. He didn't say this to Marlene but to von Sternberg, who had already declared that he wouldn't direct the film if the female lead was anyone else. He did, however, pass on to Marlene the words about her weight, and she immediately began a program of exercise and a starvation diet. She had never thought her weight a problem until von Sternberg explained to her that the camera added pounds.

"When I was a girl," Marlene told me, "we spent more than a year almost starving to death. Why do I say 'almost'? We were starving. It was during World War I. What would we have done without potatoes? I found out. I had a tendency to plumpness, but it was not a problem, except for a motion picture actress.

"I remember when Maria told me she was teased by other girls and ignored by boys because of her figure, or more correctly because she didn't have a figure. I wanted to be a perfect mother, but I overfed my darling daughter. She liked to eat, and I couldn't say no to her. Worse. I found treats to give her. The food seemed to make her happy, and I loved to see her happy. I think back now, and maybe I was guilty of eating vicariously, especially desserts, as I had to be careful about my figure.

"She said I had no idea how she felt, because I was so thin.

"Well, I hadn't always been *so* thin. Sometimes as a girl I was plump, but I didn't know it. When I was a child, it was fashionable to be a little plump. It meant your family cared about you and you were well taken care of, and that your family was prosperous enough to do so. Mama, my mother, was a little plump. When I made my first movies, I was plump by the standards that were changing. The camera preferred slimmer women.

"Jo let me know I was too plump. He made himself quite clear about it, but he really only had to say it once.

"Maria didn't seem plump to me. I thought she was perfect. And if she was a little plump, I knew she would outgrow it, the way children do. I had no idea her weight made her deeply unhappy because she didn't tell me that until many years later. If I had known, I could have helped her to diet because I certainly knew all about dieting, every kind of diet. I didn't like to give up anything, so I cut down on amounts and tried to limit myself to only one real meal a day. That works for me, and I never feel deprived, but it might not work for everyone. After a while, my metabolism seemed to readjust. Perhaps my appetite decreased, and I never had any problem keeping my figure. I think the most important reason was my desire to keep my career on track.

"Looking back, it may have been hard on Maria, because she was being compared to me. I think she looked more like her father, who was a very handsome man.

"I wanted to be a perfect mother, but there is that one guilt I have as a mother."

•　　•　　•

"PABST WANTED TO GET rights to *The Blue Angel* to star Louise Brooks as Lola Lola," Brooks's friend John Springer told me, referring to the German director G. W. Pabst. "It would have changed my life," Brooks had told Springer.

Lucie Mannheim, the leading candidate for the part, appeared for her screen test, perfectly prepared, trying to conceal her displeasure that an actress as well known as she had been asked to test. Mannheim had immediately recognized what a great part it was, and she had told friends it was a part she was determined to play and that it was hers, or virtually hers, which Jannings had led her to believe.

She arrived with another friend as her accompanist, Friedrich Holländer, a greatly respected star of the German musical theater world. It was a dazzlingly impressive entrance for Mannheim. Perhaps it was *too* overpowering, showing that Mannheim cared *too* much, something that Lola Lola never did. Marlene's nonchalance better suited the character, and von Sternberg also liked her lack of experience and her ability to take direction perfectly, *his* direction.

What no one knew, except von Sternberg, was that he had seen a young actress who absolutely fascinated him. She did not look the way he wanted her to look, nor did she have the apparent talent he desired, but she did have something. After he saw her, he couldn't get her out of his mind, and that was exactly the quality he wanted in Lola Lola. That could not be taught to an actress; it was a natural attribute, a gift. Von Sternberg was searching for an actress who could inspire obsession, and he was obsessed—by Marlene.

Mannheim's was to have been the final screen test, but von Sternberg added one more.

Marlene arrived without having prepared any special songs, and without the appropriate accoutrements of Lola Lola—the dress, makeup, the flashy, cheap jewelry—having brought only herself, slightly overweight. That was enough for von Sternberg. Marlene remembered his eyes on her legs. She hoped her legs were going to win the part, but she wasn't planning to be heartbroken if she didn't get it. She mistakenly thought the role was going to be only a small one.

"I had no idea what a great part it was," she told me almost half a century later, "or what a difference Lola Lola would make in my life, or, for that matter, what a difference Josef von Sternberg would make in my life.

"I can't say I took my screen test for *The Blue Angel* very seriously. I didn't think I would get the part. I wasn't even sure I wanted the part.

"I'd been out very late the night before, and I'd had scarcely any sleep. I never needed much sleep. Four hours was sufficient. Five hours was better. Too little sleep, not on a prolonged basis, but an occasional sleepless night, always had an exhilarating effect on me. It got my adrenaline going especially if I engaged in physical activity—dancing, for instance. Too much sleep has always made me feel groggy. I was quite invigorated when I arrived for my *Blue Angel* screen test.

"I wasn't nervous at all and didn't feel any pressure, so maybe it was better. I was totally open to being directed because I didn't know what to do. Later, Jo told me that was what he wanted—pliant, ready to be shaped by his direction. I assumed the director knew what he was doing. He wasn't at all hesitant. He wasn't the least bit nervous. He was all determination, and I felt myself putty in his hands. He did not want someone with a preconception of the part. I even accepted without a word of protest his call for a curling iron. He called for the curling iron *and* a piano player, in that order.

"Actually, that curling iron struck fear into my heart. There was nothing I despised more. I didn't like the effect it created, and I didn't think that frizzy look suited me. Worse yet, I've always had baby-fine, delicate hair, and I'd been warned that a curling iron could make my hair fall out. If I didn't believe *all* of it would fall out, I believed *some* of it would, and I couldn't afford to lose a single hair. But I thought one time couldn't do *too* much damage.

"Well, it turned out my hair was stronger than I thought."

Lucie Mannheim was to achieve film immortality in a smaller, but still memorable, part. She is forever Annabella Smith, the spy who involves Robert Donat in a spy ring when she dies in his apartment at the beginning of *The 39 Steps*. As a refugee in England, married to actor Marius Goring, Mannheim enjoyed a respectable career on stage and screen.

### Der blaue Engel (The Blue Angel, 1929–30)

Professor Immanuel Rath (Emil Jannings), a middle-aged bachelor, visits the Blue Angel cabaret. He suspects some of the boys in his high school class are frequenting that disreputable place, and he wants to discipline them. Instead, he is helplessly drawn to the featured performer, Lola Lola (Marlene Dietrich). He visits her dressing room afterward and in no time he is in bed with her.

When his students find out that their puritanical professor is frequenting the Blue Angel, they make it impossible for him to stay at the high school, and he loses his job. Thinking he has money, Lola offers him consolation, and they are soon married.

When the professor's money runs out, he has to sell provocative pictures of his wife and work in the traveling troupe as a clown to make a living. It is degrading for a man like him, and his mind is affected. Contributing to his downfall is his wife's open contempt for him and her relationship with another member of the troupe (Hans Albers).

When the troupe returns to the Blue Angel, the professor

wanders in a daze back to his high school, where, sitting in a classroom, he dies.

"Jo knew a great deal and had wonderful intuition about so much," Marlene said, "but he had a very poor crystal ball about the future of Germany. There weren't many at that time, in 1929, who had a clear crystal ball. We didn't really know the future. Rudi's and my interest was theater and films, and we weren't especially political, although we had ideas. The Nazis knew what they were working for, but no one I knew believed that they would take over.

"Jo was so thrilled to be working in Germany. He hadn't been entirely pleased by his experiences in Hollywood, and he was over the moon about the idea of filming in Germany. He didn't believe he was respected in Hollywood, and he wasn't going to respect people who didn't respect him. He hoped he would have a more brilliant future working with UFA in Germany. He didn't guess that if he'd stayed in Germany, he wouldn't have had a future in film. He wouldn't have had a future at all.

"When the Nazis took over, they immediately said, 'No Jews at UFA,' and then they said, 'No Jews.' Unless Jo, who was Jewish, had been able to escape, they would have killed him. But as we were working on our film, we weren't speculating on life and death, only on our professional life and death. You never know at the time things are happening what will truly be important in your life."

AT THE BEGINNING OF the sound era, it was assumed that films could be made simultaneously in more than one language, to keep at least a part of the international audience that silent films had always had. Garbo's first talkie, *Anna Christie*, was shot in both English and German versions, and so was Alfred Hitchcock's first complete sound film, *Murder*. In both instances, however, different casts were used so audiences wouldn't have trouble understanding foreign accents. With *The Blue Angel*, however, the original German cast was used in the English-language version. Marlene was confident her accent in English would be acceptable.

"I had studied English as a child in Berlin," she told me, "but what I noticed when I went to America, in New York and then in California, was contractions. My governesses who were supposed to teach me English didn't bother about contractions. One was German and one was French, and one was British. Well, perhaps the French one and the German one didn't understand about contractions themselves. It wasn't a very good idea to have a German teacher teaching me English who had a heavy German accent. At the time, I was a little girl and didn't understand about those things, but when I needed to speak English, I thought back, and I believe a big part of the problem was I was carefully taught to mimic the English of the person who had, I think, what was the strongest German accent in English in all of Germany.

"When I heard I would be doing the English version of *The Blue Angel*, I rationed my speaking of English so that I could surprise everyone. I did surprise them.

"Suddenly, I burst into English, very fluent. I had practiced. No one paid any attention. They weren't impressed. I found out later I did have an accent, and they just thought I was speaking German.

"Jo mentioned to me I needed to do something about my German accent. Too heavy. He needn't have said anything. I was on my way before he finished speaking to find a coach.

"I've always envied my little girl, who began school in Berlin, then went to America, and then to a Swiss school for French, and she never spoke any language with an accent. In English, she sounded just like an American should."

After *The Blue Angel* and von Sternberg, Marlene was always exceedingly conscious of light. She believed top lighting made all the difference in whether she would appear beautiful or not on the screen. Though she was always involved in her part, she was also conscious of von Sternberg and the crew and the lights.

There was one touch he taught her that seemed simple, but which she never forgot. She always had a mirror, large if possible, but a small one could serve, so that she could check her makeup under the lights.

*The Blue Angel* WAS a runaway hit in Europe in its original German-language version, but when it opened in America in the English version it was unnoticed. For one thing, it was very difficult for American audiences to understand the German actors' accents, especially on the primitive theater sound systems.

Von Sternberg had already convinced B. P. Schulberg, the production chief at Paramount, that he had found the next Garbo. The American studio went ahead with its plans to produce *Morocco*, the director's next picture with Dietrich. Only after *Morocco* became a big success and Marlene Dietrich had virtually become a household name was the German *Blue Angel* with subtitles released in the United States to critical and popular acclaim.

# II. *Hollywood*

*J*o insisted I go to Hollywood," Marlene told me. "He didn't say I owed it to him. He wouldn't do that, but I felt I did, and I felt Jo felt I did. I did not want to let him down, but I had two reasons for not going. The first was some self-doubts which I could never admit to, that I wouldn't be able to do the part and succeed in Hollywood. The word Hollywood was awe-inspiring. The idea of starring in a Hollywood film made me tremble inside, not outside.

"I told Rudi my other reason, that I would rather not leave Maria until she was a little older. He said, 'When she is a little older, you will also be a little older.' I understood.

"I thought I would be incredibly happy if I became famous. I wanted to show my success to my friends. I believed it would make my mother happy. I wanted to show my enemies. I wanted the people who didn't know I existed to know I very much existed. I wanted to show myself. Then, it happened.

"*The Blue Angel* and Hollywood.

"I had it, fame, and I wasn't ungrateful, but I wasn't rapturous as I'd expected to be. I thought I'd be floating, that my feet wouldn't touch the ground.

"Maybe it was too hard, getting there and then worrying about staying there."

Jonas Sternberg was born in Vienna in 1894. The "Josef" and "von" were later changes of his own, indicating for the world that he was of noble Aryan birth, which he felt better suited him and his manner than his small physical stature and his impoverished Jewish ghetto childhood.

Sternberg lived in Vienna until he was seven. At that time, his father, Moses Sternberg, who had preceded his family to New York, was able to send for his wife and son. Three years later, the Sternbergs returned to Vienna. Four years later, Jonas was back in America to stay.

He left school at sixteen and began to work at low-paying jobs in the garment industry, in millinery, and for a lace-making company. For recreation, he visited the art museums of New York, where a new world was opened to him. He saw artistic possibilities in the relatively new medium of the motion picture.

Soon, he was working for a film-processing company, repairing damaged prints. He noticed aesthetic and technical mistakes by the filmmakers, and brought them to the attention of his bosses. His suggestions were so good that they promoted him. He became an artistic adviser to filmmakers. With this background, he was assigned to the Signal Corps during World War I, where he made training films, a somewhat unexplored form of film at that time.

After the war, he went to California and took whatever was available then in the exciting new film industry. He found work with Charlie Chaplin at the United Artists studio, first as an assistant director and then as a director of a small picture starring Edna Purviance. Chaplin wasn't satisfied with the film von Sternberg made and never released it.

He was given another chance in 1925 at Paramount with *The Salvation Hunters*, which established him as a Hollywood director. Among the American films he directed before *The Blue Angel* were *Underworld* (1927), *The Drag Net* (1928), *The Docks of New York* (1928), *The Last Command* (1928), and *Thunderbolt* (1929). He went to UFA at the invitation of production chief Erich Pommer, who wanted him to direct Emil Jannings's first sound film. Jannings, who had starred in *The Last Command*, and for which he won his Oscar, also wanted von Sternberg as his director.

LEAVING RUDI AND MARIA in Germany, Marlene sailed from Bremen on April 2, 1930, arriving in New York a week later after a rough crossing. She was met by a Paramount photographer and a publicist who didn't know how to pronounce her first name, and by Herman G. Weinberg, an American film critic who wrote subtitles for foreign films, with whom she had been corresponding. After several days of press conferences to introduce her, she left by train for the West Coast. Her Paramount contract was for two pictures. She told interviewers she missed her little girl. At that time, it wasn't the fashion for glamorous actresses to talk about their children.

Von Sternberg had given her a novel to read, *Amy Jolly, Woman of Marrakesh*, which he wanted to make into a movie starring her. Marlene was unenthusiastic about the project. She didn't realize it was to be the basis for her first Hollywood film, *Morocco*.

In Hollywood, von Sternberg, who was also a skilled lighting cinematographer, remade Marlene with makeup, lighting, diet, and exercise. From the shabby, sybaritic Lola Lola, she became the insouciant blond goddess who could say convincingly in *Shanghai Express*, "It took more than one man to change my name to Shanghai Lily." In *Morocco*, she plays a woman who is just as comfortable in a man's tuxedo as in an evening gown.

### Morocco (1930)

Amy Jolly, a cabaret singer performing in Morocco, becomes obsessed with handsome young Tom Brown (Gary Cooper), a Foreign Legionnaire who is able to resist her charms.

When Tom is accused by his adjunct officer (Ullrich Haupt) of consorting with his wife (Eve Southern), Amy clears Tom by saying he was with her, which is not true.

Tom tells Amy he is quitting the Foreign Legion, and Amy hopes they will be together. He doesn't quit, however, and is sent on a dangerous assignment.

Amy, angry that he chose the Foreign Legion over her, turns to a wealthy artist friend, Kensington (Adolphe Menjou), and accepts his offer of marriage. Before the marriage can take place, the troops return, but without Tom.

He is assumed dead, but Amy keeps looking for him. She finally finds him in a cheap bar with a native woman. He claims he doesn't love her, but Amy doesn't believe him.

As Tom is about to be shipped out again, Amy notices women standing at the city gate, waiting to follow their men, wherever they go. She joins them, taking off her high heels as she follows Tom into the desert.

The overwhelming success of *Morocco* justified Paramount production head B. P. Schulberg's faith in Sternberg and his discovery. Marlene Dietrich did, indeed, seem to be the new Garbo. The picture immediately made a $2 million profit for Paramount and was nominated for four Oscars, including a best-actress nomination for Marlene.

"FRITZ LANG TOLD ME I could never be a spy," Marlene said, referring to the legendary German director of *Metropolis*. "He said I am too distinctive, that everyone would be looking at me. He didn't say I was too beautiful. Well, distinctive isn't so bad.

"But he was wrong about me. I was a perfect spy for just the reason he said I wouldn't be. No one would ever suspect me, because I attracted so much attention.

"In *Dishonored*, I successfully played an unsuccessful spy, a lady known as X27. Before I could be shot, I had them wait for me so I could put on my lipstick. I wasn't going to my death not looking my best. In the story, it was my very last chance to look my best."

Lang had his own opinion of how Marlene could look her best. "For me, a sexy image was to think of Marlene in a short skirt, a very short skirt, with a little apron, making scrambled eggs for me for a midnight supper."

### Dishonored (1931)

During World War I, a streetwalker (Marlene Dietrich) is chosen to be a spy by the head of the Austrian secret service (Gustav von Seyffertitz) because she is loyal to Austria and not afraid to die. Her real name is Kolverer, but she becomes X27.

In her first assignment, when she discovers that an Austrian general (Warner Oland) is passing information to the Russians, he commits suicide. She also discovers that his accomplice, Colonel Kranau (Victor McLaglen), is actually H-14 of the Russian secret service, but he escapes.

X27 is sent to the Russian side of the Polish border, where she works as a hotel chambermaid, prying information from Russian generals. Kranau recognizes her through her disguise because of the black cat that always accompanies her.

When she escapes, Kranau follows her to the Austrian border, where he is arrested and condemned to death. Realizing she loves him, she arranges his escape, but she is caught and condemned to be shot.

Standing before the firing squad, she calmly applies her lipstick and then is shot.

As soon as *Dishonored* was completed, Marlene hurried back to Germany to spend Christmas with her daughter and Rudi. "There was never a day I wasn't thinking of Maria. When I wasn't remembering my lines, thoughts of her were with me constantly. Some were memories, reminiscences. Some were plans, dreams. Sometimes I would talk with her in my head, but I couldn't hear her answers.

"I remembered her as a little girl, younger than she was when I went back to fetch her. What surprised me was she didn't really seem to remember *me*. She hadn't been thinking about me the way I had been thinking about her.

"After my Hollywood sojourn, when I went back to Berlin for my daughter, it was very shocking to me that she was not waiting for me as anxiously as I had been anticipating being with her. She was my world. I was only part of her world."

Marlene returned to Hollywood with her young daughter. Shortly afterward, as soon as he finished his film work in Europe, Rudi followed, leaving Tamara in Paris.

THE ENORMOUS SUCCESS, BOTH critical and financial, of *Morocco* and *The Blue Angel* more than compensated for the failure of *Dishonored*, but the depth of the Depression caused Paramount to be wary of any potentially expensive disappointments. Von Sternberg's reaction to the studio's understandable plea for restraint was always greater extravagance.

### Shanghai Express (1932)

The Shanghai Express, traveling between Peking and Shanghai, is stopped an hour out of the station by rebels. Their leader is one of the passengers, Henry Chang (Warner Oland), posing as a Eurasian merchant. Chang is going to hold the passengers as hostages until a rebel agent who is being held by the government is released.

Among the passengers is a mysterious adventuress known as Shanghai Lily (Marlene Dietrich), "the white flower of the China coast." A fellow passenger, Captain Donald Harvey (Clive Brook), recognizes her as Madeleine, a former girlfriend.

Chang asks Lily if she will become his mistress, and she refuses. When he threatens to blind Captain Harvey, she accepts.

One of the passengers, an American Chinese (Anna May Wong), stabs Chang and the rebels disperse, leaving the train free to continue on to Shanghai. Lily and Captain Harvey contemplate their life together.

*Shanghai Express* became the most successful Dietrich–von Sternberg film thus far, and it was nominated for three Oscars, though Marlene was not nominated. It won for best cinematography.

"THE MOST AFRAID I have ever been in my life was in 1932 when we were living in California, and I was waiting for *Blonde Venus* to begin filming," Marlene said. "I received a threatening letter, the first of several, saying that Maria would be kidnapped if we did not pay a kind of ransom to stop the kidnapping.

"We were to pay so she would not be kidnapped, and the letter warned against telling the police or we would be sorry. I was already sorry. They said they would know if we told the police. I have never known such fear in my life. I couldn't eat. I couldn't sleep.

"I didn't want to leave Maria for a moment, and I didn't want to instill my fear in her. I didn't want her to know what was happening, but it wasn't easy to hide it from her because she was such a precocious child, and I, though trying to restrain myself, was acting like a crazy woman. Maria didn't seem to notice because maybe she was used to me and thought I was always crazy. Anyway, she was never worried about anything as long as Rudi was there.

"The moment I read the first letter, I rushed to show it to Rudi. Rudi didn't want to drop off the money the way they said. Money in a box was to be left on the running board of a car, which was to be parked out in front of the house. They originally asked for ten thousand dollars and then, twenty thousand dollars."

Marlene remembered "a terrible and terrifying phrase" that had been in the letter. "It said, 'If you don't pay what we ask, the price will continue to go up, and if you don't pay at all,' and this was the terrible part, 'your daughter will only be a loving memory.'

"Rudi was upset and alarmed, but he was never given to panic. Even as I told him, I felt some of the calming effect Rudi had for our daughter.

"Rudi went to the phone. I said, 'We mustn't call the police.'

"'I'm calling Jo,' Rudi said.

"Then the phone rang. It was Maurice Chevalier. Rudi told him to come right over, and asked him to bring his gun. Dear Maurice didn't ask any questions. He came right over with his pistol and a shotgun, too. He and Jo Sternberg, who also rushed right over, took their places outside of Maria's door with shotguns and pistols and alternated with Rudi, and one of them, usually Rudi, walked around, highly visible, so that they could be seen on the property with rifles. Rudi dressed differently each time, so the kidnappers would think there were more people than we had. We only had three, but they were three men who knew how to shoot and were prepared to kill to save Maria.

"We waited and slept little. The next day, nothing happened. Same the next day. Maurice went home. The letters continued. We hired some outside bodyguards. I don't know why the kidnappers didn't come. Now I think they never planned to do the kidnapping and hoped to cash in with just the threat to a frightened, hysterical mother who would give them anything.

"What Rudi didn't tell me until long after it was all over was that he had called the police at the beginning after I told him, so that they could have surveillance on the house. I asked why he didn't tell me. Well, I knew why. I began by forbidding it and refusing to discuss my position. Rudi told me that he had perfect faith in my acting performance on stage and screen, but under the circumstances, he wasn't so sure of my performance in real life when I was under so much pressure. Rudi was right. Rudi was always right.

"The worst thing that came of it was I was permanently more frightened for Maria in Hollywood, and I never escaped that, so the letter had its effect. I couldn't smell the orange blossoms."

As *Blonde Venus* WAS being filmed, Marlene had Maria sitting by on the set, just out of camera range, so she would know her daughter was safe.

### *Blonde Venus* (1932)

Ex–nightclub performer Helen Faraday (Marlene Dietrich) is happy in her domestic existence with chemist Edward Faraday (Herbert Marshall) and their young son, Johnny (Dickie Moore), until tragedy strikes. Edward is diagnosed with radium poisoning and will require expensive treatment abroad, which he cannot afford. Helen must go back to work so that Edward can be treated.

In spite of her success as a nightclub singer, Helen cannot make enough money to support Johnny and Edward while he is being treated in Europe. Nick Townsend (Cary Grant), a wealthy playboy she has met in the club, offers to help her if she will become his mistress. With Nick at her side, her nightclub act becomes a sensation and goes on tour.

Cured, Edward returns to New York but he leaves Helen, taking Johnny with him, when he learns of her relationship with Nick, not realizing that she did it for him. At Nick's urging, Helen does not let her marriage fail, and she and Edward are reunited when Edward learns the truth.

In late 1932, after the box office failure of *Blonde Venus*, von Sternberg's contract with Paramount ran out. He announced his retirement and went to Berlin. Paramount was now free to assign another director for Marlene's next film. Marlene sued the studio for breach of contract, but lost. Rouben Mamoulian, who up to that time had a brilliant stage and screen record, became the director of *Song of Songs*.

### Song of Songs (1933)

Lily Czepanek (Marlene Dietrich), a simple country girl, is noticed working in her aunt's Berlin bookstore by Waldow (Brian Aherne), a young sculptor. He invites her to his studio across the street, and she visits him every night. He persuades her to pose nude for a statue he is sculpting. When it is finished, Waldow's patron, the Baron von Merzbach (Lionel Atwill), is more impressed by the model than by the statue.

He wants to marry Lily, but she wants to marry Waldow and have a family, a prospect the artist rejects.

Von Merzbach secretly pays Lily's aunt (Alison Skipworth) to lock Lily out of the house, and then arranges for Waldow to leave his studio. With nowhere to go, she accepts the baron's offer, becoming the Baroness von Merzbach.

When Waldow visits the baron's mansion, Lily tries to show him that she does not love the baron by flaunting her affair with a riding instructor (Hardie Albright).

During an assignation, there is a fire in the instructor's cottage. Though Lily survives, she leaves before the rabidly jealous baron discovers her infidelity.

Waldow searches for Lily, finally finding her singing in a Berlin cabaret.

Virtually every film worker at UFA, including Nazi propaganda minister Joseph Goebbels, who supervised the studio, wanted to go to Hollywood, except for Josef von Sternberg. He wanted to leave Hollywood and return to UFA, where he expected to be received with acclaim as a star director.

Marlene could never understand how her mentor, a man as brilliant as Josef von Sternberg, whom she said she worshipped, "could be such a total fool about Hitler and his gang. I suppose Jo had a blind side, because he wished to work in Germany, to return to his first language and be received in triumph. He didn't feel Hollywood had appreciated him the way he should have been appreciated. He was such a brilliant man that he was even brilliant in deluding himself.

"He didn't seem to understand what it would mean to him to be a Jew in Germany, and what it meant for his possibilities as a Jewish director at UFA. I think it was some false picture he had built up in his own mind, a dream.

"One of the first steps the Nazis took was to say no Jews could work at UFA. Some saw it coming and left ahead of that decision. Others left immediately afterward. It wasn't easy leaving the work they loved and changing to another language, and many didn't know another language. They had to accept poor jobs in other countries or never make it at all in films and theater. Hollywood could only absorb so many Jewish refugees to play movie Nazis.

"I was so lucky. I didn't have a perfect crystal ball, but even a clouded crystal ball told a negative truth which you couldn't miss. People had to leave family behind. I did. I was lucky enough to have the possibility and the money to get them out, but my mother and sister wouldn't go. Loss of family, separation from your friends, loss of your familiar world, and your possessions. Terrible. The lucky ones felt forced to go when they could still get out.

"Jo was so lucky the Nazis didn't want him as a director. Jo was more brilliant at films than at politics.

"At first, through intuition, then through experience, I understood profoundly, deep in my soul, that my director, Josef von Sternberg, knew what he was doing in films. I put all of my trust in him.

"My belief in him as my director was total—a respect, a reverence I had which was almost religious fervor. I thought as highly of him as he thought of himself, and that was very highly indeed.

"Without him, I would never have had the career I did, the life I've lived."

MAE WEST WAS A big star at Paramount at the time. She developed a friendship with Marlene.

"Marlene Dietrich was at Paramount in '33, and our dressing rooms were very close to each other, practically side by side. She was very sweet, and kinda lonely and insecure, too.

"We could tell each other secrets in German, though we had to be careful because there were other people around who might understand, especially with all the refugees comin' from Europe. They thought things would get bad there. They were right.

"My German was what I remembered from my mother speakin' with her family and friends when I was little. I learned it by accident. Marlene didn't mind my accidental German and understood it just fine. Hers was very different from the way Mother spoke it.

"When I said my first words to her in German, she laughed. I didn't mind. I sounded pretty funny to myself. It *was* her first language and my second, if you could even call it that. I asked her why she laughed. I told her German was a childhood language of mine and that it was kinda rusty.

"She said, No, it was very good, but it was the accent. It was very strong Black Forest. I told her my mother came from Bavaria. She said she knew. She was from Berlin.

"I tried to show her the ropes, to give her some of my insights into how to handle herself, so the producer types wouldn't try to handle *her* and take liberties. We exchanged what we knew about camera angles and lighting. She knew quite a bit from the German films she'd done. She liked my makeup tips, especially for drawing on lips.

"The biggest pointer I gave her was about her lipstick. I showed her how to make her lips seem fuller and poutier and sexier, by not bringing the lipstick all the way to the corners of her mouth.

"She was a real pretty girl, but very shy. I was always sensitive to shy people, because of my own shyness. There wasn't anyone in the world, except my mother, who would have said I had a shy side.

"Anyway, she said to me she was thinking of goin' back to Europe because she couldn't get rid of her accent, and she was worried she couldn't make it in America. She was more confident about what her career would be in Europe, but she didn't really want to go back there, especially she wouldn't go to Germany.

"She gave me a pair of opera glasses. Who else would give *me* opera glasses? I loved opera and had recordings of opera, but I didn't exactly need to use opera glasses in my bedroom.

"But I treasured the gift. It was one of the nicest things anyone ever gave me.

"I'll tell you something Dietrich said to me once. We used to talk a little about sex, but we never talked dirty. Most of the time, I was just givin' her advice on how to rebuff the studio lotharios. There were a lotta them with the octopus tendency.

"My technique was to try some humor, but that wasn't her style. She wasn't very funny when she was tryin' to be funny. I remember we were havin' an intimate conversation about men and about how careful a girl had to be, and she said this funny thing to me, which I didn't understand, but remembered.

"She said, 'You should only make love with a man you love or a man you hate.'

"I didn't understand. It didn't make much sense. I wouldn't've wanted to do it with someone I hated, and I was avoidin' bein' in love. I didn't think it was polite to ask her what she meant. Maybe she was just joking and I didn't get it because she delivered it so straight, and I wasn't expectin' it. Deadpan. I meant to ask her sometime, but our careers went in different directions, and we sorta drifted apart. I think of her often and she gave me a lotta gifts I still have, scarves and the opera glasses that remind me of her.

"One time I told [Jim] Timony [Mae's manager] what Marlene said. I asked him did he think she was bein' funny or serious?

"He said, 'She was being enigmatic.'

"I didn't know any more than I did before I asked the question.

"Jim explained the word to me. It's like a riddle without an answer or a joke without a tag line. So I learned another word, but it still didn't exactly answer my question.

"Marlene Dietrich was a good friend. She used to bring me food she cooked herself—soup, a beef stew—and it was good. It was substantial and full of vitamins.

"She loved to cook. She was very talented at it, like Mother. Maybe it's what girls learn in Germany. I, personally, was happy to stay out of kitchens, except as a visitor.

"Sometimes she got some bad press, and I don't think she deserved it at all. You ought to at least have the pleasure of doin' something if you're gonna get pilloried for it. I think she had the same problem I did, of the audience confusing her with the parts she played. She did them too well, so no one thought of her the way I did, a nice girl who cooked delicious chicken soup for her friends."

AFTER PUBLICATION OF HIS *All Quiet on the Western Front* in 1929, Erich Maria Remarque, who was not Jewish and not a communist, came to be considered an undesirable by the emerging Nazi Party. The pacifist views expressed in his bestselling novel were alien to the Nazis' militaristic philosophy. When the Nazis came to power in 1933, they burned his books publicly.

One evening in the early 1930s, someone Remarque respected and trusted warned him in a phone call, "They've put you on their list of *highly* undesirables. You know what that means. I'd get out if I were you."

Taking almost nothing with him, Remarque stopped only to hang up the phone. He got into his car, which he kept packed with his manuscripts, and by the next evening he had already crossed the border to Switzerland, where he stayed until he left for the United States in 1939. The year before, the Nazis had revoked his German citizenship.

Marlene first met Remarque at the Venice Lido, where she was having dinner with von Sternberg. Remarque, who had been observing Marlene from a distance, mustered up his nerve and approached their table.

He introduced himself to von Sternberg and "Madame." Generally Marlene would have resented an intrusion on her private time, but she recognized his name and was impressed by Remarque's good looks and his conversational savoir faire as he kissed her hand.

The passionate friendship that followed lasted throughout their lives. He was impressed because she was carrying a book, and he told her that he was pleased to find a beautiful woman who read, and the German poet Rilke at that.

After the meal, von Sternberg left them. "The evening was one of intellectual and emotional intensity," Marlene recalled many years later. "As the restaurant was closing, Remarque said to me, 'I have to tell you—I'm impotent.'

"He didn't seem too upset. I certainly wasn't. I said, 'Oh, what good news! Now we can be friends,' and we *were* great friends."

Remarque had been seriously wounded, five times in the same

battle, as a soldier during World War I. Each wound could have been fatal, he told Marlene.

His sister, Elfriede, was taken prisoner by the Nazis, and then tortured and killed because they really wanted *him*. It was a blow from which he could never recover. He didn't *want* to recover. His adored sister had been lost, and he blamed himself for her tragic fate.

"What I had to offer," Marlene said, "was my ear, a sympathetic ear that would listen to his deepest troubles. Fortunately, I did not have such deep troubles myself, and I always had Rudi to tell them to. It's so wonderful to have someone who's a perfect confidant, to whom you can tell anything. Rudi was never judgmental, not toward me, only toward the others, but he could be *very* judgmental if anyone wronged me."

Remarque's German experience left a permanent mark on him.

"He would keep a suitcase which was always packed," Marlene said. "I only had glimpses of what was inside. It was mostly paper. There was a clean shirt, some underwear, and I think two pair of socks. He told me, 'I always have it ready, in case I have to flee somewhere.'"

Marlene and Remarque were not as close when, some years later, he married Paulette Goddard. Marlene felt Goddard did not like to have her visit, because she thought her generous husband might give Marlene one of his valuable paintings to take home with her.

"What I really wanted," Marlene said, "was his fantastic carpet, but I don't think he was going to roll it up and have me take it away. And I never would have accepted it, but it was beautiful. He had good taste."

Remarque preferred living in Switzerland to New York. Goddard preferred living in New York and even after he suffered several strokes, she continued to travel frequently to New York. Gossips speculated that she might have a lover there.

As it turned out, it wasn't a lover. It was her hairdresser at Charles of the Ritz. She didn't feel anyone else could get her hair color just right.

MARLENE WAS USUALLY EXTREMELY punctual, but on one occasion she was the last to arrive for dinner, she said, "because of primping."

"In my private life, I was never a primper," Marlene told me. "In my public life, I was the ultimate primper. I never wanted to disappoint anyone by not looking the most beautiful I could manage.

"Eating dinner first-class at the start of the Paris–to–New York voyage of the *Île de France* is not exactly a film or stage appearance, but it isn't ordinary life either. It's in the middle, between public life and private life.

"It was 1934, and I was returning from Europe. I had planned my outfit days ahead, but at the last minute I changed my mind and changed my dress and that meant I had to change all of my accessories.

"When I arrived at the table, everyone else was seated. All of the men, of course, stood up when I arrived. As they did, I realized I could not sit down. There were twelve at the table. I would have been the thirteenth. Impossible. It could have meant terrible luck for everyone, especially me. I just stood there. I didn't know what to do. The others couldn't understand why I was refusing to sit down.

"I said, 'Thirteen. I'll be the thirteenth person at the table. I can't sit down.' And just then, the most handsome, wonderfully masculine man was there at my side.

"He said, 'If I may, I'd like to pull up a chair,' he already had a chair ready, 'and then there will be fourteen.'

"It was what my dear friend Billy Wilder would call for one of his films, a meet-cute.

"I held out my hand and said, 'I'm Marlene Dietrich.'

"He said, 'I know very well who you are.'

"He took my hand, and he said, 'I'm Ernest Hemingway.'

"It was the beginning of one of the most treasured friendships of my life, which lasted as long as he lived."

I SPOKE WITH ONE-HUNDRED-YEAR-OLD Leni Riefenstahl at her home near Munich. The controversial actress-director told me that before von Sternberg had achieved his great success with *The Blue Angel* and Marlene Dietrich, he had talked with Riefenstahl about coming to Hollywood to be directed by him. He wanted to create a project especially for her, as he would soon do for Marlene Dietrich, and he would direct the film himself. At the time, Riefenstahl was considerably more famous than the relatively unknown Marlene.

She was a star of "mountain" movies, a popular genre during the 1920s. In these films, she risked her life dangling high above the earth, supported only by a flimsy rope as she scaled jagged precipices with effortless grace, never using a double while performing her perilous stunts. Later, Riefenstahl would achieve undying notoriety by directing two documentary classics, *The Triumph of the Will* and *Olympiad*, both commissioned by the Nazis to glorify their regime. Although Riefenstahl was never a Nazi herself and produced other memorable work, none of it political, she could never escape the stigma created by those two great films. No matter how much she protested her innocence, she would forever be linked with the Nazis.

"I gave it some serious consideration," Riefenstahl told me, "but I never came close to going to Hollywood. I didn't speak English. Perhaps English would not come easily to me. That was an important consideration. Later, I learned English, and now I enjoy it. Marlene had studied English as a girl. There may not have been room for more than one German leading lady in Hollywood. If I left Germany and went to Hollywood and failed, it would have been mortifying to return to Germany a failure. It would have been more mortifying in light of Miss Dietrich's success. I was attached to my world in Germany, and I found it painful to think of leaving it.

"Most important, to me, I didn't want to go on forever being an actress. And I knew I couldn't go on forever as an actress had I wanted to. I was frequently athletic in my parts in the films, and athleticism lasts only so long. Mine has apparently lasted one hundred years, though I don't ski or mountain-climb as well as when I was twenty. I swim better now than I did then. Who knows what destiny brings? I did not know then that I would be filming underwater at the age of one hundred.

"I knew Marlene, but not well. She had one kind of fame. I had another. Mine became a mixture of fame and notoriety.

"My true great ambition was to be a director. All of my success was German success. Germany gave me the chance to be a director. I believed there was more opportunity for a woman to become a director in Germany than in Hollywood. For a time, I was right.

"I paid a high price during my long life in Germany for my mistakes in judgment. In the earliest days of Hitler, just after his election, I believed he would be good for Germany. I could not possibly have been more wrong. But I was able to save the lives of some Jewish film workers during World War II. My cameraman was half-Jewish, and I swore I couldn't make my film without him, so he was saved.

"The life I could not save was the life I cared most about, even more than I cared for my own, the life of my brother, who was a doctor. When I learned that he was going to be sent to the Russian front, an almost certain death sentence, I would have done anything to save him. Anything. I would have been guilty of everything I've been accused of if I could have saved my brother. My problem was that I had exaggerated my high connections and everyone had believed me. I believed it myself, which made what I said so believable.

"In my desperation to reach someone, when none of the men I thought would help me returned my urgent calls, I called Magda Goebbels. I had never liked her, but I knew she must have great influence through her husband. She said there wasn't anything she could do. She said she had no influence over her husband, except in bed. He only cared that she was beautiful and had a beautiful baby every year, which made him look virile and Aryan. Magda had told me she found her husband repulsive and ugly. She said it was Hitler she was really in love with, and she married Goebbels so she could be near Hitler. She told me that when she slept with Goebbels, she imagined she was in bed with Hitler. She was having babies for Hitler, and she thought of them as Hitler's children. That's why when it was over for Hitler, she was able not only to kill herself, but to kill all her young children.

"I didn't know if it was true that she couldn't help me. I only knew she didn't. I think she could have, if she had wanted to. But why should she? I'm sure she didn't like me any more than I liked her.

"Obviously my connections weren't as good as I had told people or even what I believed they were. My brother died at the Russian front. That was all that mattered. Someone who knew him and survived called me, so I would know that he had died and not hold out hope that he had been taken prisoner so I wouldn't wait in futility for his return. I was told he had died helping someone else on the battlefield. Then I knew for certain that it was my brother. It was why he had wanted to be a doctor, to help people."

As I was leaving, Riefenstahl added, "It was easier for Marlene to leave Germany behind because she didn't have so much of a career to leave behind. One film."


*The Scarlet Empress*, THOUGH a box office and critical failure, has since become the quintessential Dietrich–von Sternberg film.

Von Sternberg's brilliant pictorial conceptions, enhanced by Hans Dreier's sets, Travis Banton's costumes, Peter Ballbusch's statuary, and an outstanding cast are superbly realized by Dietrich at her charismatic best. Her portrayal of Catherine the Great, the lead role, moves from the naive young princess whose mother boasts that her daughter can make beds to the worldly empress who knows what to do in those beds. Marlene was able to make the acting transition from the innocent adolescent girl in Germany to the unhappy wife of the archduke to the supremely confident czarina.

This film follows many of the traditions of the silent cinema, which was, of necessity, more a medium of emotions than of ideas. This emotional dimension was enhanced by familiar music that gave a voice beyond words to the silent images on the screen.

A striking example of this technique in *The Scarlet Empress* is the long, elaborate wedding sequence, which is silent except for Anton Rubinstein's piano piece *Rêve angelique*, arranged for a chorus and symphony orchestra. The rest of the music in the film is drawn from the works of Tchaikovsky, Mendelssohn, and Wagner, a common practice during the silent era.

Another convention of the silent era used extensively in *The Scarlet Empress* was the lengthy intertitles, which provide the historical transitions between sections of the film.

The look of the film is also reminiscent of silent films, especially those from UFA in Germany. Much of this look is due to the lighting, of which von Sternberg, a skilled cinematographer, was a master.

Von Sternberg instructed his art director, Hans Dreier, to employ a stylistic approach in *The Scarlet Empress* that was typical of German Expressionism rather than to strive for historical accuracy. Capturing the mood of the drama and the spirit of its characters was von Sternberg's objective. He saw his film not as a history lesson, but as a universal emotional impression, which he hoped would affect every member of the audience.

The sets for *The Scarlet Empress* are among the most fanciful ever designed for the screen, yet Dreier, who during his long career at Paramount was nominated for seventeen Oscars, was not nominated for this film. (Dreier had been nominated for *Morocco*.) *The Scarlet Empress* was, in fact, not nominated for *any* Oscars.

### The Scarlet Empress (1934)

Dutiful, obedient Princess Sophia Frederica of Prussia (Marlene Dietrich) is betrothed to Grand Duke Peter (Sam Jaffe), the heir apparent to the Russian throne. As a child (Maria Sieber) she had been prepared for such a destiny, but she never quite adjusted to it, finding more comfort in her doll. She will be accompanied on the arduous seven-week journey to Russia by her mother, Princess Johanna (Olive Tell) and the Russian Count Alexei (John Lodge).

Count Alexei has been sent to escort Sophia and her mother by carriage with mounted guards to Moscow. Since much of the trip will be during winter, she is given sables to keep her warm. Her father (C. Aubrey Smith) rather unemotionally bids her goodbye, telling her they will probably never see each other again, but she has her destiny to fulfill.

The young, romantic girl is more interested in knowing whether her future husband is handsome. Alexei assures her that he is outstandingly handsome. That thought keeps her warm during the trip, during which she has to resist the advances of the handsome envoy.

In Moscow, the young princess is quickly put in her place as a Russian wife by the imperious empress (Louise Dresser). Grand Duke Peter is grotesque, totally unappealing. Disliking the name Sophia, the empress changes it to Catherine and commands her to produce a male heir for the Russian throne.

When her mother is abruptly sent back to Prussia, Catherine is left alone in a strange country. Her only friend, it would seem, is Count Alexei, with whom she has fallen in love. Catherine, however, is disillusioned when she learns directly from the empress that the opportunistic Count Alexei is having regular romantic rendezvous with the empress.

Catherine rushes out into the palace garden, where she is stopped by the captain of the night guard, Count Orlov (Gavin Gordon), who laughs when she announces haughtily that she is the archduchess.

"If you are the archduchess," he says, "I am the grand duke."

"I wish you were," she replies.

He needs no more encouragement. A lonely Catherine impulsively surrenders her preciously guarded virginity to the handsome figure in his dashing uniform.

When Catherine gives birth to a male baby, the grand duke knows the child is not his and plots to murder Catherine as soon as his mother dies.

On the empress's death, Peter unleashes a reign of illogical terror that causes the military, the Church, the nobility, and the Russian people to want him replaced by the immensely popular Catherine.

At a dinner, Peter announces to the guests that he prefers his mistress, Countess Elizabeth (Ruthelma Stevens), to his wife, and he insists that Catherine join in a toast to her. Humiliated, Catherine leaves on the arm of Orlov, who is stripped by the czar of his rank.

A coup on Catherine's behalf is successful, and Peter III is quietly assassinated. Catherine becomes a great, popular—and promiscuous—leader of Russia.

The first time the audience sees Sophia, she is a beautiful blond child who greatly resembles the grown-up Catherine, as played by

Marlene. The resemblance is quite natural because she is played by Maria, Marlene's own daughter.

During Maria's scene as young Sophia, the doll that makes its appearance was one of Marlene's own dolls, brought with her from Berlin. Whenever she could and it was appropriate, she liked to have one or more of her dolls appear in her films. She felt they were lucky for her. "I liked to travel with them."

Two months before *The Scarlet Empress* was released, Alexander Korda's *The Rise of Catherine the Great* starring Elisabeth Bergner and Douglas Fairbanks, Jr., opened. It was a more literal, historically correct portrayal of Catherine's story, although von Sternberg said he based his version on the empress's diary.

At Paramount at the same time as Marlene, her good friend Mae West had unsuccessfully been importuning production director Ernst Lubitsch, with whom West did not have a good relationship, to make a Catherine the Great film she had written.

IN 2010, LEATRICE GILBERT Fountain remembered the kindness and generosity that Marlene Dietrich showed her in the 1930s. Fountain's mother, Leatrice Joy, was a 1920s film star who had married and divorced John Gilbert, one of the most famous actors of the silent era.

In 1934, while Lewis Milestone was directing *The Captain Hates the Sea*, he gave a dinner party at his home in Hollywood. Among the guests was Marlene Dietrich. Absent was the star of the film, Gilbert. Leatrice, Gilbert's daughter, told me how Marlene happened to be there, as she heard the story and what it came to mean to her father and to her:

"Marlene Dietrich, who was fairly new to Hollywood, didn't know too many people, but through von Sternberg she'd met Lewis Milestone, and they had become friends. During the conversation around the dinner table, Milestone said, 'What a tragedy it is that

Jack Gilbert is sitting just a few miles up the road, probably drinking himself to death, and he has everything, but is so lost and nobody's doing anything about it. He still has his looks. He has his intelligence. He has his talent, his skills, his experience. How could such a thing happen to such a great star? It's so sad. It's tragic there isn't something anyone can do.'

"At that point, Marlene Dietrich rose from her chair and announced: "I shall save him.'

"Then, without finishing her dinner, out the door she went, into her car, up the hill to my father's house. She rang the doorbell and knocked on the door, but there was no answer.

"She didn't give up. She just kept pounding on the door. Jack was probably in such a drunken haze, he didn't hear her pounding.

"When he finally did get to the front door and opened it, here was this incredible apparition in her gorgeous gown, her radiant hair, her porcelain complexion. And, can you imagine, she said something like, 'John Gilbert, I have come to save you.'

"My father was a grand-style romantic, so you can imagine how pleased he was. It had been a long time since anybody cared about him like that.

"In 1926, at the same time my father and Greta Garbo were getting together, Rudolph Valentino died suddenly at a very young age, leaving his fans bereft. Thousands and thousands of *deeply* grieved women attended his funeral. As soon as they got used to his being gone, they looked around for someone else to adore, and who was there but John Gilbert?

"Then there was the romance with Garbo, and they just *loved* that. They called them 'Fire and Ice' and bought millions of tickets to their movies. Irving Thalberg created the title of 'The Great Lover' for him. My father called it garbage. People used to greet him, 'Hello, great lover of the silent screen!' He couldn't *stand* that concept, but it sold tickets, so he was stuck with it.

"When the talkies came in, most people in Hollywood thought it was a passing fad, and the producers didn't worry much about it, but the actors did. Some of the studios started giving them voice tests. And it's very interesting to me that no one gave John Gilbert a voice test. If his voice was as screechy as has been said, why didn't somebody find that out?

"So, he was very nervous. He had acted on the stage as a child, and he had listened to his mother speak with what they called 'pearlike tones.' The actors then enunciated very clearly, 'Hel-lo, how-are-you?' When he started talking in a movie, that's how he sounded, because he thought that was what actors did when they talked, and that's what they laughed at. He was saying to this young woman, 'I-love-you,' and they roared! But it wasn't the sound of his voice, it was the way he had been trained to speak as an actor. So he had to undo all that.

"Jack had an ironclad contract guaranteeing him $250,000 a picture, choice of subject, of director, and Louis B. Mayer, the head of MGM, couldn't break it. But they did manage to steer his choice of films into less than what he would have liked to do. He made some all-right movies, but they were not what his fans wanted to see.

"So, as the contract ground on, the studio did everything they could to make him uncomfortable. Under the rules of the contract, he had to show up at the studio whether he was working or not. So every day he would drive up, and sometimes the gate man would pretend not to recognize him, and he had to show identification to get in. Can you imagine?

"He was left out of all celebrations and social occasions. I think Mayer was afraid if they just let him go at the end of his contract, he could easily have gone to another studio. That would have been competition for MGM. It was logical to the studio that if they were going to get rid of their big moneymaking star, they would have to destroy him first so nobody else would want him, at least not as the big star he had been.

"He was a fragile character anyway, given to drinking, and this just ground him down, so by the time the contract finally petered out, he just went back to his house without anything to live for. So he was feeling pretty down when the gorgeous woman showed up on his doorstep and came to his rescue. She came into his life and offered him something to live for.

"Along with Garbo, Marlene was probably one of the two most beautiful women ever to be in Hollywood, and there she was, standing on *his* doorstep, with her furs, jewels, her evening gown. Everything. I have no idea what my father made of her. I was still a child when he died, so he didn't talk with me much about those things. Well, I have *some* idea what he thought. Here was this very determined German lady, and nothing was going to get in the way of her newest project, which was to save this valuable man. And by golly, she almost did!

"She came close. She got him professional help, a psychiatrist or a psychologist. She got him to stop drinking. I wouldn't have thought anyone in the world could have done that. She made him eat properly. She cooked for him.

"I think it's true that she loved a challenge. It gave her something to get up her energy for. She was very energetic and a very focused woman. She loved a challenge and caring for someone she cared about. This just had to be done, so she was going to get in there and do it. She came close. She picked him up and got him started.

"She took him out to places and social events, and made him see people again. She was even arranging for him to make a film in England with her. It was *Knight Without Armor*, and they were all excited about doing this. He really believed he was going to have another chance, a chance to come back, really, from hell to a hopeful future. His first chance had come ten years earlier.

"At the time, I didn't know all that was going on in his life. I was only nine or ten, so I wasn't told things. My parents were divorced when I was a year old, and I didn't live with my father at all. I missed having a father *very* much. He would occasionally show up at a birthday party. So I wrote him a fan letter, and I sent it to MGM. I said, 'I don't have a picture of you, and I'd like to have one. Maybe sometime I could see you. I hope we can be in touch.'

"Of course he was no longer at MGM, and it took several months before the letter got to him, so I forgot about it. I was disappointed, and just went on in school. One day I came home, and there was a huge bouquet, a floral arrangement like in a funeral parlor. I asked our maid, 'What is *that* for?' and she said, 'That's for you. Your father sent it.' I hadn't remembered seeing him since I was a little girl at the beach. I really didn't know him at all. The bouquet had a little card attached that said, 'I adored your mother. Let me adore you.' Talk about romance! Dear me!

"From then on, I would go up and visit him. He would send his car down, this beautiful limousine. It wasn't a large house. It was a lovely Spanish house on top of Tower Road, behind the Beverly Hills Hotel.

"We would talk and do things. He was very awkward and didn't know a thing about children. Gradually, as we saw each other, we saw we had things in common. Maybe it's enlarged in my imagination, but I felt a bond. I really felt we were getting to know each other.

"We spent hours and hours together trying to catch up. He tried to teach me how to play chess. Once we pulled up the rugs, and he taught me how to waltz around the living room. Then, we would just sit and talk, and he treated me as if I were forty years old. He would say, 'Now, Leatrice, what's your take on Roosevelt,' and I would give as considered an answer as I could. I tended to be liberal in my politics, even then, so I said I thought he was doing good things for the country. He said, 'Well then, how do you feel about prohibition?' and I said, 'I don't think it can ever work.' He said, 'You're right. You're absolutely right. You *are* my own daughter!" We had a lot of these funny, kind of lopsided conversations. We had so much fun together.

"Then, I went away to summer camp, and he wrote letters to me all the time while I was there, and I wrote back to him. Once he wrote, 'You know, Leatrice, you fill a great void in my life, and I hope we will be together forever.' Then, when I got back, I saw him only once more in the fall and then at Christmas, I went to spend the day with him.

"His house was on several levels, and you left one level by walking up the stairs. At the top of the stairs, there was a great, beautiful Christmas tree, decorated with the most beautiful ornaments and lit with candles. I'd never seen a candlelit tree before or since, but Marlene Dietrich had decorated it in the German tradition, and all around the tree were twenty or thirty presents, all for me. What a dream that was for a little girl! And my father sat and watched me open these presents. There was a gold watch, a silk dress, a beautiful bracelet—all kinds of wonderful stuff.

"Marlene, with her exquisite taste and generosity with her time, had shopped for every one of those gifts and bought them for my father to give to me.

"She had volunteered to do it. My father said she had told him, 'I know better what she will like than you do because you were never a little girl, and I was.'

"It was Marlene's idea, too, to get so many gifts. I was certain to like something. Actually, I loved everything. She said that opening so many packages would make a great party event that would be an unforgettable experience for both of us.

"We felt this happy closeness, like soldiers who have been in battle together. We really connected with each other. We laughed at all the same things, and if we'd had more time, I think we would have cried about all the same things.

"That day, I persuaded my father to drive home with me in the limousine. I wanted him to come in and see the Christmas tree I had decorated at our house. So, when we got in the car and we traveled to the other side of Los Angeles, I didn't tell him until we got there.

"He said, 'No, of course not. I can't do that.'

"I said, 'Oh, yes you can.'

"He said, 'Young lady, you're arguing with a Gilbert.'

"I said, 'And so are you.' He thought that was the funniest thing he ever heard.

"He came in, and as my mother came down the stairs, she nearly fainted. So I'm standing there in the hall, and there was the funny little Christmas tree.

"They were still so young, still so beautiful. I just stood and watched them for a few minutes together. It was very touching. They stood and talked for a minute, and he left.

"That was the last time I ever saw my father. He died about a week and a half later.

"He'd had a heart attack the summer before, when he was swimming in the pool with Marlene Dietrich. They pulled him out, and revived him. He survived, but he continued to have trouble with his heart, and I think he had gone back to drinking. Of course, I didn't know any of this for sure.

"We were going to see each other on the ninth of January, but I couldn't go. My mother came to get me in school, and in the car on the way home, she told me that my father had died that night.

"It's difficult for anyone to lose a parent, but I had not only lost a parent, I had lost a lot more: such hopes and all my plans in the relationship we were having and the greater one we were going to have.

"I had not had a close relationship with my mother, and my stepfather didn't like children at all, not even his own. I had created this dream image of a father who knew who I was and cared, and we were going to go on, and I would grow up talking with him. I probably put far too much emphasis on what was *going* to be, because when I was pulled away from him, it was as if the world had ended for me for a very long time. The person who came to save me and helped pull me out of my youthful grief was Marlene Dietrich. She saved me.

"More than my mother, more than anyone, Marlene understood the enormous loss I felt. Mother missed understanding that because my time with my father was short. But what she wasn't able to realize was that in my mind I had enlarged this to fill up all the vacancies. I now had this wonderful father who was interested in me. We would do things together. I had projected the years ahead in which we would be together, and I was on my way to see him in January. I spent Christmas with him, and then, suddenly, he died. I had not even known he had a heart condition. I knew nothing about his health.

"I only met Marlene a few times while my father was alive. She always hurried away, because she understood how precious the hours alone with my father were to me. She would remember an appointment and have to slip away. She was a very understanding, considerate person.

"When my father died, it was just like a total cataclysm, and Marlene was sensitive enough to pick that up when I was in *deep* grief, and she was the *only* one. She did what she could to comfort me. When she was around, she took me to theaters and to her house and sent me gifts and sent me cards and letters. She tried to get me going again. It's a rare thing she did, and I'm always grateful to her. She truly was wonderful to me.

"I remember going with her to the opening of *Snow White*. She came to meet me in this great, beautiful blue Rolls-Royce limousine, and she was all fluffy in her lovely furs and twinkling jewels, and gentle fragrance. Just to drive in a car with her was a sheer delight.

"She always talked to me as if I were a grown-up. She never talked down to children. Her daughter said that, too. She just had one voice for everybody, which is lovely, you know.

"The last time I saw her, I was about fourteen or fifteen. She lived in Europe an awful lot, especially in France. She never owned a house in Los Angeles. She just rented when she'd come to do a picture here.

"It was really exciting when packages arrived from Paris when Marlene was traveling, and the lovely things she brought from London. I'd never had such beautiful and expensive things. I'd never ever seen things like that. I saved them for years. Now, I don't know what's happened to all of them. I have some of them. Well, it's been a long time. About eighty years.

"She sent me a little charm bracelet, which was supposed to be for the coronation of Edward VIII. The coronation never happened. The bracelet has his picture in a little royal coach. She sent me a chemical set because she thought it would be good for me to know about that, and a box of geological specimens from Switzerland, including a fossil of a seashell found on the top of one of the Alps, showing that the land had once been under water. She wanted to encourage me to think, to read, and to study. She was really marvelous.

"She picked out the last Christmas presents she gave me: a beautiful little silk dress, which I still have, a little pink negligee with beautiful tucking in front, and a little pearl necklace to wear with the dresses. I remember all of the lovely gifts, some of them for Christmas or my birthday, most of them for no special occasion.

"She had flawless taste. She never overdid it. She herself never looked one inch over the top.

"It was like having a beautiful fairy godmother."

Marlene remembered young Leatrice well. "I immediately loved her," Marlene told me. "She was John's child, and she was a dear little thing. And I was missing my own little Maria terribly.

"I spent time with her whenever I could, because I knew her father hadn't spent enough time with her before he died, and then there was no more possibility. From my early life with my own father,

I understood what that was like. I'd felt the presence of my father more than I really understood at that time, when I was a small child.

"I liked to shop for my own young daughter and send her back gifts, and I could shop for John's little girl at the same time."


JOAN CRAWFORD TOLD ME she remembered her good friend Cesar "Butch" Romero telling her about his time working with Josef von Sternberg on *The Devil Is a Woman*.

"Butch thought it was going to be a fantastic opportunity, a great learning experience that would take him where he wanted to go, and not the least of it, maybe what he was most excited about was he was going to be acting opposite Marlene Dietrich.

"Butch knew he wasn't the first choice for the part of Antonio. Joel McCrea had begun filming but had stopped and left the set and the film. McCrea was enjoying success, and he had hesitated about accepting the part of Antonio because he didn't feel he looked very Spanish. Though Butch didn't speak directly with McCrea, the rumor was that McCrea felt he had been badly treated and without respect 'by an egomaniac,' and that he didn't have to accept that kind of treatment from a director McCrea considered incompetent, with no idea of what he wanted. McCrea told people that the reason von Sternberg made such a fuss was to cover his incompetence. Anyway, that was the gossip.

"Butch told me that he was determined to go in and do a really good job in this part he felt suited him, and then, he'd not only have a wonderful experience, but it would really add to his credits and put him in a new league.

"I had dinner with him, and we went dancing, right after he finished filming. I asked him how it was, working on the film. Butch had a very calm and even disposition, the exact opposite of the stereotype of Latin fire and temperament. In response to my question, he turned purple.

"He told me when he arrived, he was treated rudely, in an abrasive and cursory manner by von Sternberg, who scarcely said a word to him. Well, he hadn't expected to be treated like a big star, but von Sternberg not only didn't welcome him to the set, or thank him for stepping in, he didn't even say hello.

"Butch read a few lines, and von Sternberg talked loudly while he was saying them. He never commented, but someone took him away to get his costume, so he supposed he must have passed. Anyway, there was no one else there to play it, certainly not the funny-looking little man waving around a riding crop and wearing boots over his jodhpurs. He was the most autocratic director Butch had ever worked with, a true tyrant, belligerent, and insulting everyone, including, *especially*, Marlene. With Marlene he did it in German. Butch's other language was Spanish, but Marlene told Butch that he was calling her 'a cow.' Butch felt like physically teaching von Sternberg a lesson, but he knew it would wreck his own career and not do Marlene any good. Besides, he said he would have looked like a terrible bully picking on a midget.

"The part wasn't very challenging, he said, and the most difficult thing was running down a steep flight of stairs in high heels. Well, they weren't really very high heels, but they gave him a pair of Spanish boots and no time to practice. He always marveled at the high heels I wore, and that I danced in them. He was a wonderful dancer, and I loved going dancing with him. He said he could never have danced in high heels.

"But he was supposed to run down the stairs, which he did. 'Faster,' von Sternberg said. Butch did it again. Faster again. Faster. 'Take the stairs a few at a time.' Butch did two. Then three. 'More! More!' was the little general's command. Butch felt really awkward in those boots with the heels, and he said they were a little tight and his feet really hurt, especially on landing after about fifty times. He said he thought, no, he was sure, that von Sternberg was crazy, raving mad, but he wasn't going to let him win.

"It was while he was taking the four or five steps that he tripped in those high-heeled boots and fell, as he told it to me, flat on his face.

"There was no concern or sympathy forthcoming from the director, though there were gasps from just about everyone on the set. The director said, 'Get up. Do it again.' Butch said it was like he was cracking a whip, only he didn't actually have a whip, just that riding crop. He didn't need one. He had the power that the studio had given him. He could command everyone to do anything. Anything except to like him. He didn't have a lot of fans.

"But he told me von Sternberg had him do about one hundred takes of running down the stairs. Anyway, it *seemed* like a hundred takes to Butch.

"Finally, they finished, and Butch was able to watch those hundred takes, of him running down those stairs, including the one where he fell on his face. Then, after we'd seen them all, he heard von Sternberg whisper, 'Use take two.'

"Butch said the truth about the mythical Josef von Sternberg was that he didn't know what he was doing."

Though the film was a commercial failure, it has since become a cult classic.

### The Devil Is a Woman (1935)

Concha Perez (Marlene Dietrich) is a woman some men can never get out of their minds. Two such men are handsome young Antonio Galvan (Cesar Romero) and retired army officer Don Pasqual (Lionel Atwill). Galvan, a political refugee, has just met her at the Seville carnival, and he tells Pasqual about her. Pasqual knows her well, but his desire for her has never been gratified. He warns the young man to stay away from her. She will take but never give back anything in return.

Galvan does not heed Pasqual's warning. He pursues Concha, and Pasqual, still hopelessly in love with her, challenges him to a duel.

Galvan shoots first, wounding Pasqual.

Pasqual, believing he will take away Concha's chances of happiness if he kills the younger man, shoots into the air.

Concha visits Pasqual in the hospital, and he tells her to go to Galvan. She joins Galvan on the border, planning to marry him in Paris.

At the last minute, Concha changes her mind and returns to Pasqual.

"Jo told me I would be a great director someday," Marlene told me. "I took that as a compliment, a wonderful compliment, coming from him. But over the years, I've wondered. Was he being sincere or sarcastic? Did he mean I had *too many* opinions, ideas, and that he would like me to be more quiet? I thought about asking him years later when we met, but I didn't. He probably wouldn't have remembered how he felt at that long-ago moment. But if he did, he might not have told me the truth, not wanting to bruise my feelings.

"Jo was wrong about my becoming a great director. Jo sometimes was wrong, but he never admitted it. I don't know about being a *great* director, but I believe I could have been a very good one. There was only one thing wrong with that idea. I never *wanted* to be a director. Never. I am a performer. I don't like to tell people what to do, except as it's necessary for my own performance."

*Desire* WAS ORIGINALLY CALLED *The Pearl Necklace* and was supposed to have been directed by Ernst Lubitsch. Since he was also head of production at Paramount, he decided to limit his participation in the film to producing. He turned over the directing to

Frank Borzage. Gary Cooper was chosen by Borzage to star with Marlene. Borzage had recently directed him in *A Farewell to Arms*.

Before *Desire* started shooting, Marlene accompanied Rudi and Tamara by train to New York, where they were to embark by ship for Paris. Maria, now ten, stayed in Los Angeles.

"Rudi and Tamara and I were never a *ménage à trois*," Marlene explained to me. "Tami's appearance at just the moment I had to travel to Hollywood was a godsend. We needed her for Maria. She stayed because she was in love with Rudi.

"In addition to helping with Maria, Tami had worked in the theater and was a devoted, understanding companion for my Rudi, giving him what he needed, a sexual relationship. It was perfect for everyone, except Tami, who had to be content with last place in our little family.

"Sometimes Maria stayed with me. If Rudi was there, it worked, the three of us would be together, and Tami was in a nearby place. At first, Rudi left her in Paris when he was with me and Maria in California. When we would travel, Rudi and Maria and I would have a suite that was appropriate to my star status. Tami would have a nice room in the same hotel. After Rudi had the chicken ranch, Tami stayed there. It was her home.

"Tami always seemed frail and sad. She needed to be taken care of, and Rudi was the best man in the world a woman could get to take care of her. I know. I seem a very independent person, but I loved having Rudi take care of me and of everything for me.

"I wondered if Tami ever wanted a baby of her own? Rudi's baby. She must have. Rudi never talked about Tami with me, the same way he never talked about me with her."

### Desire (1936)

While fleeing from Paris with a stolen necklace, Madeleine de Beaupre (Marlene Dietrich) is stopped at the Spanish border for a more thorough inspection than she expects. To smuggle the necklace across the border, she slips it into the pocket of a man she has just passed on the road.

After she has crossed the border, she catches up with the man in his car and passes him. Then, she purposely wrecks her car so that he has to pick her up. He is Tom Bradley (Gary Cooper), a Detroit automotive engineer.

Unable to get the necklace away from the unsuspecting Bradley during their drive to an inn, Madeleine enlists the aid of her confederate, Carlos Margoli (John Halliday). Their attention to him causes Tom to believe that Madeleine is in love with him. Soon, she really is, and she returns the necklace and marries him, becoming a Detroit housewife.

At the beginning of 1936, Marlene started working on a film called *Invitation to Happiness* with Charles Boyer. It was based on *Hotel Imperial*, originally a play in Hungarian by Melchior Lengyel. After four days of shooting, producer Benjamin Glazer quit. He told Paramount production head Ernst Lubitsch that he could not tolerate Marlene's insistence on script changes, which, under the terms of her contract, she was entitled to make. Lubitsch took over producing the film, now called *I Loved a Soldier*, arranging with director Henry Hathaway to shoot around Dietrich until studio and star could work out their differences. At the time, Marlene was reputed to be the highest-paid woman in the world, although Mae West also claimed this honor.

Lubitsch left for a European holiday, handing over the responsibility of dealing with the star to William LeBaron. Their differences, however, could not be reconciled, so, after twenty-eight days of shooting, Marlene left the production.

She was replaced by Margaret Sullavan, and the title of the film reverted to *Hotel Imperial*. Sullavan suffered a fall after three days and could not continue. Other actresses, including Claudette Colbert and Bette Davis, were sought but were unavailable. The production cost of the film had by now reached nearly $1 million. It was finally made and released in 1939 with Ray Milland and Isa Miranda. Lengyel's story *Ninotchka* was released the same year, starring Greta Garbo.

*The Garden of Allah*, Marlene's next film, was based on a 1904 novel by Robert Hichens. It was produced by David O. Selznick, cost over $1 million to make, and starred Marlene and Charles Boyer. The director was Richard Boleslawski, who had just come from the Moscow Art Theatre, and it was shot in the new Technicolor three-film process. There was an elaborate dance sequence. Thanks to the skillful machinations and personal charm of master agent Leland Hayward, a twenty-six-year-old Joshua Logan was hired as dialogue coach.

I spoke with Logan at his New York City River House apartment. The living room was adorned with his marvelous collection of antique Swiss automatons. As I arrived, Logan had them all turned on at once. Some were dancing, some were telling fortunes, one was powdering her face.

"Part of my job was convincing Dietrich that it was a great script when she knew it was 'twash,' as she called it. She had trouble pronouncing Rs, and the script was full of them. It seemed to have been written to include the most Rs possible. Charles Boyer had trouble pronouncing virtually *every* word in the awful script, probably because he was embarrassed speaking those lines, which Selznick kept calling 'desert poetry.' I should add that Boleslawski didn't speak English.

"I was getting the unheard-of salary of three hundred dollars a week, but after a few days in the Mojave Desert heat with this script and a discontented cast and crew, I tried to quit, but Selznick wouldn't let me. I don't know why, except that Marlene liked me because I was from 'Noo Yahk.'"

### The Garden of Allah (1936)

Domini Enfilden (Marlene Dietrich) has spent years nursing her ailing father. When he dies, she is advised by her spiritual adviser, Mother Josephine (Lucille Watson), to go to Algeria, where she can start a new life with the help of a cleric there.

En route from France to North Africa, Domini encounters a gloomy, unpleasant Russian, Boris Androvsky (Charles Boyer). They meet again in Beni Mora at the parish of Mother Josephine's friend, Father Roubier (C. Aubrey Smith).

Seeking diversion, Domini hires Batouch (Joseph Schildkraut) and his brother, Hadj (Henry Brandon), as tour guides. She is taken to see the Ouled-Nail dancing girls. One of the girls, Irena (Tilly Losch), attacks Hadj in a jealous rage, and a riot ensues. Domini is rescued by Boris, who is also there. They soon fall in love.

At a bazaar, a sand diviner (John Carradine) predicts a trip for Domini, followed by sublime happiness. Then he stops predicting and will not continue.

Domini and Boris are married and leave on their honeymoon. At a desert encampment, Boris is recognized by a soldier (Alan Marshal) as Brother Antoine, a Trappist monk who has abandoned his order.

Guilt-ridden, Boris returns to the monastery to make peace with God. Domini leaves him at the gate, knowing she will never see him again.

"One day in the desert," Logan continued, "I got sunburned, and Marlene insisted on rubbing oil on my chest and back, in front of the crew. From then on, badly concealed leers and knowing smirks followed me wherever I went.

"Marlene kept pictures of John Gilbert in her location room. Each one had a burning votive candle. He'd just died, and they'd evidently been very close.

"When *The Garden of Allah* was previewed, no one could understand a word of that 'desert poetry.' But in Selznick's defense, I should add that he made a number of changes that established order, so it was possible to make something of the film, showing him to be a thorough professional. The photography won an Oscar."


DOUGLAS FAIRBANKS, JR., MET Marlene at a dinner party in London at the home of Alexander Korda. From the moment he saw her enter, Fairbanks lost interest in the menu, though Korda was a wonderful host, renowned for his sumptuous dinner parties.

Marlene was sitting on one side of Korda. Fairbanks wondered which of the men at the party was her escort. Or could it be that she was alone, as he was, in which case they were the *only* ones who had come alone. Fairbanks approached her and introduced himself.

"She had a beautiful voice," Fairbanks recalled, "a soft, low purr which held wonderful promise, even more so than on the screen, and it was exactly the voice she *should* have had. That rarely happens. Her extraordinary presence was enhanced by an *Orient Express* accent."

She was beautifully dressed, in perfect taste, though he wasn't able to remember exactly *what* she was wearing, not even the color. "Perhaps it was a mauve or a lavender. It was obvious that few women would enjoy being at the same party with her. Any man there could scarcely keep his eyes off of her.

"She did not seem to be overly aware of her beauty, nor did she seem to be oblivious to it. She moved with the grace of a dancer."

Fairbanks himself was an accomplished dancer and an extremely graceful person.

He spent the evening weighing the possibilities. What he knew was he didn't want this brief introduction to be the end. He didn't even know where she was staying. While he was considering all of this, she seemed to have left. Then he heard that wonderful voice, so close it seemed to be touching him.

"'Mr. Fairbanks, I wonder if you might be able to give me a ride home. I see you have come alone, and I've come alone, and I don't live very far away.'

"I would have driven her to the ends of the earth, with pleasure!

"In the car, I wondered if I should try to seduce her on the night we met. I didn't want the evening to end at her door, but I didn't want to rush things. I might never have another opportunity.

"While I was wondering what to do about asking her to dinner, she asked me if I would like to come up to her apartment. Of course I would. When we entered the apartment, I said, 'It's very nice of you to have me up for a drink.'

"'That wasn't what I had in mind,' she said.

"Her voice was as much of a dream as she. Magical. I never thought about her age. I assumed we were about the same age. Up to that time, I looked a bit younger than I was. I thought perhaps I looked too young, but I wasn't deeply concerned because I knew that time would take care of that, and, as you can see, it has.

"It was only much later that I learned that Marlene was eight years older than I. It didn't disturb me, and I never mentioned it to Marlene, in case it might disturb her.

"Besides, I've always been rather drawn to older women.

"Marlene had a lovely suite at Claridge's, where I would visit her just about every night when we were in London," Fairbanks told me.

"Going in was easy. No problem. Going out discreetly was another matter. Difficult. Worse than difficult. There was no other way out except to take the lift and stroll nonchalantly through the lobby.

In the early morning hours, the other exits would be locked and one would have to enlist the aid of an employee of the hotel in order to leave.

"I came up with a more ingenious answer. Priding myself on being rather agile and athletic, the answer was obvious—the fire escape.

"I wasn't exactly dressed for the role, because people really dressed up in those days in London. I wore white tie and tails nearly every night. That night was not the exception. I tied my tails behind me so they wouldn't hamper my descent. It was already getting light outside as I touched the ground and turned to get a taxi. Usually taxis were plentiful, but I'd considered the possibility that just as dawn was breaking, I might not be able to hail a taxi. Well, no matter. My own flat was not far away. A short, brisk walk.

"As I turned, I looked into the face of a very young bobby, as the British policemen are known. It was a young face, very shiny. He didn't look as if he'd shaved yet. I tried to appear casually jaunty, as though I always left by the fire escape for my morning constitutional. He had a big grin and he greeted me with a friendly 'Good morning, Mr. Fairbanks. Are you rehearsing for your next film?' Oh, the joys of fame!

"'Very practical when nobody's about, but be careful not to have an accident, sir. Good day, Mr. Fairbanks.'

"As he strolled off, he probably didn't hear my mumbled, 'Good morning.' A taxi stopped and whisked me away to Grosvenor Square. The next night, I took the lift.

"I have to admit I was pleased when a flat became available on the floor just below my penthouse. When I told Marlene about it, she dashed over and took a lease on it. She used the flat as a kind of storage room, and we used my living room and garden for entertaining.

"I preferred to avoid meeting William Paley [president of CBS]," Fairbanks told me, "who was often in the hall returning late from some festivity or other. He was interested in Marlene and had been doing his best to court her, but she hadn't responded to him except in a coolly civil way, which annoyed him. He considered himself an intense competitor, and he was accustomed to getting what he wanted.

"One night, or I should say, one morning, I saw Paley in the hall and he was walking straight toward me. He walked right up to me and in a rather angry tone, said, 'Fairbanks, I know where you've been.'

"I put my finger to my lips and whispered, 'Yes, but please don't tell Marlene.'

"Marlene Dietrich enjoyed the constant hint of scandal, more than a hint, and she did her best, in a subtle way, to enhance rumors that she was a bad girl, not a good girl. She believed bad girls were more compelling for the public's imagination than saintly women.

"She did not, however, ever want the rumors confirmed. She preferred an illusion of indiscretion. She did not want anyone to know anything, except, of course, she and her lover.

"That was fine with me. I always preferred innuendo, a whisper rather than a shout. Usually it's the man who prefers to be gossiped about when he is seen with a beautiful woman to enhance his reputation, and the woman is supposedly shy, but in this case we had the role reversal. 'Their imaginations will be very active thinking about us, Douglas,' she told me. Personally, I hoped they had something else to think about."


"MARLENE TOLD ME SHE was von Sternberg's creation," Fairbanks said. "Actually, she told everyone that. She worshipped at his feet, and she made a point of telling everyone that she did. That was Marlene. She was always a bit overdone. She loved being mysterious, unfathomable, provocative, and she was.

"She constantly perpetuated the myth of von Sternberg, and thus she perpetuated her own myth. At least in the beginning. I feel she played a part, an excellent role which suited her, or at least suited an aspect of her character. The part became her, and I think she became the part.

"But she was no one's creature. I feel she did everything von Sternberg wanted her to do, as long as it was what *she* wanted to do.

"Her face looked like marble, her features beautifully sculpted. I never heard it said that she looked like anyone else, and she didn't. She was very intelligent, more intelligent than people realized, more intelligent than *she* realized.

"She had had an affair with John Gilbert, who had had an earlier affair with Garbo.

"After Jack Gilbert died, Marlene kept votive candles in front of his silver-framed photo, and everywhere she went, the picture and the candles went with her. When our relationship began, we were making love in front of the photograph. At first, I was a little inhibited in front of the photograph and candles, but I never said anything.

"I was a little hesitant with Jack looking out at me, but I got used to it. After a while, I stopped noticing. Then the photograph and the candles disappeared."

"ONE EVENING," FAIRBANKS TOLD me, "we were to have dinner, as we usually did, and I called for her. She asked me if I'd mind if we double-dated with another couple for dinner. She said that she had already invited them. So that didn't leave much choice. I wanted to please Marlene. In those days, we spent a great deal of time together, and we would be alone after dinner.

"Well, I *was* a little disappointed, actually *more* than a little, because I'd been looking forward to the evening alone with her, for dinner, and whatever. *Whatever*, I have to admit, was the part of the evening at that age and with her that I most looked forward to.

"Before I could say anything, she added that they would be waiting at the restaurant. I could only be gracious, which I would have been anyway. I supposed that if she had invited them, the other couple would be interesting. It was more interesting than I'd ever imagined.

"When we entered the restaurant, the others were already seated at the table, a very nice-looking young man who rose as we were seated. With him was an attractive young woman.

"Marlene introduced us. 'Douglas, dear,' she said in that lovely voice of hers, 'I'd like you to meet Rudi, Rudi Sieber, my husband. And this is Tami, Tamara, his friend who lives with him.'

"At the end of the evening, when we were alone, Marlene asked me, 'Did you like them?'

"'Of course,' I sputtered. Actually, I did like Rudi, who was quiet, subdued, and seemed a little frightened, like me. I hadn't really noticed her. Rudi was charming, but, to tell the truth, which I didn't volunteer to Marlene, I would rather have had him be charming somewhere else.

"I considered myself a man of the world, sort of sophisticated in the ways of the world, and not easy to shock, though possible to shock. Well, I was at the least surprised.

"I suppose when I look back, I had a rather puritanical childhood in the sense that the Puritans had the same drives, emotions, passions as the rest of us, perhaps stronger, because they were so pent up, but the important thing was that other people didn't know. The Great Cover-Up.

"Marlene was unconventional in her lovemaking as she was unconventional in everything. She was passionate, spontaneous, imaginative, unforgettable. I certainly could never forget her. She was off the scale.

"I almost never really looked at Tamara, the person Rudi brought. I was so deeply interested in Marlene, who was such a fascinating presence that she couldn't help but dominate the scene. Even when she was quiet, her look was always captivating.

"One day someone asked me what Marlene's husband's girlfriend was like. There was gossip about the odd arrangement the three of them had, and I had become a part of it. I tried to treat it casually, like it wasn't an odd arrangement at all. I pulled it off, publicly rather successfully. Privately, I wasn't doing so well. It's easier to play a part for others than it is to play a part for yourself. I discovered that I was more of a prude than I knew. I don't think I was prudish about what others did, unless it affected me, self-centered chap that I was.

"That night I focused on Tamara, and I realized that she was a very pretty girl. She didn't dazzle like Marlene, but then who could? She didn't emanate confidence, and when she observed me looking in her direction, she looked down, and I thought she might scurry away. She seemed to be trying to blend into the background. She had a wispy quality, but she was very graceful in the way she walked and moved. Marlene told me that Tamara had danced professionally and was very talented as well as being very pretty. 'She was Russian at a time there were many Russians in Berlin, among them many pretty girls, so it was difficult to stand out,' Marlene said.

"I mentioned that Tamara didn't dress to stand out. 'It's funny that you should say that,' Marlene said. 'Everything she wears was mine. I give her whatever I tire of, or find myself not wearing.'"

"Marlene enjoyed swimming in the nude," Fairbanks remembered. "I don't know if she swam nude when she was alone because, of course, when she was alone, I wasn't there and no one was to bear witness. I know that Marlene enjoyed having some people around to watch her, admiringly.

"She never said anything about it, and she seemed not to notice that she was being looked at, but she *was* being looked at, and she was well aware of those who were taking discreet peeks.

"It was not just that she had a beautiful figure, which she did. But what added to making her so striking was that wonderful complexion, all over. She had the fairest skin I'd ever seen, pale, slightly pink, translucent, like the finest porcelain.

"She encouraged me to take it all off and swim with her. When I knew we were all alone, I did as she said, but anytime I thought there were people around, especially women, I preferred trunks. Marlene said, 'Whatever makes you comfortable, Douggie.'"


THROUGH FAIRBANKS, MARLENE CAME to know George, the Duke of York, and his wife, the former Elizabeth Bowes-Lyon. George would soon become the king of England, though few had ever considered that possibility, certainly not George and Elizabeth. It was his elder brother, Edward, the Prince of Wales, who had been destined to be crowned, and indeed who did become king, though only briefly.

From George, Fairbanks learned that Edward VIII was planning to announce his abdication so that he could marry Wallis Simpson, a divorced American. Fairbanks told Marlene of Edward's intention.

Marlene was shocked. Through Fairbanks, she had met members of the British royal family, and she was horrified that Edward, whom she particularly liked, would make such a dreadful mistake. "We must stop him," she said to Fairbanks.

"That her 'we' did not include *me* was immediately clear," Fairbanks told me.

"'I'll stop him,' she said. 'I must have a bath—and the right perfume.' She began taking off her clothes as she went.

"She took quite a while fussing with her hair. 'I'm ready,' she announced. I offered to drive her, but she told me that wouldn't be appropriate. She said she was planning to dissuade the Duke of Windsor from acting rashly and giving up his destiny for 'that homely, flat-chested woman.'

"Marlene said if verbal persuasion didn't work, she was prepared to seduce him, and to show him that Wallis wasn't the only woman in the world. 'Far from it. I'll make him forget her.'"

In the midst of their own affair, Fairbanks expressed his lack of enthusiasm for Marlene's plan.

"'Oh, darling, don't be old-fashioned. We're doing it for England, which we both love. Some sacrifices must be made.'

"She went off in her limousine, but she'd dallied a bit too long, enhancing her charms, which hadn't needed any enhancing, and the king was out when she arrived, or so she was told. She had missed her chance.

"So Marlene never found out if she could have changed the course of history. Perhaps it was just as well because she always believed, *knew*, her scheme would have worked, if only she'd been there in time."

I asked him what he thought. Did he feel she could have distracted the king of England from his great love?

"Who knows?" Fairbanks replied. "Not I. Edward was a strange duck. Not at all like his brother, 'Bertie [George],' except Bertie also found a soul mate in his Elizabeth. She was invaluable to him when he became king of England. Maybe Wallis was Edward's soul mate, and because of her, he abdicated. Maybe he felt that way at the moment, and maybe he thought he didn't like being king, but later he might have felt differently. He'd been born into the ultimate royal privilege, and it all came so easily. It had all been given to him, and it was always there, so he took it for granted. He didn't know anything else, so he may not have been able to imagine what life was like for other people. He may have thought being king was something he could take away with him.

"I wondered if he and Wallis were happy for all those years afterward. It seemed they couldn't be, because the price they had to pay was too high. Their life wasn't at all what she had wanted. She didn't want him to renounce the throne. I think she was really in love with the throne. You can only shop so much. She didn't have the state occasions to wear her clothes and jewels. If they weren't happy together, they could never admit it publicly or even to each other, or even to themselves."

ALEXANDER KORDA PAID MARLENE $450,000 to appear in *Knight Without Armor*, a film based on a James Hilton novel. This was the highest salary a female movie star had ever received. She originally hoped John Gilbert would make his great comeback with her in the film. He was replaced by Robert Donat, whom King Vidor said to me was "off screen a small man with asthma, on screen, a giant."

Douglas Fairbanks, Jr., remembered talking with Marlene about Donat, whom they both considered a brilliant actor. "Marlene had been thrilled about working with Donat, but all too quickly it became apparent that he was in extremely poor health, valiantly trying to go on with the film in spite of the asthma that had long plagued him.

"It reached the point where he could not speak his lines, even with frequent intervals of rest, and he had to be rushed to the hospital. The producers were told that it might be months before he could return to the film, possibly two months. Or it might be never.

"The producers felt they had no other option than to replace Donat, but Marlene wouldn't accept that. If Donat is to be replaced, she said, 'you have to look for my replacement, too.' The producers hesitated and decided to give Donat two months because of Marlene's stand of support for him.

"At the end of the two months, Donat returned to *Knight Without Armor*. There was a party to welcome him, and Marlene proposed the toast:

"'To our knight without asthma.'

"Sadly, it wasn't true. It was just a temporary respite."

## *Knight Without Armor* (1937)

A. J. Fothergill (Robert Donat), an Englishman exiled from czarist Russia because of an article he wrote critical of the government, agrees to stay in Russia as a British spy. In this role, he joins the revolutionaries. After an assassination, he is put in charge of delivering the Countess Alexandra (Marlene Dietrich) to Petrograd for interrogation. He helps her to escape, but she is soon recaptured by the Reds.

While they are being transported to Samara, her captor, Poushkoff (John Clements), falls in love with her and, at the cost of his own life, allows her to escape with Fothergill.

When she becomes ill in a forest, Fothergill goes for a doctor. While he is away, she is rescued by the White forces and put on a train for the border. Fothergill races to catch the train, which he just barely does.

In London, famed cinematographer Jack Cardiff, who was a camera operator on this film, told me his vivid memory of Marlene Dietrich from the filming of *Knight Without Armor*.

"If you ever want to make a crew unhappy, shoot on a weekend. Actors usually don't like to, either. It's a good time to choose if you don't want to have any gawkers. On a Saturday or a Sunday, you won't have anyone hanging around who doesn't need to be there, a rule of thumb. Actually, a rule of the whole hand. I've scarcely ever known anyone who would have chosen Saturday or Sunday to shoot except for Alexander Korda, the producer. He was very happy to work on a weekend. Any day. I don't know if he slept at all. He was so swept away by his enthusiasm.

"We were shooting this little Russian bathroom. The assistant director had us there, and they were going to do just a few close-ups. The important information he told everyone was that we would be off and away by five. Our electrician was reading a newspaper.

The lights were being set up. It was a listless crew. They were clearly working without enthusiasm. We had all shot bathroom scenes before. They were far from exciting. Lots of water. Lots of foam and an actress in a bathing suit. All that foam produced the illusion that the actress was naked in the tub. It was a yawner for the crew.

"Then, Marlene entered. She made a grand entrance followed by two maids who were carrying extra towels. Her hair was in an upsweep, a bit messy. It seemed very natural and had probably taken a great deal of time to produce that natural look. She had a cigarette in a long cigarette holder.

"She nodded graciously to us. She walked to the bath and tested the water, not with a toe, but with her finger.

"Then, she took off her bathrobe. No bathing suit. Marlene Dietrich was starkers.

"A stunned crew shot that scene. We were all hoping it would have to be reshot, but no such luck.

"Marlene exited the tub with the two maids holding up their towels to cover her. The floor was wet and soapy.

"Marlene slipped. She tried to gain her balance, but couldn't, and she couldn't get up on that wet, soapy floor. Her arms and legs were all askew, going in different directions.

"Everything she had showed. It was all magnificent. If we hadn't been worried about her, it would have been totally enjoyable. We all admired her enormously and didn't want her to be hurt. The two maids helped her to her feet and covered her with the two towels. She was fine, absolutely fine, not hurt a bit. She knew how to fall.

"And none of us will ever forget that scene. There were some who were present who weren't looking at the right moment. I don't think they've ever gotten over it."

"When Marlene was filming *Knight Without Armor*," Fairbanks told me, "she heard the Russian word *dushka*. She liked the sound of that word, and her enthusiasm for it was enhanced by learning that my friends, the Duke and Duchess of Kent, had named their dog Dushka. So, one day, Marlene announced to me, 'I'm Dushka,' explaining that she needed a private name that only we knew for when she wrote to me. She said she was sending me a little gift she hoped I would enjoy, and it would have a card from Dushka. She'd wanted to let me know, so I'd know who sent it.

"I tried to think quickly what the occasion was for the gift I didn't want, not to be guilty of forgetting an anniversary of ours that she held sacred. I couldn't think of anything. I knew it wasn't my birthday. It wasn't even Marlene's birthday. She thought it nice to give me a gift on her birthday. I had to ask her, 'Why am I getting a gift? Have I forgotten something?'

"She said, 'I'm sending you a gift because I felt like giving you something. It's the wonderful thing about being rich. You can give people you love gifts whenever you want to.'

"Marlene wasn't really so rich, but she felt rich. I've never had the luxury of feeling rich, even when I suppose I was because I could always see the possibility of the funds running out and not knowing how to replenish them. It was probably related to boyhood financial insecurity, the financial insecurity my mother [Beth Sully] felt all the while we were living high. My mother knew what it was like to have a rich family and lose all your money because it had happened to her.

"There was Marlene, who had lived through World War I in Germany and then had to uproot herself because of the Nazis, but she didn't feel insecurity. She had such perfect confidence in herself. And why not? I could never muster that kind of confidence in myself, except on a ship during World War II while in action, when I had no time to think and review my shortcomings.

"The next day, the package was delivered. The handwritten card said, 'From your Dushka.' Inside the box from Cartier was a wonderful clock."

• • •

"THE COMMISSARY AT DENHAM Studios in London was really a restaurant," Jack Cardiff told me, "with the lunch crowd sometimes including Marlene Dietrich, Laurence Olivier, Noel Coward, Orson Welles, a very young Vivien Leigh, Charles Laughton, Miriam Hopkins, H. G. Wells, George Bernard Shaw, who often visited, and Hank Fonda, when he was in town. I kept saying to myself, 'This is Madame Tussaud's, but with sound.'

"These people had great voices. Certainly, as everyone knows, these were great faces, but their voices were great, too.

"There was the constant hum and buzz of all of those fantastic voices. My business was the way the people looked, but I was always conscious of the way the people sounded. Marlene Dietrich had the most incredibly sexy voice in life, even more than on the screen. It was so enjoyable and distracted me so much, I couldn't ever remember what she said. She was always very friendly to me.

"I met Marlene in a way I don't recommend, though it worked out for me. I was late getting to the set for some of the preliminary photographic tests, and I never liked anyone being late, especially myself, so I stupidly barged in through a door and nearly knocked down the person coming out of the door. The accident was completely my fault. I felt I was a rude fool. Fortunately I kept my wits, and especially my reflexes, to reach out and catch Marlene Dietrich, so she didn't fall. I couldn't believe it. It was Marlene Dietrich in my arms. I might have injured the star of our film, *Knight Without Armor*. It could have been *Knight Without Leading Lady*.

"Marlene, who was stunned, looked very pale and white. I wasn't aware yet of how pale and white she *always* looked. I always saw more than I did in real life when I looked through the viewfinder at someone. I think it's a matter of focus and concentration, and also I can subtract my own physical self and social nervousness and become part of the camera.

"I caught Miss Dietrich while saying, 'Sorry, sorry, sorry.' In the midst of my frantic apologies, I said, 'I'm Jack Cardiff.' She said, 'I know.'

"Despite my abject misery, I couldn't help but notice her radiant beauty. She seemed beautiful in the way a goddess should be.

"I thought, what if she never forgives me for being a clumsy oaf? I might have ruined our filming.

"Far from holding our close brush on a collision course against me, it seemed to make her friendlier, like we had a secret or something intimate we had shared. I was only a callow youth, but that seemed to endear me to her.

"What really brought us close was a bad cold I caught. Marlene noticed and she actually became maternal.

"'Oh, poor boy. We can't have you sick. I can fix it, but I'll have to call Germany to get some more of my magical remedy, and you'll see, it will cure you immediately.'

"It happened just as she said. My cold was getting worse minute by minute it seemed, when the German potion appeared. With the first dose, I began immediately to recover. I soon was feeling better than I ever had.

"'Naturally,' she said.

"I wish I'd asked more questions about her magic medicine and ordered a supply for myself, but maybe it had to come from the hands of a goddess, Marlene."


"ONE OF THE SURPRISES about Marlene," Fairbanks recalled, "was how motherly she became if I ever had a cold, which I frequently did. Marlene's attentions were so delightful, it was almost worth having a cold. Anyway, if one had to be under the weather, her homemade chicken soup was very consoling. She would stroke my fevered brow with her soft cool hands caressing me.

"'Douglas, dear, you will recover very soon,' she reassured me in that seductive voice. I wasn't in a hurry.

"She absolutely loved to take care of people. No one, not even my mother when I was a young child, had been so—I can't think of a better word—motherly.

"She was always ready to rearrange my closets. She did a masterful job, or should I say a *mistressful* job? My closets looked beautiful. It was just that I couldn't find anything. I had become familiar with my own disorganization. I didn't stop her, however, because it seemed to please her so much. She explained to me that her mother had been the most wonderful housekeeper in the world. Her description of her mother's work ethic sounded more to me like an obsession than an accomplishment, but the pleasure for her mother may have been in the finished result. I never felt the need to see my face reflected in a pot on the stove.

"She wasn't just happy when she had cleaned my place, but while she was doing it. She could look sexy while she was doing it, even wearing her hairnet."


WHILE SPENDING A HOLIDAY in Paris, Marlene realized her German passport was about to expire. She needed to renew it until she could become a U.S. citizen. It was important, however, that the Germans did not suspect what she had in mind. They had been sending high-placed Nazis, German generals, and even old German royalty to visit her and pay court. All of them brought personal greetings from Goebbels and Hitler, who were anxious for her to return to UFA. Grand promises were made as to the privileges she would have in selecting scripts, directors, whatever pleased her. Marlene reassured them that she would be coming back.

Then she personally went to the German embassy to renew the

passport that would allow her to return to the United States. She paid as great attention to her appearance as she would for a film role, and rehearsed her part, so she could be calm and charming, in German, and a bit nonchalant.

Embassy officials must have believed her, because her German passport was renewed, allowing her to leave France and return to America. Then on March 6, 1937, in Los Angeles, California, she was sworn in as a U.S. citizen.

ERNST LUBITSCH PRODUCED AND directed *Angel.* It was based on a Hungarian play by Melchior Lengyel. The idea, that a woman could have two lovers, offended the Production Code, even though one of the lovers was her husband and even though in the end she chose him over the other.

### Angel (1937)

Maria Barker (Marlene Dietrich), feeling neglected by her husband, Sir Frederick Barker (Herbert Marshall), leaves London for a secret trip to Paris. There she meets Anthony Halton (Melvyn Douglas) at a salon for sophisticates, and they become romantically involved. Since she won't tell him her real name, he calls her Angel.

Fearing complications, she returns to London and her husband. All goes well until Halton shows up in London and turns out to be an old war buddy of Sir Frederick's. Faced with a choice between her husband and her lover, she chooses Sir Frederick.

The Production Code board especially objected to the sophisticates' salon, which was originally shot as what it was in Lengyel's play, a sex club. Lubitsch had to reshoot this sequence at great cost to Paramount after prints had gone out to theaters.

"MARLENE WAS AWARE OF the danger of 'Hitler and his gang,' as she called them, long before anyone else," Fairbanks told me. "She was very upset by the idea that [British prime minister Neville] Chamberlain had gone to meet Hitler to try and appease him and get along. She was enraged. 'How could he believe Hitler?' she asked me.

"'Well, I don't think he did,' I said. 'I'm only speculating, but I don't think he believed Hitler. My guess is that he was just playing for time. A lot of people think war is inevitable, and he was stalling to get England better armed and in hopes of the United States entering the war.'

"Marlene seemed persuaded. 'You have such wonderful British connections, Douglas dear,' she said. I started to explain I didn't really have special knowledge, it was just my guess, but then, I thought, I usually say too much. I decided to just leave well enough alone.

"We met one day to have lunch. I'd missed breakfast, my own fault, by sleeping late, so I was starving. But when I saw Marlene, I forgot all about food. She was wearing a filmy ecru frock in sheer layers. There was the illusion that you could see through the dress. You couldn't. I can vouch for that, because I looked. But the illusion was there, and that was exciting enough. As though that weren't enough, she was sitting there with those beautiful legs crossed. The skirt wasn't short, but because of the way the layers fell, one could see a great deal of leg.

"She wasn't often early or even on time for social meetings, though she was extremely punctual for the set, whenever she was working. I made it a practice to be a little early whenever we met, because it seemed to be the correct way, for the gentleman to arrive first. This time, I'd miscalculated.

"It turned out she was early because she had something to tell me. She began speaking after just a quick peck of a kiss. She said, 'Douglas, I've an idea.'

"That wasn't unusual. She had a very active mind. She had ideas within ideas. And she was full of surprises. I was never surprised anymore. I would only have been surprised if I *hadn't* been surprised.

"She leaned close and almost whispered in that glorious voice of hers: 'I want to kill Hitler.'

"'Don't we all,' I said. Hitler was running rampant over Europe.

"'I've been thinking about it, and I feel I must do something. The thing is I think I can do it or at least I can make a good try.'

"I said, 'How would you get close enough to Hitler? No one can do *that.*'

"She said, 'I know how to get close to a man. I've heard that Hitler likes me. Leni Riefenstahl has been telling it to people. Goebbels and his cronies are always wanting to get me back, with their promises. I have to agree only to do one film until I see whether I want to do more, and they are offering me the world. "The Queen of UFA" is a phrase they like. I could say I'm ready, but a condition of it is I want to be alone with the führer. It would be the condition of my return. I would explain that it's because I admire him so much, "worship him," I would say. I would go so far, gushing over how I feel about him, intimating that I am desperately in love with him. I would make it very clear that my staying in Germany to make UFA films is conditioned on my simple personal request to be with him. I'm certain that Hitler would agree.'

"I said, 'But you would be searched. Hitler must be unbelievably well guarded. There will be guards who want to search you *very thoroughly* to protect Hitler, and because they would enjoy searching *you!*'

"She said, 'If necessary, I would go in and visit him naked. I mean I would be naked.'

"'That should get you in,' I said. 'But how would you kill him?'

"'I wouldn't have any trouble killing him. It would be a pleasure. It's like war. I think killing him would save thousands of lives, even millions.'

"'But what murder weapon would you use and how could you get away? They'd never let you escape.'

"'I would not expect to escape. I would go there prepared to die. I don't want to die. I want to live. Life is wonderful. But to kill Hitler would be wonderful. We all have to die sometime, and that would be something to die for!'

"I said, 'If you are naked, or wearing little, and you are thoroughly searched, what weapon can you smuggle in?'

"'It's the only thing I can't solve, so I'm turning to you. I know you know about British mysteries, that kind of thing, and you have a wonderful imagination. I thought of a hairpin specially made to be very sharp. Poison seems the most possible. And you have contacts.'

"I couldn't imagine what she meant. My reading was a little dated, Wilkie Collins, that sort of thing.

"I never thought of anything, but if I had, I don't know what I would have done. How could I send the wonderful woman I loved into a situation fraught with danger, with no chance of her returning and virtually no chance for success? Fortunately, her idea didn't go any farther because she didn't figure out how to complete the assassination of Hitler. She was a very brave girl, and I know she would have gambled her life if she thought she had a chance of success.

"I think that something I said to her during our conversation may have influenced her. She didn't respond when I mentioned it, I think because it was something she'd already thought about. As long as her dramatic wish to kill Hitler remained a whim, an unsatisfied impulse, that was one thing, but had it gone farther, she would have to think about the repercussions to her family, especially her mother, about whom she was most concerned and whom she hadn't been able to persuade to leave Germany. Perhaps her mother later thought it an ill-considered decision to stay, but only after it was too late to leave Germany. No one could have imagined how bad it was going to be in Germany. Marlene might not have hesitated to give up her own life, but her mother's life—she could not have done that.

"In 1938, Marlene rented a chalet near Salzburg in Austria for a few weeks. While we were staying there, she was invited to a formal party at a wonderful place, almost a castle and I was her escort. Inside, the halls were lined with marble busts, suits of amour, and full-length portraits of royal Austrians. The furniture was gilt and silk, and it blended perfectly with the exotic tapestry wall hangings.

"I knew a few people there, but Marlene knew a great many, and it seemed everyone knew her, or wanted to. It was a glamorous formal event belonging in a film. The beautifully attired guests were, for the most part, Austrian, and there were a number of Germans.

"A bearded man motioned for me to leave Marlene and the group surrounding her and follow him to a corner room. Before closing the door behind us, he looked about furtively. He began speaking in a low tone, quickly—in German. I didn't understand a word, but I was so intrigued, I just listened, occasionally punctuating my silences with what I hoped was an appropriate *natürlich*.

"It was clear that he was transmitting information he considered of the greatest importance. When he had finished, I felt the need to assure him that he had conveyed his message, so I uttered an especially knowing *natürlich*. He looked astounded.

"We returned to the ballroom and I rejoined Marlene. I looked smug. I felt smug because of the way I had played my own personal *natürlich* game.

"My assumption was that the Austrian gentleman was unsympathetic to the Nazi Anschluss and wanted to preserve the separate identity of his country. I had been invited there, the only American present, by Marlene who was well known for her anti-Nazi sentiments.

"It was a few years before I learned what I had been told. I had been entrusted with information about the timing of the Anschluss, the takeover of Austria as it had been discussed by the most important Austrian Nazis, Prince von Stahremberg, and Hitler. It had been assumed that I would pass this information on to Washington, but when I said *natürlich* at the end, they had assumed that the powers in Washington already knew, and that *I* knew they knew.

"What would have happened if I had understood every word. Or, if I had taken the situation seriously and confessed that I didn't understand a word? I don't know.

"My personal guess is nothing would have happened. I didn't really have as good access as they thought I did. I probably didn't have as direct access as *I* thought I did.

"The main reason for telling me was there was still hope on the part of some for a policy of appeasement. A little later, all was different. I never told Marlene the story. By the time I found out the possible serious implications, we weren't together as much and weren't as close, although we remained friends. I cared what she thought about me, and I didn't want to lose her respect. I didn't want to lose my own respect for me, but, oh, well . . .

"I've never liked unpleasantness, especially in a love relationship, and I've tended to avoid any sort of emotional breakup," Fairbanks told me. "I wasn't able to avoid it with Marlene. In truth, it was my fault. It was in the California house that was Marlene's home, a rented house with much more room than my own. It had a lovely pool.

"*The Prisoner of Zenda* had been a success beyond anything I'd imagined. My father and Marlene had been right in urging me to accept the part, even though I would only have third billing. Each felt the picture would be very popular, that my role was juicy, and that above all it was better to be in a film which was certain to be successful than to be sitting at home waiting by the telephone, which never rings when you're watching it.

"I felt quite at home at Marlene's, and one afternoon I went to her desk to look for some writing paper. I had no intention of prying or violating her privacy, but I saw a packet of letters loosely tied with a piece of blue ribbon. That was, of course, when I should have stopped. Until that moment, I had always considered myself a gentleman. After that moment, I was never quite so certain. Apparently, I was a gentleman as long as the circumstances were conducive. I saw a few words of the top letter, and I realized it was a love letter. I didn't go too much farther. I read a few lines without disturbing the blue ribbon. Passionate, erotic. I went into an instant jealous rage and awaited Marlene's return, which happened almost immediately before I had the time to examine my own ungentlemanly behavior and realize that my behavior could jeopardize our loving friendship.

"Marlene examined my behavior for me. She dissected it. I'd never seen her so angry. Usually she had a great deal of tolerance for people's mistakes, but I'd done something that was intolerable for her. Actually it was intolerable for me. I was sorry, but I fumbled and couldn't quite get the words out. If I had, I don't know if she would have heard me. Her pale skin was red. I'd never seen that before.

"'I'm so disappointed in you, Douglas,' she said. Usually she called me 'Dear Douglas' or 'Douglas dear,' even 'Douggie dear.' I'd come to consider 'dear' a part of my name. There was a tone of finality in her words. 'My husband, Rudi, would never have looked at my personal papers.'

"Rudi was a nice fellow, but I didn't like being compared to him, especially unfavorably. I didn't at that moment appreciate her comparing me unfavorably to any man. I was having a bit of a tantrum myself. At my worst, I could behave like a very spoiled chap.

"I believe the reason both of us allowed our worst selves to emerge in ridiculous tantrums was because the fire of our passion had cooled to faint embers. We didn't hang on harder because we had already lost the passion of our romance.

"What we hadn't lost was the friendship, and the bond of what we had shared. We never made up because we didn't have to.

"With the distance of a few days, I called her and tried to apologize. She didn't allow me to embarrass myself and her. She cut me off, saying, 'It doesn't matter, Douglas. You don't need to say anything.' That was the sad part of it. It didn't matter. There wasn't anything I could say. At the time I thought if I said how sorry I was and tried to explain, I might be able to make her feel better. I might be able to make myself feel better. But a wonderful friendship remained and endured.

"I never found out who the letters were from. Maybe they were years old. The strange part was it didn't really matter anymore. I was replaced as a lover by the writer of *All Quiet on the Western Front*, Erich Maria Remarque.

"She did everything with such enthusiasm, it could be overwhelming," Fairbanks said. "She was a libidinous girl, and so much passion could confuse a man. She made me feel like I was the only man—the first, the last—who could ever inspire such passion in her. I came to believe that. Very flattering, very cheerful to accept.

"I was wrong. The drive and passion were more than one man could find himself the unique object of. I'm sure of that now.

"It was great while it lasted. It ended because I was the one who forgot the part I was supposed to play. Actually, I didn't even know I was playing a part. I only acted naturally, but at the end, I behaved badly, and I was not forgiven as a lover. I believe it was because she was getting tired of me. No surprises.

"With a brief pause between our intense relationship and our new friendship, we became good friends, a friendship which remained.

"There were two Marlenes I knew," Fairbanks said. "There might have been some others, but for me, it was two.

"The first was beautiful, glamorous, mysterious, sensual. Her sensual personality made her seem more remote and unattainable. Her voice had that smoky quality. You could feel it. Anyway, I could feel it.

"My friend John Springer wrote a book called *They Had Faces Then*. I thought an interesting book would be *They Had Voices Then*.

"The other Marlene I called 'Marlene the Hausfrau.' This Marlene did not mind looking frumpy, although no matter what she did, she could never quite be that. She was beautiful, even with that hairnet on. She always kept a hairnet handy, which she could whip out on a moment's notice to cook or clean. I said to myself, though not for anyone else, a person doesn't know Marlene unless he knows her in flat shoes."

"MEMORY IS SHORT IN America," Marlene told me, "and even shorter in Hollywood. There, you are what you are doing today. Legendary is of little importance."

"'It isn't bankable,' Billy Wilder told me. Billy and I would talk about it. Billy said to me, 'In Europe, you are as good as the best thing you ever did. Not in Hollywood.'"

In early 1938, the *Independent Film Journal* published an open letter to the Hollywood studios from the National Theatre Distributors of America. It had a list of stars the writer of the letter, Harry Brandt, called "box office poison." Marlene Dietrich was on this list, which included Katharine Hepburn, Bette Davis, Joan Crawford, and Greta Garbo. Brandt, the owner of a chain of theaters in New York City, asserted that any one of these famous names was enough to keep audiences at home, that they were box office poison. The Hollywood studios took the letter quite seriously.

Each one of these stars was able to come back from this attack with a subsequent hit—Hepburn with *The Philadelphia Story*, Davis with *Dark Victory*, Garbo with *Ninotchka*, and Marlene with *Destry Rides Again*.

*Destry Rides Again* was loosely based on a novel by Max Brand. The book had already been made into a film for Tom Mix in 1932. It was the cowboy star's first talking picture. Universal owned the rights to the novel and could remake it anytime it desired.

Hungarian-born Joe Pasternak, who had become a producer at

Universal, told his friend Billy Wilder that he needed a change from Deanna Durbin films. These musicals had earned the profits that had secured his position at the studio.

Pasternak wanted to make a western, but not a regular western. He was able to obtain James Stewart from MGM as the star, and he gave the co-writing job to Felix Jackson, a refugee from Germany.

Jackson suggested an idea that Pasternak told Wilder "tickled" him. Destry would be the new sheriff, who didn't believe in guns. Wilder said that his friend saw that as a wonderful twist. Wilder told me that he was glad he didn't have to direct the film because the idea didn't tickle him at all.

A female character was added to the script, and Pasternak wanted a woman who would be special, the equal of Stewart. He thought of Marlene Dietrich. Pasternak was committed to it. She became for him the only actress who could play that part.

Universal preferred Paulette Goddard. They were insistent. Pasternak was happy when he learned she was unavailable.

At Universal, there were executives who didn't like the idea of James Stewart as a western hero. Someone said he was "too skinny" and didn't seem like a western hero. "He's no Tom Mix," Pasternak was told.

The casting of Marlene Dietrich was even less popular. "What was this European type doing there in the West?" he was asked.

"He really put his neck on the chopping block," Wilder told me. "Pasternak chose as director George Marshall in an effort to save his neck."

Considerable rewriting was deemed necessary, and when filming began, the script was not yet finished. Most noticeably, the ending had not as yet been decided. The deadline for a complete script came and went, while the film went over-budget.

## *Destry Rides Again* (1939)

The frontier town of Bottleneck is run by Kent (Brian Donlevy), a crooked gambler who owns the Last Chance Saloon. With the connivance of Frenchy (Marlene Dietrich), a dance hall girl, he has cheated most of the town's cattlemen out of their ranches at the gambling table. When Sheriff Keogh (Joe King) tries to defend one of these ranch owners, he is shot dead and his body disappears.

The town drunk, Wash Dimsdale (Charles Winninger), is named sheriff by the town's crooked judge (Samuel S. Hinds). Then, Dimsdale surprises everyone by swearing in Tom Destry (James Stewart), son of a great lawman, as his deputy. It turns out that Destry doesn't even carry a gun.

Destry, however, finds Sheriff Keogh's body and unites the townspeople, including Frenchy, against Kent and his gang. In a shootout, she steps in front of Destry, taking the bullet Kent intended for him. She dies, and Destry finally takes up arms, killing Kent. Law and order are restored to Bottleneck.

"*Destry Rides Again* was a big moneymaker and a great popular success. Joe [Pasternak] was saved from the guillotine," was the way Marlene expressed it. Marlene was pleased with herself because she had been successful not only for herself, but for von Sternberg and for Pasternak, for the more rarefied *Blue Angel* audience, and for Destry's mass audience, those for whom Pasternak had produced the Deanna Durbin films.

"I am known for being self-centered," she told me, "and I am. But I have to admit I had very strong feelings about wanting not to let down Jo and Joe. Each one had risked a lot for me, and never said that to me, but they didn't have to say a word. I understood. They had gambled on me. And I hadn't let them down. I didn't put it into words any more than they did. But I felt very good about Lola Lola and Frenchy—not just for myself."

Tennessee Williams told me that Marlene Dietrich was his favorite actress and that he had seen *Destry* more than once. He loved the songs by Frank Loesser and Frederick Hollander, especially "The Boys in the Back Room." Marlene's rendition of the song is one of the highlights of the film. It has often been imitated. Tennessee did a funny imitation of Marlene singing it.

MARLENE TOLD ME, "WHEN I first met James Stewart, I thought, 'What a nice man!' I liked his open, innocent, so American way. I immediately trusted him. We were attracted to each other. He was a bachelor. We began having an affair. It was not a *love* affair. It was an affair of mutual liking. Those are some of the best. Sometimes they last a lifetime as a friendship. This one lasted as long as filming.

"Then I discovered I was pregnant. It was his baby, too, so I told him. He looked shocked. He said, 'Jeez, what are you gonna do about it?'

"I noticed he said 'you,' not 'we.'

"I would have liked another child. I'd had a terribly difficult time having Maria, but enough time had passed for the memory of that to be fainter. Somewhat fainter.

"Now, the 'gentleman,' and I use that word a little loosely, had certainly never talked about marriage. Our affair was not that kind of torrid event. It was fun. He had never said, 'I love you,' or anything like that. One rather expects that kind of thing, those words, even if delivered in perfect insincerity.

"I knew he liked me, and I liked him, and that was enough for me and obviously enough for him.

"I wondered what I should do.

"I thought about Rudi. Of course, he would say he was the father. I knew what he would say to me. He would ask me, 'Do you love the father, Stewart?' If I had answered yes, he would have been terribly hurt, but he would have acted the part of the father. I told him the truth. No, I didn't love Stewart. It had been true at the time of the affair. It was more true after I'd observed his reaction to my news. Rudi would have been happy that I didn't love Stewart. That was what mattered to him.

"I thought about Maria. She'd always told me she wished she'd been part of a big family. When she came to know the Kennedy family at Cap d'Antibes during holidays, she'd thought they were the perfect family.

"But at this stage, would she really be happy about having a brother or sister, a new member of the family? She had always been our precious only child, *everything* to us.

"Having the baby would have involved living a lie, lying to Maria. I wouldn't have been able to tell her that Rudi was not the baby's father. She would never have thought anything else."

Marlene would never have told her daughter the truth because that might have broken the bond between them, jeopardizing Maria's feelings for her, and for her new little brother or sister.

"It would have been a torment," Marlene said.

"What happened?" I asked.

"Nothing," she answered. "It was a mistake. No baby. Just a mistake.

"When I believed it was true, I saw a lot of problems. When it wasn't true, I felt sad."


ON THE EVE OF World War II, Marlene had a relationship with Joseph Kennedy during summer vacation at Cap d'Antibes in the south of France. At the time, Kennedy was the U.S. ambassador to Great Britain.

She was staying at the Hôtel du Cap. Rudi, Maria and Tamara, and Erich Maria Remarque and Josef von Sternberg, were part of her group. Kennedy was there with his wife and children, staying in a compound on the same property.

"I enjoyed my relationship with Joe Kennedy, and obviously he enjoyed his with me," Marlene told me. "I know he enjoyed it because I knew him well enough to know he never did anything he didn't want to do.

"There were people who suggested he had pro-Nazi sympathies. Absurd. If he had any such feelings about Hitler and his gang, I could never have been close to him. He was totally American and patriotic, but he had a different perspective from mine. He was strongly opposed to the entry of the U.S. into a European war. As the U.S. ambassador to England, he was very influential with President Roosevelt, and he was working against the U.S. sending ships to England or against any aid that could bring the U.S. into a European war.

"He told me and everyone that he was in no way sympathetic to Hitler and the Nazis, but he did not want any American boys dying in a war. I didn't either. Americans did not want it. But I believed that America would not be able to escape, that Hitler would attack America. I was wrong. It turned out to be Japan.

"I had a secret personal mission in mind when I was with Joseph Kennedy. I believed I could shift his thinking, that I could persuade him that the United States could not escape Hitler and could not remain isolated from Europe, and soon from England. Even some of his older children felt that way, but they didn't argue with their father.

"I was in a difficult position. He listened to every word I said. Or he seemed to, but it made no difference. I couldn't budge him in his viewpoint. Eventually, it made him very unpopular in America. That made him unhappy because he thought he was a person everyone liked. Well, far from it, but he didn't know, so he was happy. The truth was, most people *didn't* like him. The reason was because he was unlikable, though I liked him.

"Well, there wasn't much he could do about that. Powerful people are often disliked. Not always. But personality shouldn't be everything, the way it is. Smart people sometimes do stupid things. Joe was smart, but he believed some things that weren't smart. He was rigid. I tried to tell my view, and he just got more rigid.

"He was a very rich man, but he never gave me even a simple token, like a scarf. Some people thought he watched his money very, *very* closely. They said he was stingy when it came to spending money. Personally, I think he wanted to be sure you really liked *him*, just for himself alone. He wasn't a very comfortable man when it came to women."

"The first woman I was in love with was Marlene Dietrich," Senator Edward Kennedy told me. "She was the first love of my life, the most beautiful woman in the world, but she preferred my brother Jack. He had a gift with women. But she liked me, too. She was always very warm and friendly to me and despite my awe, I came to feel very comfortable with her.

"Jack was older, which made him more attractive. Well, he was more attractive, and he was mature for his age. I was immature for mine because everybody treated me like the baby of our family, which I was.

"Everyone called me Teddy. At the time, I guess I was almost seven years old.

"Our family was spending our summer holiday in Cap d'Antibes, as we often did, and Marlene Dietrich was there, too. My brothers and I admired, worshipped our father, and it was clear that he liked her *a lot*. That enhanced her glamour for us.

"Whenever I saw Marlene with my father, I knew he was very pleased. Young as I was, it was clear that he enjoyed her company.

"My father and my brothers never explained anything about sex to me. I think they thought it just came naturally. Well, it did to them, but I was puzzled.

"My brothers understood perfectly the relationship between

Marlene Dietrich and my father. As a child, I asked Jack about it, and he just said, 'They're very good friends.'"

MARLENE HOPED HER MOTHER would come to America, but she could not convince her that it was the best thing to do.

"I don't know if my mother knew why she *had* to stay in Germany, but her mind was made up and it couldn't be changed. She may have felt closer to Liesel than to me, although Liesel told me she believed I was our mother's favorite. She said our mother had referred to me as her 'treasure.' She certainly never referred that way to me when I was present.

"She spoke enough English, so that was not a reason for staying in Germany. But she was so independent, she would not have liked being in America dependent on me. Then, there was Hasso, who had inherited most of the family business and was still very young.

"I believe my mother couldn't leave Felsing's, which she loved like a child—maybe more. And with clear signs that expensive, fragile clocks were in trouble, as was everything and everyone else, my mother couldn't desert Felsing's."

Marlene understood that her mother felt a duty toward her nephew Hasso, who was still a minor and her ward, and who had inherited the major share of Felsing's. Marlene knew that her mother regarded Felsing's as her ward, too.

Her mother was immensely proud of the family business on Unter den Linden, with its history and tradition. It was her mother's source of income, which gave Josephine the independence for which she yearned. It was possible to take Hasso with her to America, but it wasn't possible to take Felsing's.

Marlene knew that her mother could not go against her principles, her duty. She also knew that love was a part of it. No matter how much her mother spoke of duty and principles, she *loved* Felsing's.

• • •

LIKE *Destry, Seven Sinners* was produced for Universal by Joe Pasternak, and the songs were again written by Frederick Hollander and Frank Loesser. In this film, which is clearly intended as a sequel to *Destry*, Marlene plays the same character, a bad girl gone good, who doesn't get the man at the final fade-out. The man she doesn't get is John Wayne.

### Seven Sinners (1940)

Bijou Blanche (Marlene Dietrich) is a cabaret singer who has to keep moving from island to island in the South Pacific because of complications with men.

Aboard a freighter looking for a new island to land on, Bijou decides to try Boni-Komba, where the governor may not remember her. One of the passengers aboard the ship is the governor's daughter, Dorothy Henderson (Anna Lee).

On Boni-Komba, Bijou is hired by the Seven Sinners Café. While she is singing, Bruce (John Wayne), a naval officer, enters to round up errant sailors who are supposed to be at a reception for Dorothy. He, too, quickly falls under Bijou's spell and loses interest in Dorothy, who is falling in love with him. Bruce's invitation to Bijou to sing at an official naval reception is vetoed by the governor (Samuel S. Hinds), who is watching her suspiciously.

After a stabbing in the Seven Sinners, the governor arranges for Bijou to leave the island. At sea again, Bijou looks forward to a relationship with the captain (Albert Dekker), providing he can control his drinking.

Pasternak cast Marlene again as a dance hall girl in *The Flame of New Orleans*. This time, the legendary René Clair would be the director. The moment that Pasternak learned that Clair was coming to America from Paris because of World War II, the producer, who was a great admirer of Clair, immediately signed him to a contract.

### The Flame of New Orleans (1941)

A dazzling wedding gown is seen floating down the Mississippi in the middle of the nineteenth century. In flashback, the audience learns why.

Claire Ledoux (Marlene Dietrich), posing as a European countess, has really come to New Orleans in search of a wealthy husband. She thinks she has found him in Charles Giraud (Roland Young), a banker. Giraud asks her to marry him.

When Giraud overhears her making remarks that indicate she is only a fortune hunter, she blames her "cousin," whom she explains looks and sounds just like her, but is a tart. Since the cousin is nonexistent, Claire must assume her bawdy identity from time to time to allay Giraud's suspicions.

Meanwhile, she has met a young man she likes, Robert Latour (Bruce Cabot). He is acquainted with Giraud, and they both are struck by the uncanny resemblance between Claire and her low-life "cousin."

Latour finds out the truth, but doesn't tell Giraud. Uneasy about the cousin, Giraud offers to pay Latour to take her away in his boat.

During the wedding ceremony, the bride-to-be disappears after fainting. All that's left is her wedding gown floating in the Mississippi.

"Bruce Cabot," Marlene told me, "was someone I would have preferred not to work with, and even more not to know. He had an extremely high opinion of himself, which I did not share. He came ill prepared to the set, not knowing his lines. I never determined if he was that stupid or didn't care. Probably both.

"René Clair did not speak English well enough to direct the film. I was the only person who spoke French, but when I spoke French with Mr. Clair, he didn't seem to like it. Maybe he took it as a criticism of his English. Maybe he thought other members of the cast wouldn't like it. Later, when I knew him socially at dinner parties where there were many French people, he was always very happy to speak French with me. He never made me feel that he appreciated me professionally, but he certainly appreciated the French bread I found for him in a wonderful little French bakery in Los Angeles.

"I think Monsieur Clair did not feel comfortable in English, and he didn't feel comfortable in Hollywood. He was so known and so respected in France, and he had great freedom to choose his projects and make films that reflected the essence of his unique René Clair vision."

While having lunch at the Paris Ritz, René Clair told me, "When I was offered *The Flame of New Orleans*, I wasn't very impressed with the script, but I told myself that it was better than it was. I believed I could work on it and improve it, as I was accustomed to doing in France. When I tried to make changes, it was resented, and I found out very quickly that the director does not have the final word.

"Marlene was a delightful person, totally sincere and totally professional. I could not have asked for more from her, but I don't think the leading man [Bruce Cabot] was right.

"She found a bakery that did wonderful French bread and some delightful croissants, as good as any in Paris. She brought them with a pleasure that almost surpassed the pleasure of the eating.

"At the time I was making films in America, I believed they weren't as good as what I might have done in France, but looking back with the passage of time, I feel they are different, but not less good. Not so long ago, I had a chance to see *I Married a Witch*. Wasn't Veronica Lake good? May I say, 'bewitching'?

"People thought I took the job directing *The Flame of New Orleans* because I wanted the money. Well, that's true, too, but what I really wanted was to keep working at what I want to do, direct films.

"Being a legend is no substitute for working. Having the chance to do what you want to do and then having it taken away from you is worse than never having had it at all.

"It doesn't stop all at once, because you don't know that your last film is the last one until a long time afterwards. I think the moment I actually realized that everything was over and I was only a legend was when Henri Langlois [founder of the Cinémathèque Française] wanted a pair of my old socks for his museum."

MARLENE WASN'T SURPRISED WHEN George Raft greeted her in perfect German on the set of *Manpower*. Mae West had told her that both of Raft's parents came from Germany. His real name was Rapf.

### *Manpower* (1941)

Close friends Hank McHenry (Edward G. Robinson) and Johnny Marshall (George Raft) are electric company linemen. While they are working in a storm, a co-worker, "Pop" Duval (Egon Brecher), is electrocuted.

Duval's daughter, Fay (Marlene Dietrich), a hostess in a clip joint, is unmoved. Her father deserted her and her mother. Johnny has no respect for Fay, but Hank falls in love with her. Even though she tells him she doesn't love him, Fay marries Hank to escape a bleak present and a bleaker future.

Johnny is hospitalized after an accident, and Hank insists he recuperate at his house with him and Fay. Fay confesses to Johnny her unhappiness with Hank. She really loves Johnny. He rejects her advances because of his friendship for Hank.

Fay decides to leave Hank and go to Chicago. When she visits the club to get a suggestion for a club in Chicago, she is arrested in a police raid. Without telling Hank, Johnny bails her out. Then, he slaps her because of her treatment of Hank.

Hank is on a dangerous job during a storm. His crew refuses to work, but Johnny agrees.

Hank is heartened by Fay's appearance until she tells him she is leaving him because she loves Johnny. Enraged, Hank tries to kill Johnny as they climb to repair the wires. But Hank can't let Johnny fall to his death. In trying to save his friend, Hank falls.

Dying, Hank tells Johnny, "Take care of her like I tried to do."

Later, Fay stands in the rain, suitcase in hand, waiting for the bus. Johnny watches as the bus stops to pick her up. The bus departs, but Fay is still there.


Marlene Dietrich met Carroll Righter in Hollywood at a dinner given by Charlie Chaplin. They were sitting next to each other and immediately enjoyed each other's company. He had attended school at Heidelberg, which intrigued her.

Marlene began telling him how disappointed she was feeling because she wasn't getting the offers she had hoped to get. She wasn't even getting offers she *hadn't* hoped to get. She was not receiving scripts, and her agent was about to drop her.

In 2010, Tom Pierson, Righter's friend and associate, talked with me about the role Righter played in Marlene's life.

Carroll told her, "You've been trying to take a sunbath at eleven o'clock at night." After discussing something about astrology, he told her that she was about to have two offers of films, and that it was of the greatest importance which one she took. It wasn't a matter of which was the better film, or which was the better part for her. It was a matter of which film would be made. "One of the two films will not be made, and that would be *very* bad for your career."

Marlene had Righter make her astrological chart. She soon had two offers, and the film she chose was made. The other wasn't. She had followed Righter's advice.

### The Lady Is Willing (1942)

Although musical comedy star Elizabeth Madden (Marlene Dietrich) knows nothing about babies, she wants to adopt the one she has found. To do so, she must be married.

She asks pediatrician Corey McBain (Fred MacMurray) if he will marry her, and he agrees to a marriage in name only. Eventually, they fall in love as they plan their marriage.

Their happiness is threatened by the appearance of McBain's ex-wife (Arline Judge). Suspicious of their relationship, Elizabeth takes the baby on tour with her.

When the baby gets sick, she calls Dr. McBain, who comes and treats the child. Their differences are resolved, and the couple is married and lives happily with their baby.

Marlene became an increasingly dedicated believer in the astrological charts that Carroll Righter regularly made for her. Someone who didn't know her well said flippantly, "Does Righter tell you when you can brush your teeth?" Marlene remembered her own icy silence. She resented anyone who "dared to cast aspersions on the unique ability of Righter," in which she believed. Marlene meticulously followed his advice, particularly in heeding his warnings, after the experience she had while working on *The Lady Is Willing*.

While *The Lady Is Willing* was filming, Marlene received an urgent message from the astrologer warning her not to go to work on a particular date or she would have an accident. As it turned out, that date was one in which all of the scenes involved Marlene. She considered pleading illness and not reporting for work, not letting director Mitchell Leisen know the real reason. It would have been unacceptable for him to cancel everything or have to work around her. It would cost the studio a fortune, and Leisen was already behind schedule. Priding herself on being a professional, Marlene decided to take the risk.

She tried to persuade herself that Righter could make a mistake, just this once, but to no avail. After all, she knew he had never made a mistake. She called the chauffeur the studio had provided and asked him to come early so that he could drive more slowly than usual.

When she left the car to enter the studio, she was especially careful. When she sat down to wait for her scene, she looked to make certain the chair was there under her. She remembered once when she sat down and it wasn't there. She was so careful that she remembered thinking that such extreme caution could be how people in old age might feel.

She rose to play the scene in which the Broadway star carries the baby she has found. As she did, she stepped on a toy on the floor and felt herself falling. She was holding a real baby. She had to protect the baby as she fell, which caused her to fall in a particularly awkward manner. The baby was not injured. Marlene said that she was happy and proud that she had protected the baby. After the fall, her first words were, "Is the baby all right?" But Marlene had fractured her ankle. She had to wear a cast that went from her foot to her thigh in order to protect her fractured ankle. Her last scenes were filmed in close-up, not showing her leg.

After that experience, Carroll Righter's words became even more sacred for her.

A MONTH AFTER PEARL Harbor, Marlene joined John Wayne, Randolph Scott, and director Ray Enright at Lake Arrowhead, California, to shoot exteriors for the fourth version of a Rex Beach novel, *The Spoilers.*

### The Spoilers (1942)

Cherry Malotte (Marlene Dietrich) owns a dance hall in Nome, Alaska, during the gold rush of the 1900s. She is in love with Roy Glennister (John Wayne), co-owner with Al Dextry (Harry Carey) of the Midas mine. The new gold commissioner, Alex McNamara (Randolph Scott), causes a rift between the partners when he requests that the mine be shut down until a claim-jumping accusation can be settled. Roy agrees, but Al doesn't. Cherry suspects Roy has been influenced by Helen Chester (Margaret Lindsay), niece of the judge (Samuel S. Hinds), who is setting up Alaska's first U.S. court, and she is jealous. When the ruling continues being postponed, Roy realizes that Helen has been conspiring with the judge and McNamara to keep control of the mine. Roy and Al send their lawyer (William Farnum) to Seattle to appeal the case.

When the town's marshal (Bud Osborne) is unintentionally killed in an attempted robbery, Roy is falsely imprisoned. A plan by McNamara and the judge to kill Roy in an escape is foiled.

An attempt to regain control of the mine, which has been seized by the court, is successful. In town, Roy and McNamara have a long fight over Cherry. Roy wins.

In the original 1914 screen version, William Farnum played Roy, but in this 1942 version he appears in the small part of the lawyer.

•   •   •

*Pittsburgh* WAS MARLENE'S SECOND consecutive film starring her with the same two leading men. Both pictures were successful, so the casting worked, but in wartime pretelevision America, there were always lines at movie houses no matter what the film. She plays a "Hunky," a derogatory term for eastern Europeans.

### *Pittsburgh* (1942)

Josie Winters (Marlene Dietrich), a "Hunky" with ambitions beyond what her coal-mining father was able to provide, has become the mistress of fight promoter Mort Brawley (Douglas Fowley). She now calls herself "Countess."

At one of Brawley's fights, she attracts the attention of two miners with ambition, Pittsburgh Markham (John Wayne) and Cash Evans (Randolph Scott). They get to know each other better when they all rush to help in a mine accident in which a friend, "Doc" Powers (Frank Craven), is trapped.

After they save him, Josie lets the two men know that she isn't interested in going back to that life. To win her, they start their own coal company.

The company is so successful that it merges with a much larger steel company. Josie falls in love with Pittsburgh, but he is even more ambitious than she, and he marries the steel company owner's daughter, Shannon (Louise Allbritton). Because of his overpowering ambition, Pittsburgh loses all of his old friends, including Cash and Josie. Then Pittsburgh disappears.

Cash starts his own business, which is successful, and he marries Josie. Then one day Pittsburgh is found working in one of Cash's shops. Success was too much for him, and he felt compelled to return to being a skilled workman with pride in what he did while contributing to the war effort.

When Marlene first saw John Wayne just before they worked together, she was struck by his looks, "broad shoulders and flat behind," and charmed by his accent. She said, "What pleased me most was he wasn't vain or arrogant. Far from it, he was insecure as an actor, worried about his talent, or what he felt was a lack of it. As a man, he was a little insecure and vulnerable. I was able to help in both respects.

"We had a small affair, a small friendship, which we both enjoyed. I don't think it's what a man his size would like to have said about him, but he brought out the maternal side in me, which is a very strong part of me. I felt I could help him professionally and personally because all he needed was more confidence, and I know I gave him that, professionally, and personally, too.

"I feel our friendship would have gone on more strongly if our films together had been better, even if he did prefer women who had dark hair and whose first language was Spanish rather than German."

*Follow the Boys* (1944) was a Hollywood revue in the style of *Stage Door Canteen* and *Hollywood Canteen*, except that the "plot" was kept to a minimum, and there were more stars performing. Marlene's contribution was to be sawed in half by Orson Welles. In the dramatic sequence that introduces the acts, George Raft plays a dancing star who starts the Victory Committee after the army rejects him. The organization joins the USO, and the film is the story of what the stars do to entertain the troops going overseas.

IN *Kismet*, MARLENE IS rejoined by William Dieterle, who directed and acted with her in the 1923 *Der Mensch am Wege*. Dieterle, then Wilhelm, had appeared as the star of an early UFA German silent version of *Kismet*.

### Kismet (1944)

Hafiz (Ronald Colman), flamboyant poet, magician, beggar, and thief, seeks a prince for his daughter, Marsinah (Joy Ann Page), to marry. She is wasting her time with a gardener's son, while Hafiz is having an affair with Jamilla (Marlene Dietrich), queen of the grand vizier's castle.

Stealing some finery from a bazaar, Hafiz approaches the grand vizier (Edward Arnold) as the fabulously wealthy Prince Hassir in hopes that he can convince him that he should choose Marsinah as his new queen. Before he can present his proposal, however, Hafiz is arrested for theft and sentenced to have his hands chopped off.

Before the sentence is carried out, Hafiz receives clemency on the condition that he will kill the young caliph, who now threatens the despotic reign of the grand vizier. In return, Hafiz will keep his hands and the grand vizier will marry his daughter, making her the new queen.

In his attempt to kill the caliph, Hafiz kills the grand vizier instead, and is arrested. The young caliph (James Craig) turns out to be the gardener's son who loves Marsinah. Hafiz is pardoned on the condition that he leave Baghdad forever, which he does, with Jamilla.

Bette Davis invited Marlene to participate in the Hollywood Canteen, an organization founded by Davis and John Garfield. It was affiliated with the USO (United Service Organizations), which was created to provide a center for off-duty servicemen away from home. Besides offering a congenial atmosphere, there were meals and dances and other recreational activities. The Hollywood Canteen was the most famous USO center because Hollywood stars appeared there. Besides performing, some of the actors waited on tables while the most glamorous actresses danced with the servicemen and acted as hostesses.

Immediately, Marlene said yes. Orson Welles, who liked to perform his magic act for the servicemen, asked Marlene if he could saw her in half, and she was delighted, as was the enthusiastic and appreciative audience.

"Fortunately," Marlene said, "Orson was a very skillful magician, because here I am with no seams.

Orson said, 'Don't be afraid. If I make a mistake, we know how to put you back together.'"

She also played her musical saw for the troops, as well as volunteering to cook, clean, and wash dishes, tasks which Marlene and Hedy Lamarr especially sought out. Marlene remembered hearing Bette call out to someone, "Get those two Krauts out of the kitchen!"

"Miss Dietrich really impressed me," Bette Davis told me. "When I called her to ask her if she would participate in organizing the Hollywood USO, she accepted in that call, and never needed to be reminded about the importance of what we were doing. The servicemen loved being served by a beautiful Hollywood actress, sitting and eating a sandwich with a Hollywood star, and especially dancing with one of their dream girls.

"But the most striking image of Miss Dietrich was one I saw regularly. She would be wearing her hairnet, and she would be down on her hands and knees scrubbing the floor of the kitchen. When she cooked, I could understand. I liked to cook myself. I don't mean I like to cook *myself*. I'm not a cannibal! I mean I like to *cook*, and I'm a very good cook, if I say so myself, but fortunately, I'm not the only one who says it.

"She never worried about dishpan hands or scrubbing-floor knees. She really worked with elbow grease. When she wasn't working on a film, she never missed. I have a lot of admiration for Marlene Dietrich."

Marlene, however, wanted to do more. After *Kismet* wrapped, she left Hollywood believing that she could make a more substantial contribution to the war effort elsewhere.

# III. *The Postwar World*

$\mathcal{I}$ come from a military family," Marlene said, "but I have no illusions about the glories of war. I lived through one terrible war, and I knew that this one was far worse.

"I looked around wartime America, protected from these horrors by two wide oceans, and I saw complacency. People didn't really understand what we were sending our boys out to face.

"I couldn't do much, but I had to do *something*."

When Marlene left Hollywood to make a contribution to the war effort, she sold nearly all of her possessions, keeping only her jewelry, the most valuable pieces going into safe deposit boxes. A few paintings had been given to her by Erich Maria Remarque. Her best paintings were safely stored "for the duration," a frequently heard phrase during World War II.

She sold almost all of her European porcelain collection. She was surprised by the number of pieces she had collected, one by one, since she was a girl. It was a strange thing to have collected so much beautiful porcelain when she knew it wasn't in keeping with the kind of life she had chosen and the life that had chosen her, but each piece, by itself, had been irresistible.

This "porcelain rapport" from her childhood had reflected the world of her grandmother and of the Felsings. "It represented beauty and stability," she said. "Porcelain needs stability." Marlene sold all but two or three pieces, needing money to support all of the people in her life. "Those porcelain figures represented something from my childhood that made me feel secure."

Marlene went to the USO headquarters in New York and volunteered her services. A USO show was formed around her that toured the United States and then flew to Casablanca by way of Greenland and the Azores. One of the members of her troupe was a young Danny Thomas.

Marlene learned that her regular thirty-six pieces of Vuitton and Hermès luggage would have to be replaced by a total of no more than fifty-six pounds of luggage. She said, "That is no problem."

She took dozens of sets of false fingernails from Woolworth's with her. "I would never have parted with my fingernails. I could more easily have parted with my own real fingernails because the Woolworth nails were more dependable. I had to buy whole sets, because fingernails are not interchangeable, and I never could know which of them I might damage. Fortunately, false fingernails don't weigh very much, and I could have carried all of them myself, and would have.

"I was in Africa, Sicily, Paris." Marlene recalled. "We were in Anzio waiting for the breakthrough into Rome. Americans, if they weren't there in the armed forces, didn't realize how fierce the fighting was in Italy."

In Bari, Marlene was taken to a base hospital with viral pneumonia. There was concern that her illness could be fatal. She was told, and believed, that penicillin saved her life. Penicillin was new at that time.

Marlene's hands and feet were frozen in the Ardennes. "It was very cold and rainy," Marlene remembered. "Unforgettable, and my hands and feet remind me. Once you have had severe frostbite, your hands and feet always remember and let you know. Many soldiers lost toes and fingers, but I was lucky."

The worst lingering injury that Marlene endured as a reminder of her World War II experiences with the U.S. troops at the front was flashback memories of what she had seen. "Those horrors recur and run in my mind. I've never been able to rid myself of them."

When U.S. troops arrived in Paris, Marlene was with them. She appeared at the Hermès store on the Faubourg Saint-Honoré dressed in a bespoke American officer's uniform. She signed autographs until she wore out the shop's small supply of scarce pencils. Then she signed using her lipstick, until it, too, ran down.

A photograph of Marlene standing in front of Hermès on that day shows French flags flying from balconies reflected in the shop windows. The elderly doorman at Hermès is wearing his decorations from World War I.

As the American forces moved through France, large numbers of German soldiers surrendered. Marlene said that she wanted to entertain the German prisoners as well as the Allied troops. She explained that most of the soldiers were not Nazis and that very few of them wanted to do what they were forced to do. "These boys aren't hardened Nazis. Many of them are only children."

When she performed for them, there were some who were hostile to her, but usually only among the officers, some of whom were committed to the Nazi ideology. After she sang "Lili Marleen," a favorite song of both sides, one of the young German soldiers came up to her and said, "You *are* Lili Marleen!"

She was asked by the U.S. military what she might be able to learn from the German prisoners that could help them at that stage of the war. She said that the very young and very old enlisted men had no secrets to divulge. "It had *all* been a secret from them. But it was different with the officers. Some of them understood the war was over for them, anyway, and they really felt no allegiance to the Nazis."

She said she felt proud that she was able to bring back some useful information. "Many of the officers came to be comfortable with me when they thought about it, and German was, after all, my first language, and most important, I could understand what they told me.

"I remember when we were surrounded. I was pretty happy to see General Gavin arrive with his paratroopers."

As THE END OF the war drew near and it became clear that Germany would not be victorious, Himmler announced that Germans who were not faithful to the cause, especially any military who were considering deserting, would not only face their own deaths when caught, but their families would also pay the price. There was no need to elaborate on what the price was.

Marlene was in Germany and hoped to be allowed to enter Berlin with the first U.S. forces. She was desperately anxious to find her mother, and she was extremely fearful about her mother's fate. Not only would her mother have had to endure the terrible conditions in Berlin—bombing, hunger, street warfare, and finally a pall of sadness—but Marlene understood that everyone knew that Josephine was her mother. When Marlene became "an enemy of the state," it meant that by the Nazi standard her mother was as guilty as she.

Marlene feared not only that her mother might have suffered through misery and even died in the bombing, but she was tortured by the thought that she personally might have contributed to her mother's suffering and even caused her death.

Marlene did not receive letters from her mother during the war, even before America entered. She did not write either because she felt her mother might be endangered by receiving mail from a daughter who was deemed a traitor by the Third Reich.

"During the early days of World War II," Marlene said, "I was able to hear about my mother from refugees pouring out of Berlin. Then they didn't pour out anymore because they were barely able to get out with their lives, so I had no news for a long time."

At the end of World War II, through her military connections, Marlene learned that her mother had been found alive in Berlin, and that she would be able to be with her.

During World War I, in Germany, young Marlene had noted that it was a woman's world. There were women everywhere. One rarely saw a man, only boys and old men. As the war ended, crippled and blind young men appeared in the streets.

When she returned to Berlin at the end of World War II to reunite with her mother, Berlin was again a city of women, as Germany was a country of women. Another generation of young men had been killed and crippled. Vivid memories of her own youth in Germany during World War I came back to her. She remembered the death of her stepfather, an army officer, and how sad her mother had been.

Marlene was horrified at seeing the total devastation of the German capital. She was able to ask Josephine how she felt about what she, Marlene, had done during the war. Did her mother feel she had betrayed their country?

Marlene's mother told her she understood and that what Marlene had done was right. Her mother told her that she had not been arrested, but that she had been questioned by the police, and a great deal of the time she felt she was under surveillance. She told her daughter that she began to go out less because of this feeling she had that she was being followed. She wasn't certain. She said she would have preferred knowing to wondering. She began to think it could be only in her mind. She couldn't talk about it with her neighbors because no one would dare discuss anything even remotely political. Your neighbors might report you. They would be afraid you might report them. Even if they weren't in sympathy with the Nazis, they wouldn't want to be seen with anyone who was under suspicion of something.

"I was so happy to see my mother, to know that she had lived through the horrors of the war, that she had endured it all, and survived. I was desperate to apologize to her for what I had put her through. I had placed her life in jeopardy. I had made her an outcast, a pariah, for all of those in Berlin who believed I was a traitor to my homeland, and there were a good many of those. I think, however, there were more of them in the early days when Germany seemed to be winning than when the bombs were falling and so many young men were not returning from the Eastern Front.

"I didn't know what my mother would say to me. I wanted to be forgiven for putting her at risk. But it was better than that. It wasn't a matter of forgiveness. My mother said, 'I am proud of what you did. You did the right thing.'

"She didn't live long after that, but she had given me a gift. I could hear her speaking those words to me in my head, and I know I always would for all the years of my life, as long as I live, I shall be able to call on that voice in my head. That was the best Medal of Honor I ever received."

Before she died, Marlene's mother explained to her daughter why she thought she hadn't been arrested. Josephine believed that she had the protection of the German army.

The army was only partly loyal to the Nazis, and she was the Widow von Losch. Her husband, Marlene's stepfather, was a lieutenant colonel, an officer who, on active duty, had died of his wounds at the front. Hitler seemed all-powerful against the helpless, but he needed the army, and he did not casually go against their codes.

Not long after Marlene saw her mother, while she was thinking about what she might do to make her mother's life more bearable, she learned that her mother had died. Through her privileged position with the American military, Marlene was able to provide a wooden coffin for her mother at a time when wood was almost impossible to obtain. A small supply was obtained from some school desks that had survived the Berlin bombing. The school had not. Marlene was afraid to ask about the children. "I could only hope that no one was in the school at the time."

She was able to organize a small funeral for her mother.

"MY SISTER AND HER husband and their little boy stayed in Germany, as did my mother, when I went to Hollywood. I tried to persuade them to leave Germany and come to California. Rudi tried, too.

"My sister's husband could not imagine what he would be able to do working in California, and he didn't want to be dependent on me for his livelihood. He and I were never compatible.

"I don't know if my sister was happy with her husband. She never said she wasn't, but we weren't that close by the time we were each grown up and married. But even if we had been the closest of sisters, she would have done her duty toward her husband, as our mother had taught us to do."

Through her military connections, Marlene learned that her sister was in Bergen-Belsen, a notorious Nazi concentration camp. Just the information that Liesel might be there terrified Marlene. As soon as she could after reuniting with her mother, Marlene went to find her sister, not knowing under what circumstances her sister was there, not knowing what she would find.

There had been a typhus epidemic that had taken many lives in addition to those victims who had been murdered in the camp. Everywhere there were ominous signs with large black letters, spelling out TYPHUS. The signs did not deter Marlene. The records of the camp had been destroyed or were in disarray when the British took over from the fleeing Nazis and German soldiers. Marlene looked at some of the corpses, terrified that she might find her sister, despite the British officer in charge wanting to protect her from the horrors of what she might see and the threat of contagious diseases.

Marlene was overjoyed when her sister was located, not in the camp at all, but living with her husband nearby in a small modest flat in the town near the concentration camp. Her husband had been managing some theaters in Berlin and was transferred to Bergen-Belsen. He had told his wife that he felt it was a punishment for his relationship to Marlene, and his inability to persuade her to appear in German films.

The theater her husband managed showed films to the German officers and guards who worked at the concentration camp. Marlene's influence enabled her now to plead for her sister, who would not leave her husband. Marlene asked that they be transferred to Berlin, where she would be able to help them. Her sister and brother-in-law were not guilty of war crimes. If her brother-in-law had refused to manage the movie theater, that decision might have cost him and Liesel their lives.

Marlene had promised her mother that she would go to Austria to identify her mother's ward, Hasso, who was there with a group of German prisoners of war held by the Russians. Marlene went there and identified the young German soldier to prevent his being sent to Russia.

"In Berlin," Marlene said, "I was able to do something for Rudi. My celebrity, my connections, and whatever I brought to the table, allowed me to save Rudi's much loved parents.

"My Rudi had lost touch with his parents, and he was terribly worried about them. They were in Czechoslovakia, their home, which they hadn't wanted to leave when we wanted to bring them to California.

"They were not rich and had lost much of what they had. They said they were too old to start again, and they had family and friends in Czechoslovakia. They thought they would only be a burden for Rudi, and for me.

"They spoke German and were Catholic, not Jewish, and like my mother, they had believed that the whole thing with the Nazis would not last long. How could it? They had no thought at all of the Russians.

"The last Rudi heard, they were in an internment camp. We heard that from people who knew people who had seen them. In Berlin, an introduction was arranged for me to a Russian general. I was told he was a fan of mine. He located Rudi's parents, and it was arranged for them to be brought from the camp to the American sector of Berlin, where they could be together, free, be better nourished, and where Rudi and I could support them. They preferred that to coming to America.

"Rudi was especially happy, because my celebrity could do that. It was a reward because of my service to America as a front line entertainer. The greatest reward for me always was in the reception by 'my boys,' the look in their eyes. But who knows if Rudi's mother and father could have survived through the end of the war, and then the Russian occupation. I don't think so.

"But we must not go on fighting the war after it has ended. The bitterness hurts the one who is bitter."


MARLENE MET JEAN GABIN in Paris before World War II, but they did not get to know each other well until the French actor reached Hollywood in the early 1940s. They were brought together by their mutual friend Marcel Dalio, who had starred with Gabin in *La Grande Illusion*. Dalio was a refugee from the Nazis. In America, he appeared in *Casablanca* with his wife, Madeleine Lebeau, also a refugee from the Nazis. Dietrich and Gabin were immediately attracted to each other.

"Jean and I had a marvelous affair. It was not without pain on my part, but the pain was worth it, for a time, while I had hope for our passionate friendship becoming even more. It was the only relationship in my life when I was the one who loved more than the other person. It was the strangest experience. My emotions were out of control. It allowed me to understand better how the men who had loved me had felt.

"Perhaps Jean was less intense about me because he knew he had me in his pocket. I was his all of the time, but he only wanted me part of the time.

"I tried to act as blasé as I could, but I've never been an actress in my personal life.

"There was no one who threatened my relationship with my husband as much as did Gabin. I don't know if Rudi knew that, but he must have sensed something, because he was a very sensitive man, especially where I was concerned.

"I understood something different was happening when I realized I wasn't writing to Rudi about everything I was feeling. It was the first time that had happened. I thought Gabin looked like a lion, and I fantasized about being his mate, permanently.

"We didn't have all the same interests. I love the opera and concerts. He didn't. He fell asleep. The ballet, too. I loved it. He slept. We both loved riding horses. And he liked my cooking.

"He was an earthy man, just the way he looked. The studio billed him as 'the French Spencer Tracy,' and he did resemble Tracy. I could always understand how Katharine Hepburn felt about Tracy.

"Gabin had been a star in France, but if an actor loses his language, it is a handicap from which he can scarcely recover. He can learn the language, but rarely, if ever, can he lose his foreign accent.

"I tried to help Gabin in every way, as I did for so many European refugees escaping the Nazis. He was unhappy because he didn't speak English, certainly not up to a standard adequate for a career in Hollywood films.

"I tried teaching him English. You think that's really funny, I suppose. Me, a teacher of English. Actually, I understand the language, its rules and usage, the grammar, all of it, well. The only thing I could never master was the loss of my accent. That may have been because I didn't try. I would have felt naked without my accent, and no one ever wanted me to lose it. It was only important to say a word clearly so the audience could understand it. Any director could take care of that.

"I did not teach my German accent to Gabin. That would have been terrible. No chance of it. His own natural French accent was too heavy. He wasn't a good pupil. He didn't really have a strong desire to learn English, only enough to earn his living as an actor. And he did not miss France, because he never really left it. He had a wonderful time in America, as a visitor.

"He was fascinated by everything he saw here—flashing neon signs, billboards, swing music, sports and movies, soda fountains, drive-in restaurants, big cars, everything that was different from Europe. He was like a child in an amusement park, or maybe better, an explorer in a strange land, his eyes always open to new vistas, but always planning to go back to France.

"When he felt France needed him, he went back. He never stopped being a loyal Frenchman. He made contact with the Free French forces. He told me he was leaving. I went to New York with him. He left bound for Morocco. The ship was sunk, but he survived, and from Casablanca he joined the Free French. For a time, he was in the tank division. It was the worst place for him to be. He had claustrophobia and he was desperately afraid of fire.

"He escaped the war without injury, but many times he could have died. I find that men who have the experience of being close to death in war, even if they aren't injured, they bear the scars. I have a few invisible scars myself.

"When the war ended, Gabin went back to Paris. He hoped to continue his career. It wasn't the same. He looked older, but he wouldn't color his hair. Not manly, he believed.

"We had one brief meeting, he and I, during the war. I was close to the front, near Bastogne. There was a rumor that a tank division of the Free French army was near. I was able to find him. He embraced me a little stiffly. All of the other French soldiers in their tanks were cheering. I kissed him.

"I heard the orders for the tanks to move out. It was an impossible dream. It happened so fast, sometimes it seems my memory played a trick. But it was real.

"He escaped without injury, but there were many times when he could have died. Death in a tank is one of the most horrible ones one can have. If you are lucky, you are killed instantly. More likely you are burned alive until a welcome death releases you.

"In 1946, I returned to Paris to make a film with Gabin, *Martin Roumagnac*. This time, it was Gabin who was able to help me with my French. The picture was a failure and part of the responsibility was mine."

*Martin Roumagnac* WAS BASED on a novel by Pierre-René Wolf. Gabin had bought the film rights in 1937 as a vehicle for himself, but no producer or director was interested, even with France's reigning international star as the lead. After the war, the addition of Marlene Dietrich to the cast changed minds.

### Martin Roumagnac (1946)

Martin Roumagnac (Jean Gabin), an architect and builder, is employed by Blanche Ferrand (Marlene Dietrich) to design and build her a house in the French provinces. Roumagnac is fascinated by this mysterious woman of worldly sophistication, as she is by his straightforward sincerity. Soon, they become lovers looking forward to a life together.

Then he finds out that she supports herself as a high-priced prostitute, with a pet shop as her front. In a rage, he kills her.

At the trial, it becomes clear that she really loved him very deeply. The jury, understanding his temporary anger and sympathizing with his permanent sorrow, acquits him.

One of Ferrand's former admirers (Daniel Gélin), a shy schoolteacher, does not agree that justice has been done, and he kills Roumagnac.

This film was released in the United States as *The Room Upstairs*. This version was twenty-eight minutes shorter. The Legion of Decency threatened a boycott unless certain scenes having to do with prostitution were cut.

"I WASN'T AWARE OF a deep need Gabin had to settle down in Paris, to marry, to have children," Marlene said. "I would happily have lived with him in Paris, but I couldn't desert my financial responsibilities, and I was too old to have children.

"Jean married a young actress. It was hard for me to accept, but I wanted him to be happy. He believed the only way for us to end our intimate relationship was to end everything and all contact. He chose to do that exactly, the opposite of what I wished for. It was a total and terrible break. I had great difficulty getting over him. In truth, I never did."

MARLENE RETURNED FROM PARIS to make a film called *Golden Earrings*. Since she claimed to have done some research in Europe on how Gypsies dress and behave, she insisted on going barefoot. This conflicted with the costume designs, but director Mitchell Leisen was well known for giving in to stars' demands, so Marlene appears barefoot—but her double does not. Leisen believed no one would notice. At least, he hoped not.

### Golden Earrings (1947)

Shortly after World War II, Major General Ralph Denistoun (Ray Milland) receives a box containing golden earrings at his London hotel. He rushes to Paris.

In flashback, Colonel Denistoun and Captain Byrd (Bruce Lester) are intelligence officers in wartime Germany searching for a German scientist, Professor Krosigk (Reinhold Schünzel), who has invented a new poison gas and doesn't want it to fall into the hands of the Nazis.

Denistoun is helped to survive by a lone Gypsy woman, Lydia (Marlene Dietrich), who guides him through the Black Forest by integrating him with her fellow Gypsies. He virtually becomes a Gypsy himself, wearing golden earrings and learning to read palms. He reads death in Byrd's palm, and afterward Byrd is killed searching for Professor Krosigk near Stuttgart.

Disguised as a Gypsy fortune-teller, Denistoun approaches Krosigk in Stuttgart. At first Krosigk doesn't believe Denistoun, then, as the scientist is being arrested by the Gestapo, he pays the fortune-teller with a five-mark note that contains the poison gas formula.

Lydia helps Denistoun back to the Allied lines, and then leaves him. Flashback ends.

In the present, Denistoun returns to the Black Forest, where he is reunited with Lydia.

I talked with Ray Milland many years later at a Lincoln Center gala. Among his leading ladies, as we spoke, he singled out Marlene as being "difficult."

"She was distinctly unfriendly toward me. When I was working with her at Paramount on *Golden Earrings*, I was studying German rather seriously, and I asked her some technical question about the language. She became enraged and treated me as if I'd accused her of being a Nazi, saying she never spoke 'that accursed tongue' anymore. Then, she'd go off somewhere with [Reinhold] Schünzel or Billy Wilder, who was making *The Emperor Waltz* next door, and chirp away in 'that accursed tongue.'"

WHEN MARIA TURNED EIGHTEEN in December 1942, she became unofficially engaged to British actor Richard Haydn, who was thirty-seven. The couple wanted to get married right away, but Marlene blocked the ceremony, saying they should wait until the end of the war.

Maria broke the engagement and, against her mother's wishes, married Dean Goodman, a drama student who later became a professional actor. The marriage took place on August 23, 1943, at the Hollywood Congregational Church. After the war, they were divorced and Maria married William Riva on July 4, 1947, in New York City. A year later, Michael, Marlene's first grandchild, would be born.

BILLY WILDER HAD LONG wanted to have his friend Marlene in one of his films. Finally, he had the perfect part.

The film was *A Foreign Affair*. It was set in Berlin and Marlene was to play the girlfriend of an important Nazi who apparently was no longer with her. Her life in postwar Berlin would be an important element of the film.

Marlene had dreamed of working with Wilder, but when she heard the idea of the film, she was uncertain. She decided she didn't want to play that part.

Wilder remembered it well. "'Billy, my darling,' Marlene explained to me, 'I want so badly to work with you but I just cannot play a woman who either was a Nazi or who was such a political opportunist that she didn't care who she slept with, as long as she got nylons.'

"'Do it for me,' I said, looking into her eyes. 'Yes,' she said, looking into my eyes. She always told me she only did it for me, but I think she did it for herself, too.

"If she meant no, no one could persuade her. She was like a mule. I think she knew all the time that she was going to say yes, but she enjoyed being coaxed."

The film, also starring Jean Arthur and John Lund, began shooting in December 1947.

### A Foreign Affair (1948)

In postwar Berlin, visiting congresswoman Phoebe Frost (Jean Arthur) investigates a singer in an off-limits cabaret, Erika von Schluetow (Marlene Dietrich), who has had Nazi connections and is now being shielded by an unidentified American officer. She doesn't realize that the officer assisting her in her investigation, Captain John Pringle (John Lund), is Erika's lover.

As Phoebe starts to fall for Pringle, she abandons her natural reserve in a wild night at the cabaret and is arrested in a raid. Erika uses her influence to help Phoebe save her reputation. Phoebe then finds out about Pringle's affair with Erika, not realizing that he has been ordered to draw her jealous ex-Gestapo lover out of hiding.

As she is about to leave Berlin heartbroken, Phoebe learns the truth and rushes back to the cabaret, where the Gestapo fugitive has been shot, and she and Pringle are reunited.

Marlene appeared briefly in an independent film called *Jigsaw* (1949), written and directed by Fletcher Markle and starring Franchot Tone. Markle was a CBS radio director who had just directed Marlene with Van Heflin and Claude Rains in *Madame Bovary* for the radio Ford Theater. Other walk-ons in *Jigsaw* were done by

Henry Fonda, John Garfield, Marsha Hunt, Everett Sloane, and Burgess Meredith. The theme of the film is anti-Semitism, daring for its time.


WHEN I ASKED MARLENE about *Stage Fright*, she said, "Oh, which one was that, dear?" I reminded her that it was her Hitchcock picture, and she laughed. She said that most people thought *Witness for the Prosecution*, in which she also starred, was her Hitchcock picture. I asked her how the two directors, Wilder and Hitchcock, differed.

She explained that she never knew Mr. Hitchcock in the same way she knew Billy Wilder. "What a charming, funny, and kind man Billy was," she said. "Mr. Hitchcock was a very intelligent director, and he was a gentleman, an English gentleman, though personally I found him very European. I never cooked chicken soup for Mr. Hitchcock the way I did for Billy, but I gave him some recipes. He was interested in cooking, but more in eating. I told him I always wore a hairnet when I cooked. He did not have to worry about that, though, because he did not have so many hairs.

"We talked about food. He loved European restaurants, and luxe hotels. Mr. Hitchcock and Billy both knew French. Both men were gallant. They never 'interfered' with me as I remember.

"I was with Tyrone Power in the Wilder film and with Richard Todd in Mr. Hitchcock's picture. They looked alike. They were both very handsome men, and it is always a pleasure to look at a handsome man.

"When I first thought about working with Alfred Hitchcock, I was quite thrilled. I thought I would learn a lot from a true master. I'd heard he was a technical genius and I'd always had a great interest in the technical part of making a film. I'd heard that Mr. Hitchcock always made friends with the technicians and worked closely with them. Just what I did. And that he was a demon where lighting was concerned. I have always been a student of lighting, which means the world to an actress.

"I was familiar with his British work, that wonderful 39 *Steps* with the beautiful Madeleine Carroll. I hoped he'd like me the way he obviously liked her. He'd been at UFA early in his career, and I was told he spoke pretty good German. In German, we could have very private conversations. I had a good feeling that we would establish an immediate rapport.

"The only hesitation I had was what I saw of the script. I didn't like the script, and I didn't think much of my part. I expressed my feelings to representatives of the producers and my agent, but I was reassured that Mr. Hitchcock understood all of that. My part would be built up, and the script would be much better. Mr. Hitchcock kept his word about my part. As for the script, they did the best they could."

Alfred Hitchcock told me, "She [Marlene Dietrich] wouldn't do anything until she consulted her astrologer. He should have received a credit."

Richard Todd agreed. "Dietrich was ruled by the stars," he told me. "She didn't do anything without talking to her astrologer. When she realized I was newly married, she asked me to give her my wife's date of birth. About a week later, she said, 'You know, it's no good. You've married the wrong person.' She'd gotten in touch with her chap in America, and he'd looked it up, and it wasn't right at all.

"We proved her wrong—for twenty years."


### Stage Fright (1950)

Eve Gill (Jane Wyman), an aspiring young actress, shelters a fellow acting student, Jonathan Cooper (Richard Todd), from the police. He is suspected of murdering the husband of his mistress, Charlotte Inwood (Marlene Dietrich), a famous singer. with whom Jonathan claims he became implicated when he tried to help Charlotte destroy evidence.

Eve's eccentric father, Commodore Gill (Alastair, but billed as Alistair Sim), agrees to hide Jonathan in his house while Eve proves his innocence. To do this, Eve becomes Charlotte's temporary maid.

Eve's father devises a plan to force Charlotte to confess in front of the inspector investigating the case, Wilfrid Smith (Michael Wilding). When the plan doesn't work, Eve tries blackmailing Charlotte into a confession while the police listen outside her dressing room. Charlotte agrees to pay, but insists that Jonathan is the real murderer.

Jonathan lures Eve into the basement of the theater where he admits not only to killing Charlotte's husband, but to another murder. He is ready to kill her, but Eve escapes. Jonathan is trapped on stage by police and killed by the falling fire curtain.

Smith and Eve, in love, leave together.

An unexpected dividend for Pat Hitchcock, who was making her film debut in *Stage Fright*, was some advice from Marlene Dietrich: "I was able to give his young daughter some valuable advice based on what I had learned about camera lighting," Marlene told me in Paris many years later. "The wrong lighting, the wrong lens, being photographed from the wrong angle, this ages you. The wrong lighting could have taken away her freshness.

"She listened with great attention, but I think she was not very vain, about makeup or wardrobe, either. She was more deeply involved with her acting. For me, acting is only part of it."

Wilkie Cooper, director of photography for *Stage Fright*, said that the greatest challenge was filming Marlene Dietrich's scenes.

"Mr. Hitchcock gave me special instructions, which really surprised me, especially it being Mr. Hitchcock and all. He said that for any scenes with Miss Dietrich, I was to listen to her instructions, and—this was the part that really took me aback—to do it the way she said. Needless to say, I didn't question Mr. Hitchcock's instructions, but I prepared myself for the worst. Perhaps seeing the expression on my face, he reassured me, saying, 'Miss Dietrich is quite expert and knows what she's talking about,' and he said, 'Don't argue about it with her. Just discreetly let me know.' No one knew more about his camera than he did. Mr. Hitchcock knew more about the camera than I did.

"Well, he was right about it. Miss Dietrich certainly did know a great deal, especially about camera lighting. Mr. Hitchcock had mentioned that she had learned from Josef von Sternberg. What she had to offer was very professional, and she knew what she was doing, for herself.

"What worried me was that she would look like she was in a different film. I needed to make it all match.

"The other problem was Miss Wyman. She could see that Miss Dietrich was getting all of this attention, which certainly must have seemed to her to be preferential. Well, it was. I can't say Miss Wyman was exactly a good sport about it, but she did her best not to complain.

"Miss Dietrich was pleasant enough to work with—as long as she got her way. She considered herself to be the director and the camera director for her scenes. I think Mr. Hitchcock must have made some kind of special agreement with her in order to get her for the picture. Though she didn't say it exactly, it was clear that there was only one concern she had, and that was that she look as young as possible. Actually, what she really wanted was to look younger than was possible for any camera or any lighting to achieve."

Hitchcock wanted Marlene Dietrich for the part, he told me, because she really was a great character, and he wanted her to bring that character with her to *Stage Fright*. He preferred actors who didn't require constant direction, and she certainly was one of those.

"Dietrich was very much herself," Hitchcock commented.

NEVILLE SHUTE, AUTHOR OF *No Highway in the Sky* (and later *On the Beach*), was an aeronautical engineer before he started writing novels. In the film based on his novel, Marlene basically plays herself. "You have no idea how hard it is to play a character just like yourself," she told me. "You have nothing to lean on. Nothing to hold on to.

"In the case of Monica Teasdale, I have the added responsibility of convincing not only the other characters, but the audience itself that I am qualified to give a life-and-death opinion on a subject I know nothing about—airplane design. But people listen to celebrities and believe them, so you have to be careful what you say in public.

"In the case of Monica Teasdale, I think she was right to worry about the safety of her fellow passengers and to use her celebrity to protect them if she could. I'm no politician, but it's how I felt about Hitler and the Nazis."

### No Highway in the Sky (1951)

Dedicated aeronautical engineer Theodore Honey (James Stewart) has found a serious flaw in the tail section of a passenger plane he designed and is on his way to Labrador to investigate a crash that might substantiate his theory. When he learns that the plane he is on may have this flaw, he insists they land immediately. Nobody believes Honey except Monica Teasdale (Marlene Dietrich), a movie star, and Marjorie Corder (Glynis Johns), a flight attendant.

In Gander, the plane is thoroughly checked, and no problems are found. Just as the plane is about to go on to Labrador, Honey wrecks the undercarriage so it cannot take off.

Honey takes his case to company executive Dennis Scott (Jack Hawkins) and the company owner, Sir John (Ronald Squire). They are not convinced by Honey, but they are swayed by the intercession of the legendary Monica Teasdale, and they open an investigation.

Meanwhile, Monica and Marjorie have come to know Honey better. He is a widower with an adolescent daughter, Elspeth (Janette Scott), who has suffered because of his neglect. The two women help Elspeth, socially and emotionally, while Honey's theory is proven correct.

"If I could have been anyone in the world," Marlene said, "I think I would have been Sir Alexander Fleming. He discovered penicillin. I tried to imagine what it would be like to walk around knowing you had done something like that. How proud he must have been. He was the person I most wanted to meet. When I did meet him, I asked him what it felt like to have done something so important for mankind, and womankind, too.

"I made him feel uncomfortable. He was flustered. He acted like no one had ever asked him that question before. Maybe no one had.

"Sir Alexander was a genius doer, not a talker, but he did have his wits about him. He said to me, 'How would *you* feel?' I didn't miss a beat because I knew. I answered, 'I'd be so proud and my chest would be out so far, I'd pop all the buttons off my blouse.'

"Then, I behaved like the most gauche fan. I asked him for an autographed picture. He sent me one. It's one of my most treasured possessions."

•   •   •

Marlene plays a daredevil aviatrix in *The Ship of Lost Men,* 1929, one of her last German films. (Collection of Paul Morrissey)

Marlene with Willi Forst in *Dangers of the Engagement Period,* 1929. She acted with her eyes. (Potsdam Museum)

Marlene in her breakout role as Lola Lola in *The Blue Angel* (1930). According to director Josef von Sternberg, Marlene won the role because she didn't seem to care whether she did. (Potsdam Museum)

Until it was released, *The Blue Angel* was referred to as an Emil Jannings movie. Afterward, it was a Marlene Dietrich movie. (Potsdam Museum)

Publicity shots of Marlene when she first arrived in Hollywood showed her as she had appeared in German films. Josef von Sternberg, however, had different ideas about the new Dietrich screen persona. (Collection of Tim Malachosky)

Von Sternberg liked to cast Marlene as a worldly sophisticate, as here in *Morocco* (1930). (Collection of Paul Morrissey)

Marlene denied rumors of an affair with Gary Cooper during the filming of *Morocco,* her first American film. (Collection of Paul Morrissey)

In *Blonde Venus* (1932), Marlene plays a part parallel to her own life, that of the celebrated performer who manages to have an affair while never intending to leave her child (Dickie Moore) and husband (Herbert Marshall). (Collection of Paul Morrissey)

"It took more than one man to change my name to Shanghai Lily," Marlene told Clive Brook in *Shanghai Express* (1932). (Collection of Paul Morrissey)

In *Blonde Venus* (1932), Marlene plays a celebrated performer who has affairs while never leaving her husband and child, exactly the situation in Marlene's personal life. Not even Cary Grant, here in one of his first major roles, could change her film character's mind. (Collection of Paul Morrissey)

In *Desire* (1936), Marlene was reunited with Gary Cooper, this time without rumors of an extramarital affair for both of them. Ernst Lubitsch was scheduled to be the director but produced instead. (Collection of Tim Malachosky)

Producer David O. Selznick called the dialogue in *The Garden of Allah* (1936) "Desert Poetry," but it was so full of sounds Marlene and Charles Boyer could not pronounce that a dialogue coach was necessary at all times. It was Joshua Logan's first job. (Collection of Paul Morrissey)

Marlene as Catherine the Great in *The Scarlet Empress* (1934). (Collection of Paul Morrissey)

Sam Jaffe as Grand Duke Peter with Marlene in *The Scarlet Empress*. Jaffe claimed that everyone on the set hated von Sternberg as much as they loved Marlene. (Collection of Paul Morrissey)

*The Devil Is a Woman* (1935), Marlene's last film with von Sternberg. (Collection of Tim Malachosky)

Marlene with Douglas Fairbanks, Jr., in London, 1937, during their long affair. Fairbanks was surprised to be introduced to Marlene's husband and his mistress. Marlene thought the arrangement "not especially irregular." (Douglas Fairbanks, Jr.)

Marlene was well known for the extraordinary amount of luggage she took with her on ship voyages, but when she went to entertain the troops in Europe during World War II, she gave it all up except for her packages of dime store false fingernails. (Collection of Tim Malachosky)

Mae West and Marlene. They were good friends at Paramount. During her childhood, Mae had learned German from her mother, which greatly amused Marlene. (Collection of Tim Malachosky)

Marlene appeared with John Wayne in three films. She said they were "very close friends." (British Film Institute)

With James Stewart, her costar in *Destry Rides Again* (1939), a comeback film for Marlene. (Collection of Tim Malachosky)

Marlene entertained American troops in Paris when they liberated the city. Here she is at Hermès, her favorite Paris shop. (Collection of Jean-Louis Dumas–Hermès)

The only man who ever seriously jeopardized Marlene's marriage, Jean Gabin. She said this was the first time that she wanted a man more than he wanted her. (British Film Institute)

Costume epics like *Kismet* (1944) reminded Marlene, she said, of the overblown kitsch of her days at UFA. The director, William Dieterle, had directed her in her first important role in a German film and had himself starred in an early silent version of *Kismet*. (Collection of Tim Malachosky)

Alfred Hitchcock directed Marlene in *Stage Fright* (1950). He told the crew that Miss Dietrich would be in charge of her own makeup and lighting because she was the expert. (British Film Institute)

Jean Cocteau visiting with his friend Marlene backstage when she appeared in Paris during the late 1950s with her nightclub act. (Collection of Tim Malachosky)

Marlene relaxes on the set with Charles Laughton, who is contemplating a cup of coffee, during the filming of *Witness for the Prosecution* (1957). (Collection of Billy Wilder)

Marlene with Spencer Tracy in *Judgment at Nuremberg* (1961), a film to which she was able to add authentic detail and even some dialogue. (British Film Institute)

"When Burt said, 'Terrific, baby, terrific,'" Marlene recalled, "I could have died of happiness." Marlene with Burt Bacharach during their extremely successful Russian tour. (Collection of Burt Bacharach)

Marlene as she appeared in her highly successful Las Vegas musical act.
(Collection of Tim Malachosky)

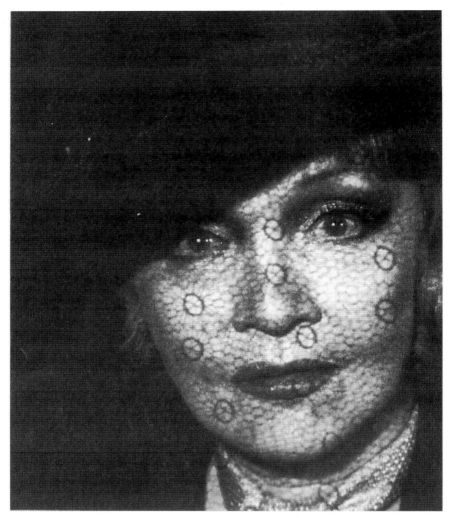

Marlene as she appeared in her last dramatic film, *Just a Gigolo* (1978). The German producers had to recreate their Berlin sets in Paris because Marlene would work only in Paris. (Photo by Emilio Lari)

UNTIL 1952, MARLENE AND Fritz Lang had never made a film together, so it should have been an auspicious occasion when the creator of *Metropolis* and Hollywood's most famous German star joined to make *Rancho Notorious*. It was not.

When I first met Fritz Lang, a quarter of a century after he had worked with Dietrich, his thoughts and dreams were still occupied with plot ideas, scripts, and the hope, though faint, that there was at least one more film in his future. That film, he said, meant more to him than all of the films in his past.

Directing films was the essential element in his happiness. "When you can't work anymore," he told me, "it's better to die. But I have to wait, because I don't believe in suicide." He still had the need and the drive, but no longer the physical ability, especially with his failing sight, to do the thing that gave meaning to his life.

In our conversations, he would intersperse bits for films he was trying to work out in his mind, and he would make up characters and stories about the people sitting around us in restaurants.

Sitting next to him whenever I visited at his Mulholland Drive home in Beverly Hills was always the ubiquitous Steiff German sailor monkey doll that had accompanied him from Berlin. Peter, as Lang called him, wore a turtleneck sweater, a sailor's cap tipped at a rakish angle, trousers, and a gold earring in one ear. The expression on Peter's face was suave and urbane, looking as if he knew Hamburg's St. Pauli district well.

Lang had imbued Peter with many of his own qualities, especially those he most esteemed, such as being able to consume an impressive number of martinis. Whenever Lang drank, Peter was served one, too. Then, Lang drank it for him.

Lang confided that Peter had a mysterious past, the facts of which Lang said he would never divulge, nor would Peter. He was concerned about Peter's future and had thought about willing him to Joan Bennett, the star of some of his favorite American films. There were several actresses Lang said he had considered willing Peter to because, he said, "Peter likes actresses.

"The only one I would never consider is Marlene Dietrich, because I don't like her and she is too old."

What Lang didn't know was that Marlene had also brought her own doll with her from Berlin to Hollywood, an African-appearing, long-legged black doll with a bright yellow skirt made of felt. She called her doll Zula. "She's my lucky doll."

Marlene was just as unhappy working with Lang as he was with her.

"I had the utmost respect for Lang's German work," she said. "His American work was never up to his German films, in my opinion.

"I didn't like his arrogance, which I think came from insecurity. I don't think he ever adjusted to America. America never adjusted completely to him. Many people didn't like him. Professionally, he didn't get many wonderful scripts."

Marlene did not like what she felt was Fritz Lang's directorial manner. "Teutonic," she said, "in the worst sense of the word. He screamed at people who didn't do something just the way he wanted it done the first time. He was horribly impatient. He expected you to read his mind. No matter how quickly you did what he said, you were late.

"He never treated me that way. I would not have accepted it, and he knew it, so that means he was fully aware of his temper tantrums and could control them if he wanted to. He used the tyranny of the director to terrorize people. I sympathized with his victims, and it upset me.

"We never spoke German together. It would have been rude to other people on the set. They were expecting to hear at least a few sentences in German, but it never happened."

## *Rancho Notorious* (1952)

After his fiancée is raped and killed in a robbery, Vern Haskell (Arthur Kennedy) sets out on a one-man crusade to find her murderer and bring him to justice. His only clue is a missing brooch she was wearing that he had just given to her.

In his travels, he meets a stranger named Frenchy Fairmont (Mel Ferrer), who leads him to a horse ranch owned by a lady friend, Altar Keane (Marlene Dietrich), a fabulous and notorious dance hall girl of the Wild West. The ranch is really a hideout for wanted men, and Frenchy is one of the most wanted. Vern, pretending to be an outlaw himself, believes he has found among the outlaws hiding out there the murderer of his fiancée. He brags of his prowess with women and mentions a robbery that could have been the one in which Vern's fiancée was killed. He also has recent cuts on his face that could have been inflicted by a desperate woman's fingernails.

Vern's background is as a cowboy, not a gunslinger, so he is not equipped to take on anyone. He studies the techniques of Frenchy, the fastest gun in the West, and soon becomes an expert gunslinger himself. Meanwhile, he has been taking Frenchy's place in Altar's heart. Then he sees her wearing the brooch and assumes she is involved in the fatal robbery.

In a rage, he leaves her and seeks revenge in a shootout. It turns out, however, that he is gunning for the wrong man. It was Frenchy's sidekick, Kinch (Lloyd Gough), who raped and robbed Vern's fiancée. A coward, Kinch refuses to engage in a shootout, but is later killed in a gun battle.

Back at the ranch, Altar is packing to leave but is stopped by some of her associates who have just returned from a bank robbery. They believe she and Frenchy are leaving with their share of the money. Vern appears on the scene, and a shootout occurs in which Altar is killed.

Fritz Lang told me that he found Marlene Dietrich "very difficult" to work with. "Marlene got younger every scene, or so she wanted you to believe. I don't know if she believed it herself. She acted as if she did, and maybe she did believe.

"One of the irritating things Marlene did," Lang told me, "was when she didn't agree with what I was doing, she would say to me that von Sternberg would have done it this or that way. She would say, 'Jo would have . . .' and then she would go into detail about what von Sternberg would have done. I tried to shut her out and not listen, but I wasn't successful because she was so insistent. She was successful in annoying me, but not in affecting what I did. I was not Josef von Sternberg. I am Fritz Lang."

The film was shot at Howard Hughes's RKO. Marlene received only $40,000 and told everyone that it was clear how Hughes became so rich. Marlene did a tour after the film was finished to promote its release. Her personal appearances were a tremendous success. Apparently, even many people who didn't want to see the film wanted to see her.

LANG TOLD ME THAT he wanted to make a film called *Blue Martini*. He asked if I had ever had a blue martini. I admitted that I'd never had even a regular one. Savoring his recollection, he explained that it had been his infallible seduction technique. He would invite a girl he was in love with "at the moment" to his place and mix blue martinis. "She would be mystified, intrigued, enchanted, and fall into my arms. Do you know what made the martini blue?"

I didn't.

"Blue food coloring. I never told a girl that before. If you write a book about me, I want you to call it *Blue Martini*. It always worked, every single time, so that proves it was the greatest seduction technique. They never could resist my blue martini."

I suggested that maybe the reason the blue martini was so effective was that the women couldn't resist him—that he was the blue martini.

"There is something I want to ask you," he said. "Would you like a blue martini?"

In 1953, MARLENE WAS invited to join other celebrities in a special cerebral palsy benefit by the Ringling Bros. and Barnum & Bailey Circus in New York's Madison Square Garden. She agreed, but only if she could be the ringmaster. This led to a lucrative invitation for her to appear at the Las Vegas Sahara Hotel, which she also accepted. Its success meant the beginning of a new career for her on stage. First, however, she still had films to make. The next one was a fleeting but profitable appearance.

### Around the World in 80 Days (1956)

British gentleman Phileas Fogg (David Niven) makes a £20,000 bet that he can circle the earth in eighty days, a seemingly impossible feat in 1872. With the assistance of his butler, Passepartout (Cantinflas), Fogg overcomes obstacle after obstacle to win his bet.

Marlene plays a dance hall queen in San Francisco. The film won five Oscars, including best picture. For the first run, the film was shown in theaters specially equipped for the Todd-AO widescreen process. (The AO stands for the American Optical Company, inventor, developer, and manufacturer of the special camera lens.) Marlene found Mike Todd "brilliant, generous," and she liked him personally.

•　•　•

*The Monte Carlo Story*, made in Italy, was directed by Samuel A. Taylor, who was better known as a writer, having written the screenplays for Billy Wilder's *Sabrina* and Alfred Hitchcock's *Vertigo*.

### The Monte Carlo Story (1957)

Count Dino della Fiaba (Vittorio de Sica) lives on a small decrepit boat, the *Speranza*, in the harbor just below Monte Carlo's grand hotel and gambling casino. He regularly visits the casino, hoping to win back the fortune he lost at roulette five years earlier. He avoids roulette, however, until one day he hopes he can discover the magic number of a winning system.

He is supported by his former servants, who now work in the hotel. Mildly impatient, they suggest he use his irresistible charm to find a wealthy wife. He chooses the Marquise Maria de Crevecoeur (Marlene Dietrich), presumed to be the wealthiest of all the hotel's guests because she gives no tips.

But she also has lost her fortune gambling and is looking for a rich husband. She is interested in the count until he admits he is penniless. Meanwhile, she has to return her jewelry to the shop owner who has followed her, and his jewelry, to the hotel.

When the *Speranza* is hit by a yacht, the owner invites Dino and Maria aboard his boat as guests until repairs can be made. He is Mr. Hinkley (Arthur O'Connell), an American millionaire.

Believing Maria is the sister of Dino, Hinkley falls in love with her while his teenage daughter, Jane (Natalie Trundy), becomes infatuated with Dino. When Dino hears that Jane is nineteen, he rushes back to the casino with what he believes is the magic number for winning at roulette.

He wins until he learns that Jane is really eighteen, about to turn nineteen. Before he loses everything, his former servants stop him. He repays them with interest, and he still has something left.

Hinkley proposes, asking Maria to come to Muncie, Indiana, with him, but she leaves to join Dino, who is returning to his ancestral Naples.

Marlene was surprised to find out that at the time all Italian films were dubbed, whatever language is used. "People complain when an Italian film is dubbed into English," she observed. "They don't realize that Italian films in Italian are dubbed, too. It's so funny."

"I DIRECTED *Witness for the Prosecution*," Billy Wilder told me, "because Marlene asked me to, and I liked the story. Very Hitchcock. She wanted to play the part of the murderess, and if I was directing, she was more likely to get it. She liked to play bad girls because they were more interesting than good girls, and she preferred real-life love scenes to the ones on the screen. In pictures, kissing embarrassed her, but I do not think so in real life."

Producer Arthur Hornblow, Jr., had approached Dietrich about playing Christine, but his producing partner, Edward Small, who had bought the film rights to Agatha Christie's long-running play, was not certain she was right for the part. He did, however, readily accept Hornblow's suggestion for a director, Billy Wilder. It was Hornblow who had given Wilder his first chance to direct in Hollywood.

"Billy wanted Marlene Dietrich," Lenore Hornblow, the producer's widow, told me. "Marlene was coached how to speak: cockney by Noel Coward, who was a close friend of hers. He came to the set.

"She made a marvelous mushroom soup. Billy was absolutely crazy about it. She would drop it by his home for him in a covered pot with a copper lid on it. The first time it arrived, Billy was very pleased, and he and Audrey [his wife] planned to have it as the first course of their dinner. When Audrey went to heat it, she saw that there was only a very small amount, not enough for two, only enough for one bowl.

"She served the mushroom soup to Billy, who offered to split it with her. Audrey said no, she didn't like it as much as he did, and, she said, 'Marlene meant it for you.' After the one-bowl delivery, Audrey probably liked it even less, and it didn't end there. Whenever the pot got left off with its contents of mushroom soup, there was always just enough for one bowl. I tried to explain to Audrey that I didn't think Marlene did it deliberately, but it was just that Audrey didn't exist for her. She said, 'Does that make it better?' I suggested to Marlene that Audrey wasn't going to like her, and why didn't she just leave more, say enough for two bowls. But though the deliveries continued from time to time, there was just enough for Billy."

### Witness for the Prosecution (1957)

While convalescing from a heart attack, barrister Sir Wilfrid Robarts (Charles Laughton) defends a man, Leonard Vole (Tyrone Power), accused of murdering a wealthy widow (Norma Varden) for her money. The chief witness for the prosecution is the man's German wife, Christine (Marlene Dietrich), who can testify against her husband because her marriage to him is not legal.

Christine's testimony, however, is discredited by love letters to another man in which she outlines her plan to implicate Vole falsely in the murder. Vole is found not guilty and released.

Triumphantly, Christine admits to Sir Wilfrid that she was the mysterious cockney woman who sold him the letters discrediting her own testimony, and that Vole was guilty of the murder. Vole appears in the courtroom with a young woman (Ruta Lee), saying he is going away with her. Enraged, Christine stabs him.

Despite his bad health, Sir Wilfrid makes plans to represent her defense.

Billy Wilder, speaking about Marlene Dietrich many years after *Witness for the Prosecution* was made, told me, "Marlene Dietrich was an aristocrat who had to leave her title behind, but she took her nobility with her. She didn't actually have a title, but she should have.

"She was one of the two most intelligent actresses I ever knew, but you have to promise you won't write that until after I'm dead."

MARLENE CAME TO KNOW Orson Welles during World War II when he sawed her in half for servicemen at the Hollywood USO canteen. She always said he was a genius, as well as a dear friend.

The part of Tanya, the Mexican bordello madam, was not in the *Touch of Evil* script submitted by Welles to Universal for their approval. Only after the finished film was screened did the studio's promotion department understand that Marlene Dietrich was in the movie, even if only in a cameo.

After Marlene agreed to be in the picture, Welles created Tanya to help explain and amplify his character of Hank Quinlan.

### Touch of Evil (1958)

Mexican narcotics detective Ramon Miguel Vargas (Charlton Heston), and his wife, Susan (Janet Leigh), escape injury when their car is blown up at the U.S. border. In an attempt to capture the Mexican he thinks is responsible, Vargas appeals for aid from Hank Quinlan (Orson Welles), the chief of police of the Texas border town.

When Quinlan uses the situation to imprison illegally a Mexican suspect involved in a different case, Vargas realizes that the situation is more complicated than he realized. At every turn, his investigation runs into the wall of Quinlan's unethical methods and special interests.

Meanwhile, the narcotics gang Vargas has been pursuing threatens Susan if he continues his investigation. Now Vargas finds himself in a battle with both Mexican drug dealers and the corrupt American lawman who is their ally. In the end, the physical disintegration of Hank Quinlan, witnessed by his longtime mistress, Tanya (Marlene Dietrich), decides the outcome.

As soon as Marlene signed, Welles wrote the sequences with Tanya. For one night's work she received $7,500.

At the time of its theatrical release, *Touch of Evil* went largely unnoticed. Since then, it has gained in critical respect.

WHEN ROBERTO ROSSELLINI'S *Open City* opened in Paris, Marlene was eager to be first to see it. She was. She was also the second to see it. And the third. Friends had told her it was a genuine masterpiece. "They were right," she told me. "I wish I knew a stronger, better word than masterpiece."

She wanted all of her friends to see *Open City*, and she went back with some of them. "You can't see *Open City* too many times. I was enchanted by Rossellini's neorealism."

When she came to know him a decade later, she found him to be the ideal intellectual, with a sense of humor, an artist, very romantically appealing. "He had such an intelligent look in his eyes. I watch for that look in the eyes," she said.

"I can understand how Ingrid Bergman felt when she met him and became so enamored. It would have been impossible for her *not* to feel that way. He could speak French, but I felt a loss for our not having a true language together. He made me wish I knew Italian, so

I could communicate with him in his own language. I felt like the character I played in *Morocco*, that I would follow Roberto Rossellini into the desert."

"My father very much admired Marlene Dietrich," Isabella Rossellini, daughter of Ingrid Bergman and Roberto Rossellini, told me. "He was so moved by what she had done before the war, to come out so strongly against the Nazis while she was still a German citizen; and then, during the war, to go to the front, very near to the action, risking her life to entertain the soldiers. He found her very intelligent, beautiful, brave, and a wonderful entertainer, but he was most impressed by her as a person."

When Isabella was a little girl, she was taken by her father to a Paris bar for a special occasion. She was to meet Marlene.

"I remember Marlene Dietrich's coming toward my father and me at that hotel bar in Paris. I was a very little girl and my father never took me anywhere like a bar. I wasn't even allowed to see movies yet."

As Marlene approached them, Isabella noticed her stride. "It was wonderful, graceful, dramatic. I've always remembered that stride from my meeting with her when I was a little girl."

She also remembered Marlene's dress. "It looked sewn on. At the time, it seemed to me like her skin."

Marlene invited Rossellini to come to hear her sing that night, and he accepted, but not for his little daughter. Instead, he took his little boy, Roberto, who was only a few years older than Isabella. "It was not a matter of age," Isabella remembered, "but my father's feeling about what a man could do. At the time, I was so jealous."


STANLEY KRAMER, WHO WAS not afraid to tackle difficult screen subjects, found *Judgment at Nuremberg* almost impossible to finance. Potential backers thought the subject matter too somber and the staging in a single courtroom too static. Kramer intended to send a second-unit film crew to Germany for exteriors that would offer some variety to the film, but bombed-out cities were considered even less appealing than a courtroom. His answer was star power, even if only in cameo roles. Consequently, he was able to obtain Burt Lancaster, Montgomery Clift, and Judy Garland for small, uncharacteristic parts, and Marlene Dietrich for a substantial characteristic part.

Marlene's character, Mme Bertholt, did not appear in Abby Mann's original 1959 CBS television *Judgment at Nuremberg* script. Stanley Kramer said that he had Mann add her role to his film version "because Marlene existed." The addition of the widow of a German general also gave Kramer opportunities to open up the teleplay. Her inclusion in the film provided interludes away from the courtroom drama as well as introducing a possible romance.

She was added to embody "the other Germans," those who did not support Hitler, especially after more people understood by what means he intended to accomplish his goals for Germany. She represents an aristocrat of pre-Hitler Germany and their code. Being well qualified by her own background to speak for such a character, Marlene made some contributions to the script after consulting with Kramer.

The film was a boon to Hollywood's European character actors, such as John Wengraf and Otto Waldis, who had scarcely worked since the war.

Maximilian Schell was the only actor held over from the television version, which had been directed by George Roy Hill. The film established Schell as an international star.

### Judgment at Nuremberg (1961)

As interest in the Nuremberg war trials wanes, Judge Dan Haywood (Spencer Tracy), a Maine judge, retired not by choice but because he lost an election, agrees to preside over the trial of four German judges accused of having knowingly conspired with the Nazis to commit war crimes. Three of the four plead not guilty. A fourth, Ernst Janning (Burt Lancaster), refuses to make a plea. Janning is the most respected figure of the group, his philosophical work going back to before the time of Hitler.

During the trial, Judge Haywood stays at the mansion of Mme Bertholt (Marlene Dietrich), her property requisitioned by the occupying Allied forces. Even though her husband, a German general, was hanged as a war criminal, she and Judge Haywood become friendly. She is shocked when he suggests the possibility that Germans like her could have been aware of the Nazi atrocities.

As the trial progresses, even the clever German defense lawyer, Hans Rolfe (Maximilian Schell), cannot hide the guilt of the four judges. He maintains that they were only doing their duty according to the law and that they had no other choice but to cooperate with the Nazis or become victims themselves.

Finally, Janning speaks, admitting that they acquiesced far too readily to Nazi demands at a time when they should have united against Hitler, when it was still possible to stop him.

Before the judge renders his verdict, he is urged by a U.S. general (Alan Baxter) to be lenient because of the Berlin Blockade, which has just begun, and the U.S.–German relationship, but the judge sentences them all, including the sympathetic Janning, to life in prison.

Before Judge Haywood leaves, Janning thanks him for being honorable and just, while Rolfe bets him that all of the defendants will be free in five years. His words will come true.

Mme Bertholt refuses to take Haywood's farewell call, sitting in the shadows in front of the portrait of her husband, as the phone rings for a long time. At her side is a bottle of liquor.

While *Judgment at Nuremberg* was only barely profitable in its theatrical run, it was well represented in the year's Academy Awards voting. Maximilian Schell won as best actor and Abby Mann won an Oscar for his screenplay. Other nominations included Spencer Tracy for best actor; Judy Garland and Montgomery Clift for best supporting actress and actor; Stanley Kramer, two nominations, for best picture and best director; Ernest Laszlo, best cinematography; Fred Knudtson, best editing; Jean Louis, best costumes; and best art direction, Rudolph Sternad and George Milo. Burt Lancaster's fine performance was ignored, as was Marlene's. She performed with seeming ease, causing many to suggest she was just playing herself.

*Judgment* premiered in Berlin just before Christmas 1961. It did poorly in Germany, both in theatrical release and later on television. Wherever the film played in the rest of the world, it was treated with respect. A few critics were annoyed by the all-star cast, which they felt was inappropriate in view of the seriousness of the subject.

"I couldn't tell if Mr. Tracy was lonely or a loner," Marlene told me. "We didn't connect personally. Of course, he was too sick to concentrate on anything but his work and staying alive. Or, how to finish the film and not let us all down! I'd like to have worked with him earlier. But I would never have even tried to compete with Miss Hepburn. She and Tracy were made for each other. Luckily, they found each other and their unique relationship, which worked for them.

"As for *Judgment at Nuremberg*, I was disappointed by my part. I don't want to go as far as saying Stanley misled me, but let us say he made it possible for me to mislead myself. I thought my part would not only be bigger but more important. But I don't regret doing it.

"Tracy must have been a wonder in his prime, and his prime was as long as his health was good. Outliving one's health is a terrible thing. I do not want to outlive my good health. Worse than outliving one's money. Money you can always get more of.

"It's important to keep your money safely in what you know. For me, that has been jewelry. I had been well enough educated during my visits to Felsing's to know that fine jewelry bought from the best stores never goes down in price. I believed I had inherited an intuition for jewelry that came to me through generations of my family.

"Real estate never goes down in value, but you have to pay to support it, and more important, you can't wear it, so that never appealed to me."


MARLENE TOLD ME THAT Burt Bacharach was one of the greatest people in her life, and that for the last part of her career he was just like Josef von Sternberg had been in the first part of her career.

"One of the things I liked about Burt," Marlene told me, "was his strength. Nothing wishy-washy about him. He always directed me with certainty in my musical appearances, even in the beginning, when he was only thirty, and I was about twice his age and many times his experience. Actually, I like everything about him. He's perfect, the perfect man for me, except for one thing. Too young. Not his fault."

In 2010, Bacharach, whose *Promises, Promises* had just opened in a Broadway revival, again a great success, reminisced with me about his long and unique professional and personal relationship with Marlene Dietrich.

"I got to meet Marlene in a routine way," he told me, "but after that, it wasn't ever ordinary because *she* wasn't ordinary.

"I was on my way to Los Angeles in 1958, and my friend Peter Matz, who conducted for various musical acts, as I did, was able to find me in the airport. He had a major conflict in his schedule. He had agreed to accompany Noel Coward at the same time he was supposed to work with Marlene Dietrich. He asked me if I could help him out and work with Miss Dietrich. I said it would be a pleasure.

"When I arrived in Los Angeles, I called her and she was waiting for my call. We arranged to meet. She was staying in a cottage at the Beverly Hills Hotel.

"I don't think meeting her now would intimidate me as much as it did then. I'm worldlier, I've met a lot of famous people, and I've even become a little famous myself. I'd probably still be a little intimidated. She was a real star.

"It certainly was with a certain amount of awe that I went to meet her. She's legendary, you know. She had an aura. I went there nervous, but she made me feel very comfortable and at ease.

"I began to work with her. I think I played her a song during that time that I'd written. I told her I wanted to be a songwriter. She liked it, and she said, 'It's Frank Sinatra,' and she sent it to him. He didn't like it, I don't think.

"We started working together in Los Angeles to get ready for Las Vegas. As I remember, we only had about ten or twelve days to get ready, but it was enough. There was a lot I was able to do right away, because I could see where it was needed. Simple stuff, like go slower on a particular word, not to rush it.

"The biggest thing I had to have was her respect, and once I got that she would listen intently to everything I said. That didn't mean she just did everything I said. But she listened, and she heard. She really listened, and she treated me with a lot of respect.

"Sometimes she incorporated what I said the next time, after she thought about it. As her confidence in me grew, she did just about everything I suggested. I wanted her to question and not just accept. She had to feel good about it and with it. She was the one who had to go out there and do it. She loved music, but she wasn't a totally musical person. She was glad to get help.

"The image I have in my mind of Marlene is from not long after I met her. We'd gone from Los Angeles to Las Vegas. She was staying at the Sahara, where she was performing. I was at a local motel, and I was playing tennis when I saw her get out of a car. She had this great big bag of groceries, and she went straight to the motel office. She asked for my key and got it and went to the kitchen of my suite.

"She'd bought six really big top quality sirloin steaks and she cooked them, draining off the juices to make a drink she said would be good for me. I drank it. It was hot outside, and I'd been playing tennis for a long time, so I told Marlene I was going to take a shower. When I get out of the shower, you'll never believe what I found.

"It was Marlene washing my sweaty clothes. I was impressed, grateful, and kind of embarrassed. But not Marlene. She was matter-of-fact. Why did she wash my things? Because they needed washing. That's the way she was. I was really surprised that first time. After that, I wasn't ever surprised. Marlene just loved taking care of people. When I think of Marlene, I remember her with that bag of groceries heading straight for my kitchen. She was a very direct person. She did what she thought was right.

"I worked with her for more than a decade. I would go back and forth from working with her and back to New York. Sometimes we'd be together pretty intensively. Sometimes there'd be longer spaces between our bookings. Looking back, it's hard even to say how much time we spent because it was big in my life. It was a great experience seeing so much of the world through her very European eyes. It was also like going back in time.

"I remember Quincy Jones coming backstage in Germany and telling Marlene how wonderful she was, and then he came over to me and took me aside and said, 'What are you *doing*?'

"I was conducting and arranging and playing piano, directing her musically, and I was already having really a lot of success.

"Out there with Marlene, I was working with music that was pretty different from what was happening in the United States at that time. I began to have a lot of R & B hits at the same time I was conducting Marlene singing 'The Boys in the Back Room.'

"I said to Quincy, 'There's more to life than just writing music.

I'm getting to see the world.' And I was seeing it in a different way than if I'd gone there with friends or something."

IN APRIL 1960, MARLENE appeared on stage in Berlin, Bacharach with her. German film director Helmut Käutner introduced her as a woman who had stayed true to her principles. She sang some songs by German composers who were Jewish.

"Our trip to Germany in 1960 was really something," Bacharach recalled. "Marlene was kind of apprehensive about it. She felt the German people would be fine, but she was worried about the press. She thought a lot of the press people might be negative, and she was right.

"It was like a kind of a silent boycott, you know, particularly at Wiesbaden. I got the feeling that it meant, 'Stay away.'

"In Germany, a girl broke through a police line to spit in Marlene's face and say, 'Traitor!' She was a teenager.

"It wasn't just spit. There was something else mixed in. I was terrified that there was something in it, like acid. Whatever it was, it was scary because it was Marlene's face.

"When I thought about it, I realized how terrible it could have been, because whatever it was, the girl had it in her mouth, so it couldn't have been anything like acid.

"In Düsseldorf, there was a bomb scare. They didn't find a bomb, but it was hard on the show, as you can imagine.

"Then, in Wiesbaden, Marlene broke her shoulder. In the middle of a song, she fell off the stage. She was singing, 'I got one for my baby, one more for the . . .' Then she fell and landed right at Jo von Sternberg's feet. He'd come to see her perform, but it was a pretty big shock when she fell at his feet.

"It seemed she fell very hard, but she got up and went back on the stage. She sort of rearranged her shoulder and finished the song. I don't remember if she began the song again or if she picked up from where she'd left off. It would be like her to remember the note when she fell and continue from right there. She was so brave.

"Her shoulder was really hurt, but she wouldn't let anything stop her, especially not there in Germany. I don't know if it was broken, but I knew it was at least sprained.

"The audience was pretty much with her, but she knew there were more people who were not in the theater, who hadn't come and who didn't wish her at all well, and some who might even have been glad to see her have an accident. Marlene wasn't going to give anyone that satisfaction of knowing she'd hurt herself, even though she really had.

"The best place for her was, strangely enough, Munich. It had certainly been an important Nazi place during the thirties and the war. That was where the audience was the most enthusiastic for Marlene as measured by the incredible number of curtain calls."


"ISRAEL WAS TREMENDOUS. Marlene sang German on the stage in Tel Aviv. First time anyone did that after World War II. She did some Richard Tauber songs at the end. She did, I think, nine songs in German. She melted that audience, you know.

"I'd describe the scene in Israel for you, except it was indescribable, especially the last part. We'd arrived in Tel Aviv, and the streets were filled with people driving Volkswagens, but German wasn't allowed to be spoken in the theaters. No German films in the cinema.

"Marlene was very clever, very intelligent. The promoter in Israel cautioned her about singing in German. We already knew the rules, that no one was allowed to sing in German or speak in German on stage or on screen. 'Not one song,' he said to us.

"Marlene said, purring softly, 'Not one, but nine!'

"Maybe he wasn't listening. Sometimes when people first met Marlene, they were so dazzled by the way she looked that they scarcely heard what she said, and if they heard it, they couldn't remember what she'd said.

"Maybe he thought she was joking. She wasn't.

"When she got on stage, she sang 'My Blue Heaven' first, I think, and then, 'You're the Cream in My Coffee,' both in English, and the audience was loving it. Then she announced that her next song was going to be the lullaby 'Mein blondes baby,' and she started singing, in German, just the way we'd rehearsed it.

"It was a tremendous surprise, a shock to everyone except me. There were a lot of tears in the audience, but people seemed glad she'd done it, not angry. After that there could be German music played and German films and German spoken on stage. Marlene was the one to break through all that, and she went on for the rest of the performance, and had Richard Tauber at the end. The audience wanted encores, and Marlene didn't disappoint them.

"I'll tell you what I think happened, I say *think* happened, because it's what I remember and all I can tell you is what I remember. Sometimes you don't remember things exactly like they were. I was telling this story to someone, and I said for her encore she did all nine songs. Well, maybe the event looms larger in my memory than it was. Or maybe she *did* do all nine. It was really a moving thing."


"EVERYWHERE WE TOOK THE show, wherever we performed, there were always veterans of World War II, many of whom had seen her perform for them during World War II, sometimes practically at the front. There were a great many, especially when we were in Las Vegas. It was wonderful to see the way she was with those guys. It was an emotional thing, but she never cried, except maybe inside when someone was in a wheelchair, or there was someone who had lost a leg. The important thing she said was never to cry. She wanted to make them happy. No one was ever turned away from her dressing room or the get-together afterwards with them. She'd stay for hours with them, because they had such a special place in her heart. She had unbelievable stamina, but she said she didn't have to have stamina because, 'They are my boys,' and she loved making them feel good. Some of these men had traveled a long way to see her again. Some of them had missed her during the war, and wanted to grab the opportunity."

"I LEARNED SO MUCH from her. I don't even know everything I learned from her. It sort of rubs off and becomes a part of you. She had a tremendous desire for perfection and what she meant by perfection was the best you could do. She could be hard on someone if she thought they weren't making their best effort, especially if they were doing something they'd done so many times before.

"She never busted my chops, but the lady could really do it, if provoked. I knew how to get out of the way, but I didn't have to, because she never yelled at me. I never gave her any reason, and she wouldn't have, anyway. It was hard to believe the vocal range she had when she yelled.

"She was pretty wary about delegating anything, and I mean *anything*. She said her mother taught her that. I understand her mother would redo the housecleaning and the cooking after the servants did it because it wasn't up to her standard for her husband and family. She certainly wasn't lazy. I guess she had energy like Marlene's.

"Marlene would say, if you want to get things done, especially things done right, which is the only way things should be done, you have to do them yourself. I don't think she *could* delegate. If she did, she fretted and suffered, so she said it was easier to just do it herself.

"I'll tell you something that was really funny and challenging for me. It was my trying to keep our orchestra interested after we'd performed in several cities, and after we'd given several performances of the same program. After we'd given six performances somewhere, repeating exactly the same material, the musicians didn't understand if it had to be thoroughly rehearsed again and again.

"Marlene liked as much rehearsal time as she could get. It was never *too* much. It was, at best, enough.

"Singing, she didn't have a tremendous range, but it was enough, and I understood how she could best make her voice work for her. Marlene understood, and we worked together very intensely when I was there. In between, I'd go back and forth to pursue my own career in America.

"I not only got to Germany, which wasn't as exciting for me, because I'd been stationed there, peacetime, but it was special with Marlene. It was so important to her. I got to Poland twice, and to Spain and Russia. The places we went were all different doing them with her.

"Wherever we'd been, as soon as we got to Los Angeles, the first thing Marlene wanted to do was to see Rudi, even before she went to her place. She would go to see him and clean his house.

"She didn't see him much, but she certainly cared about him.

"She liked to see my success. She really enjoyed it, even though she understood very well that the greater my success, the more likely it was I'd be unavailable to be working with her. But she was a generous spirit, even when it was against her own interests. She knew what was right, and she would go above and beyond that.

"You know, you mentioned *Promises, Promises*. She was always wanting me to stay and conduct for her, endlessly, and she was also very proud of what I was doing. When *Promises, Promises* opened successfully on Broadway, she clipped copies of the Clive Barnes review from the *New York Times* and sent them to about fifty people she knew, basically saying, 'See? I told you so.'

"That didn't mean she could really face my going. I was her moral support and morale support. I was someone to do it with and someone to do it for. She needed the company, too, someone who understood, so she wouldn't be alone. She felt alone even when she was with a lot of people.

"Marlene told me nobody would ever be married to me. I don't think she was joking. She just wanted me for herself. She just wanted me to lead the single life and not be tied down to a woman. She was very protective of me that way.

"She certainly wasn't beyond sneaking a girl up to her room for me. She was great that way.

"Sometimes, after we went our different directions, when I called her in Paris from wherever I was, she answered in French, with a German accent, saying she was the maid. It didn't sound like her maid. It sounded just like Marlene. I said, 'Marlene, cut the shit. It's Burt.' Then, sometimes after I said that, she talked with me. And sometimes she hung up.

"In those last years, Marlene wasn't exactly dependable, with her health failing and that lonely life she'd made for herself. After a while, I didn't call so often. I think she called me once. But I'd call her when I could because I didn't like the way she was leading her life. Being stashed up there. She'd say, 'Well, Burt, I'm getting older.'

"She wanted to make one more record, one more song. She wanted to do a song called 'Any Day Now.' She described how she wanted it to be, with the tympanis coming in, and she'd sing a little bit. It was kind of wonderful. I wish I had a recording of a conversation with her. I remember she liked a song I did called 'The Look of Love,' and she said she'd like to record it.

"After she was living pretty much in isolation there in her apartment in Paris, I told her I'd find a way to slip the equipment under her door. I was joking, but I could have found a way for her to stay inside with no one seeing her.

"Looking back, I have no regrets about the time I spent with Marlene."

•  •  •

"I WAS IN WASHINGTON to do a show," Marlene told me, "and Jack Kennedy was president. I wasn't certain how well he remembered the summers at Cap d'Antibes with his family and mine. I remember the time as if it had just happened, but I understood that it might not have been as memorable for President John Kennedy, who was about twenty-one at that time. I wrote to him to invite him to my show.

"Word came back by phone from the White House, telling me the president would not be able to accept my invitation, but that he appreciated it and that he would like to extend his invitation to me to visit him at the White House.

"I was thrilled. When I arrived at the White House, I was totally expected. I was told that the president would be receiving me in his private quarters. I was escorted there and left alone with the president, who clearly remembered those relaxed days in the south of France. Most of him was relaxed, but not all of him. We were alone together. He didn't leave any doubt as to what he had in mind.

"I can't say I was caught completely by surprise. I had considered this possibility. He was, after all, his father's son, and I was curious to see if Jack Kennedy made love like his father. I had considered the possibility that it might have meant a formal meeting, with other people present. If anything did happen, I gave thought to what my response should be. I had only one problem. I felt too old for the young president. He might not be attracted to me. My age had never been a secret. He might be disappointed. I wished I could be younger and my most beautiful for the occasion.

"I don't remember most of what happened because it was all so quick. Afterwards I remembered saying, 'Please don't muss my hair.' I kept my professional focus, and I knew I had a show to do later that night.

"I think he was even faster than his father. He seemed satisfied. Maybe much of it happened in his mind before I got there. He had an even busier schedule than his father, I suppose. They both kept their watches on. I was glad I'd pleased him.

"As I was dressing, Jack said to me, 'There's something personal I'd like to ask you, if you don't mind.' After what we'd just done, I couldn't imagine what he could ask me that would be too personal. I said, 'Ask.'

"And he said, 'Did you really go to bed with my father?'

"I hesitated a moment. I thought about what he wanted to hear.

"'No, your father tried, but I didn't agree.'

"The president smiled, so I suppose what I said was right for him.

"Jack said, 'The old fox. I knew he was lying!'"

"I LOVED EDITH PIAF, professionally and personally. From the time Piaf and I met, in the forties after the war, we became great friends.

"We liked to walk together on the wonderful streets of Paris. She was so famous and such a visible celebrity that people stared at us wherever we walked.

"We were strolling along the Faubourg Saint-Honoré with our arms linked. She always took my arm when we walked together. I said to her, 'People will talk. They will say we are of the sisterhood; that is, we are lesbians.'

"'Would you mind if they said that?' she asked me.

"I said, 'It wouldn't bother me. Would it upset you?'

"'I would enjoy it,' she said. 'I'd be honored.'"

Edith Piaf was born in 1915 as Edith Gassion. Her father was an acrobat. Her mother had deserted her as an infant. As a small child, she was temporarily blind. She had little formal education. She traveled with her father as his assistant. Sometimes, she made money singing in the streets or in cabarets. She was nicknamed

"Piaf" or "Sparrow" and was known as "Little Sparrow." She was four feet, ten inches, and weighed ninety pounds.

Her child died in infancy and the man she loved, Marcel Cerdan, a French boxer, was killed in a plane crash. She composed many of the songs she sang, the most famous among them, "La Vie en rose" and "Non, je ne regrette rien."

Marlene said that during Piaf's last illness, all requests Marlene received to sing "La Vie en rose" were refused. She told everyone that she wouldn't sing that song until Piaf recovered.

Piaf did not recover. She died in 1963.

Before Piaf died, Marlene gave her a gold cross with emeralds to bring her luck. "'I have so much luck,'" Marlene said she told her. 'Now it's your turn. You'll see.' But it didn't work out.

"Piaf was like a little hurt bird. I wanted to take care of her. I felt certain I could help her. I was wrong. Drugs could do more for her, or rather *to* her, faster than I could.

"She had no patience. She was not prepared to suffer, but her actions made a commitment to only suffering. The drugs took over.

"If you have a friend who is totally, *uncontrollably* addicted, you don't really know the person, and you don't really have the friend you believe you have. Friendship is not something you can turn on and off, like a spigot.

"I loved her talent, but it broke my heart to see her always seem so unhappy. She said maybe if she found happiness, she would lose her talent. I said, 'Wouldn't it be worth it?'

"She said, 'No.'

"I believed I could help her. I wanted to. She had many lovers, but her real love became liquor and drugs. I couldn't compete with them. She felt *she* was in control, but they took over totally, and then she was gone. It was a loss to the world, but the greatest loss was to her. Life is precious is what I always say.

"I feel that now, even as my own life is running down, not what it once was.

"She always looked so frail. So, when she was really sick, I think no one noticed."

"IN BERLIN," MARLENE TOLD me, "among people in the theater and among a good many people not in the theater, Sapphic sex was quite common, even taken for granted among performers and artists, what you might call the bohemian world. And by *bohemian*, I don't mean people from Czechoslovakia.

"The wearing of tuxedos by women of the theater had implications of this, although some of the female performers who wore the tuxedos were not in the least lesbian, while others who wore pink ruffled things were. You really didn't know who was who—until they made themselves known to you. And making themselves known to you was certainly something they knew how to do, but you had to be on the same wavelength to receive the message.

"I was an innocent girl, and my mother was a watchful guardian, but I was a curious girl. I didn't believe in rejecting anything until I knew what it was. You can say easily, 'I'm not attracted to it,' but it's not true until you know what it *is* you aren't attracted to.

"I've been asked who I had my first lesbian experience with. Well, the truth of it is, I don't remember her name. She was a girl in school, a little older, and a little taller than I was. I was allowed to spend an overnight with this girl, whose name I certainly knew then, but it doesn't come back to me now. She was the initiator of some gropings. She didn't seem to know much about what she was doing, but she seemed to enjoy her fumbling.

"I had a 'brief encounter' with Mercedes De Acosta, who had been a friend of Garbo. I have always been fascinated by Garbo.

"One thing I immediately liked about Mercedes De Acosta was that, though she spoke a great deal about her friendship with Garbo, she never revealed anything about a physical relationship with her. That was *their* business.

"People said I had an intimate relationship with Romy Schneider. Dear, beautiful Romy. I loved her, but not in that way. I felt about her like a sister, and we had much in common.

"We were actresses. Our first language was German. We both loved France and wanted to live here. We loved each other as dear friends, but not physically."

IN JULY OF 1964, during her South African tour, Marlene and the group from her show were having dinner in a Johannesburg restaurant with the local press. As they were being served, Marlene noticed that someone was missing, "Where is our driver?" she said. "Why isn't *he* having dinner?"

One of the local press people explained to her that he was waiting in the car, unable under apartheid law to enter a white restaurant.

"Hasn't anyone thought about him being hungry?" she asked. "I want two heaping full plates with everything, as much food as they can hold." It was evident that she intended to carry the food out to the driver herself.

She took the two plates out to the car and to the surprise of everyone got into the car and ate her dinner there. The second plate of food was for her.

# IV. *Paris*

*Judgment in Nuremberg* was Marlene's last substantial appearance in a theatrical film. Except for celebrity walk-ons and appearances as herself in documentary films, her performing career was now limited to stage performances, punctuated by long periods of inactivity.

One of the films in which she made a brief appearance was *Paris When It Sizzles*, starring William Holden and Audrey Hepburn, with Tony Curtis, Mel Ferrer, and the voices of Frank Sinatra and Fred Astaire, and directed by Richard Quine.

## *Paris When It Sizzles* (1964)

Screenplay writer Richard Benson (William Holden) must write an adventure-mystery film in three days. To speed up the writing process, he hires typist Gabrielle Simpson (Audrey Hepburn) to work with him nonstop in his Paris garret until the script is finished. As they have ideas, the action comes to life on screen, with the couple as protagonists. By the time the script is finished, they are in love.

In this film, William Holden plays a character very much like Joe Gillis in *Sunset Boulevard*, a Hollywood hack trying to create a salable script with the help of an attractive young woman. "The difference was Billy Wilder," Marlene said.

"Billy Wilder is a greater personality than any of his characters, even the ones who live forever in that wonderful movie *Sunset Boulevard*. Those characters will live forever within their two hours. William Holden is dead at the beginning and dead at the end but he lives forever. The dice have no memory."

TAMARA NIKOLAEYEVNA DIED ON March 26, 1965, after being stabbed by a lunatic in the institute to which she had been committed by Rudi.

"It was important that Tami came into our lives," Marlene said. "She was a pretty little thing, but she had a waiflike quality. She looked like she was never truly happy. Maybe she never was. Maybe she hadn't had much experience in being happy. You have to have known happiness to give yourself over to it.

"Tami was a Russian girl and many Russians had come to Germany after the Russian Revolution. She was always a little foreign everywhere, but she loved Maria and Maria loved her. What a blessing for us! It really made my trip to Hollywood possible, so Tami played her part in the fabled career of Marlene Dietrich.

"We might have found someone adequate to be a housekeeper for Rudi and a nursemaid for Heidede [Maria], but we found a person to be a dear and loving friend to both of them, Rudi and our daughter, a companion.

"Tami, whose full name was Tamara, was in love with Rudi, but that was only to be expected. Women were always falling in love with Rudi. He was so handsome, intelligent, charming, funny, nice, the best company. Tamara had dreamed of a career in the theater, and she had danced in choruses in Berlin. She might have had more of a career because she didn't suffer from a lack of talent, but she suffered from a lack of confidence.

"When I was very young, I thought talent was everything. I learned that confidence was more important. If you were certain you were good, other people came to share your opinion. Tami was beyond shy. She seemed ashamed of not being good enough.

"When we first added her to our family, we noticed she was a little fragile. I thought if we fed her well, she would grow stronger mentally, but it didn't go that way. I gave her all my clothes as I finished with them. They were always in beautiful condition, only lightly used. Fortunately, she was as slim as I am. Slimmer. Rudi never had to buy her anything.

"I have a theory as to part of what tipped the balance of Tami's mental health the wrong way. I believe she wanted to be me. She was in love with Rudi. Rudi was always in love with me. Rudi did love her, but in a different way that wasn't the way she wanted. She could never be the great love of his life because that place had been taken by me. She was frustrated."

During the 1960s, Tamara's mental health became increasingly fragile. She became withdrawn and more afraid of people. She wanted only to be with Rudi, as always, but to the total exclusion of all others. She had delusions about her whereabouts. Marlene encouraged Rudi to take her to a good psychiatrist. Marlene believed psychiatrists could help people, though she could never imagine herself going to one.

Tamara was unwilling to venture forth from the chicken ranch in the San Fernando Valley that had become her home with Rudi, but she could never say no to him. The visit to the doctor only unsettled her more. She seemed to feel, despite all reassurances, that she was going to be given back, like a dog or a cat that has been rescued temporarily from the pound, but didn't quite measure up to expectations.

She stopped speaking and refused food. Rudi told Marlene he was losing Tami as a companion. "Sometimes she sat in a corner, crying without tears, moaning softly like a wounded animal," Rudi wrote to Marlene, describing what was happening, saying that he was afraid she might injure herself.

In the mid-1960s, Rudi was persuaded by doctors that it was in the best interest of Tami that she spend some time in the Camarillo State Mental Hospital. It would be, they said, her only chance to return to him, cured and as she had been.

"While she was there, she was stabbed by a crazy woman who thought Tami was her enemy when Tami was never anyone's enemy," Marlene said. "It was tragic.

"All of us who knew her were sad, but Rudi was saddest. I don't think he knew how much she meant to him until she was gone and he realized she wasn't ever coming back.

"There were people who thought I might be envious of what Tami meant to my Rudi. I always knew I was first in Rudi's heart, first, second, and third.

"What I did envy was all that time Tami had with Rudi. Lucky girl. My career took me away.

"She'd wished to be known professionally as Tamara Matul, but she wasn't known at all except as Marlene Dietrich's husband's mistress.

"Instead of her birth date, which Rudi probably didn't know and maybe Tamara didn't know, either, he put on the tombstone 1930, the year Tami moved into his and Maria's life, when I went off to Hollywood."

JUNE SPRINGER, WIFE OF publicist John Springer, remembered an afternoon when Marlene called her husband. "Marlene had something she wanted to ask John about. John had a terrible cold. Marlene only heard him say a few words. He was sneezing and coughing and his voice was terrible. The call only lasted a minute. I asked John what she said. He said, 'She said she'd be right over.'

"And she was. Marlene lived near us, but not *that* near. I let her in. She didn't bother to say hello to me, but only rushed past me. I was used to that. She went straight to John.

"'I've brought you my chicken soup.' She took out a big thermos of chicken soup. 'I'll have you well in no time.'

"Then she remembered I was there. 'You have to leave, June. No wives. Go out and do some shopping.'

"And I did."

June said that Marlene did this whenever John had the faintest hint of a cold, sometimes when he didn't. "Sometimes, I could smell the cooking chicken soup, and it smelled wonderful. John always said it was delicious. I never tasted it. She never made enough for me."

Speaking with me, John Springer referred to Marlene as his "chicken soup friend."

ACTRESS DOLLY HAAS, WIFE of artist Al Hirschfeld and a contemporary of Marlene in their Berlin days, lived on the Upper East Side of Manhattan, not far from where Maria Riva and her children lived. She would eventually have four sons. Dolly told me that she would see Marlene in the park pushing her first grandson's buggy and wearing a baby nurse's outfit.

"Marlene told me," Dolly said, "people never recognized her. She said, 'People never look beyond the uniform at the face of a nanny or someone in service. No one ever looks at my face. They just look at the baby in the buggy and exclaim, "What a beautiful baby!"'"

AS MARLENE GREW OLDER, her extravagance didn't diminish, but her ability to earn money did. Marlene's youngest grandson, David Riva, who made the acclaimed documentary films *Marlene Dietrich: Her Own Song* and *Marlene Dietrich: Light and Shadow*, talked with me about his grandmother's propensity for living and spending in the present, and letting the future take care of itself.

"Mass, that's what we called her—we couldn't call her Granny—had no idea that she was going to live so long, so long without being able to work, not being in demand, and not being able to perform up to her own standard, if anyone even made her an offer. She didn't understand about losing energy. She'd been able to go on so long, it seemed to her it would always be that way.

"I think if she'd recognized how long she was going to live and known about the accidents she'd have, she would've been more frugal. Anyway, I think so.

"If she got forty thousand dollars—intellectually she was a very smart lady, but in practice she believed the forty thousand was hers to spend, and she spent it. She always spent part of it on our family. We lived very well, and she was totally generous. She wasn't a thinker about taxes, or about rainy days. That just wasn't her frame of mind.

"My grandmother always believed the money she got was hers, without thinking how much she would have to pay in tax. It had all been explained to her, and she had a good mind and understood, intellectually, but emotionally she just didn't feel it, even when once the tax people took some of her jewels for security. She thought the people who made their fortunes in the film business before all the taxes were very lucky.

"She was totally generous to her family. Us. I don't think she ever thought she would live to be ninety-one. Who does? If she had even considered that possibility, I think she might have lived her financial life a little differently, if she had thought about a day when she might not be able to work, or when no one would be ready to pay for her work, or pay so highly for it that she could keep up her living standard.

"She didn't ever seem to think about her retirement or old age. They weren't pleasant ideas for her to contemplate, and after my grandfather died, she didn't have anyone to retire with anymore. She rarely saw Rudi, but as long as he lived, she counted on the possibility that they could get together to share their old age.

"My grandfather advised her to buy things that would keep their value, even when it came to children's stuffed toys. Whatever her feelings were about Germany, she still bought me Steiff animals. Steiff, the German company, was the one that had the stuffed animals that kept their value after they were bought, and they even went up in value over the years.

"I saw her very often because my mother, Maria Riva, was her manager, so we traveled around the world with her during her last tours.

"Pretty much *London* was the first show I really remember, although I know I was at others before that. That one is in my mind. *London*, at the Queen's Theatre. I was actually the kid who handed her flowers at the end of the show. It was my job. I thought it was a lot of fun. I guess that's what made it memorable for me.

"It was interesting to see that Marlene not only had this stardom and everything else that went with it, she also had a great deal of support because of her work against the Nazis and for the Allies during the war. What she did was hugely appreciated. She was almost a folk hero as well as a great performer. That was true especially in England that they felt that, whereas in America it wasn't quite the same emotion.

"She felt her performing during the war was the most important work she ever did, there in the Ardennes Forest and the USO shows. When I was about twenty, I told her I'd like to tell my friends what she did in the war.

"She smiled and said, 'Be sure to tell them what side I was on.'

"There were always famous people, like Noel Coward, around. Carroll Righter, the astrologer, was there. Roddy McDowall, Al Hirschfeld and his wife, Dolly. They were pretty much together, often. Of course during the late seventies, Yul Brynner was around quite a bit, a late romance of my grandmother's. I remember Alexander Korda was a friend.

"Douglas Fairbanks, Jr., was there when I was very young, but I don't really remember him well. He belonged more to my oldest brother's time.

"The last time I saw my grandmother was, I'd say, about four months before she died, in '92. I had just made a trip over to Paris to see her, based on the report that she was in very poor health, and that her health was going downhill fast. My mother was either there or she was being constantly informed. I had been Marlene's agent twice, when I worked at the Robert Lantz office. I did a contract for her, and I worked with some books, articles, other stuff of hers. We were a lot in contact. Into my thirties, we were close. I admired her. I admired the famous star and public person of such strong character—who was my brave grandmother.

"Paul Kohner, Robbie Lantz, they were the émigré agents in America for the Germans, French, and British, too. Marlene went to Robbie occasionally, depending on what project it was. Robbie was from Berlin and that was where he'd spent his childhood. Marlene wasn't easy to work with. I remember that. She fired people every twenty minutes. It was almost a badge of honor to be fired by her. Almost.

"I think the thing I remember the most is her not conforming. She didn't want to conform unless she thought it was to her benefit. She could conform if she felt it was useful, but she never did that out of what we consider concern for normal behavior.

"For me, personally, it would have been nice to speak other languages. I remember Marlene was pretty serious about German *not* being spoken, so in my family, we never spoke German. We did speak some French around the house, and could read it. My father was Italian. But the pervasive language in our house was English. My mother fell in love with this country when she got here, and as far as she was concerned, she was American, one hundred percent.

She raised her kids with a fierce dedication to the United States. Marlene didn't get in the way of that, though she preferred to live in Paris, especially toward the end of her life. But France, Paris particularly, had been her favorite place since she was a child. As a tiny child, she idolized French people and the culture, because she had a French teacher she adored, and ever since then France was the symbol for her of everything wonderful, beautiful, refined. But I also think, in a strange way, it was close to home without its actually being her home. Her home was Europe. Her first home, where she was born, where her mother lived, was Berlin, but Germany let her down.

"My own experience going to France to see her was a difficult situation. When I was a kid, I would go annually to visit her and spend about a month there. There were other trips, too, but those were the big ones. Across the street from her apartment is the Plaza Athénée, this grand hotel, where we would stay. We'd go across the street every day, and spend time with Marlene. In those days, she still went out. She still did her tours. She was still even doing a movie. So she was there, but not there all the time like she was later and when she became a recluse. When I was a kid, maybe eight, or even younger than that, I used to go there, and then she would take me on what she considered the proper grandmother thing to do, on outings, which would have been a great idea except for how old she was and how famous. Trying to get out of her apartment and have a shopping trip under the circumstances was really quite impossible. We would sneak out the door to get to a taxi to the garage to get into the car, and then the paparazzi would be waiting on the streets. She loved the area around the Madeleine, and we'd always spend time there.

"I remember going into a toy store on the Champs-Elysées. It was the only toy store she knew, I guess. We went in there, and I bought an almost life-sized stuffed lion. We were in there for maybe ten minutes before it was seen that she was there, and all the paparazzi gathered outside, and it started to get really ugly, pushing and shoving. So she decided to just grab a cab, because she couldn't find the car, and she didn't want this to turn into a disaster. I guess she sent someone back for the car. It would have been fine if I hadn't been there, but she was worried about me. She was so worried about me getting trampled or something. So she hailed a taxi.

"I remember trying to stuff this lion into the taxi, because it was so large it almost didn't fit. But it made it. I remember us driving away with this lion in the back of the car. We were just laughing hysterically because the paparazzi couldn't believe the scene. We couldn't move, because we had this big stuffed lion.

"I don't have my lion anymore. Too bad. It was lost in the earthquake here in San Vicente, California. It got completely soaked and ripped apart. But I still have a couple of the stuffed animals she bought for me. Pretty much that was always our outing, coming back with a stuffed animal or a few.

"She refused to let me choose anything but Steiff. She really felt Steiff had the real quality. It wasn't so much that it was German. She bought it in spite of its being German. She knew it would hold its value. She was very much like that. She encouraged me to buy Steiff, having learned that from her husband, because he always told her to buy things that would hold their value, and she had the greatest faith in his financial advice, which she would tell me. I wish he had told her to buy real estate.

"It turned out the jewels she bought came in handy later when she needed money, when she outlived even her wildest expectations for longevity. She not only outlived her money, but she outlived her ability to make it. Besides the jewels, there were a few really good paintings. She ran out of money a good fifteen years before she died. All of that stuff did help her to survive reasonably comfortably.

"I was there and my brother Peter was there when she decided to do her last film, *Just a Gigolo*. Two days of work. She was desperate for the money. The apartment she lived in in Paris for about twenty-five years, she never bought that apartment. Even in the seventies, it was $750 a month, and of course that went up. She didn't have a lot of money from her work.

"You know, when she was at Paramount, she was the highest-paid actress in the world. It was amazing. She always had a lot of money. *Really* a lot of money. But she always *spent* a lot of money. She really did. She didn't save anything, she didn't buy anything just because it was an investment of money. She just bought what she wanted when she wanted it. The only things she ever bought that were of value later were a couple of paintings. But some of that amazing jewelry was really something. In general, she just spent her money when she wanted to and on what she wanted.

"She lived very comfortably, and, as I've said, she spent a lot of money on our family, too. Not that my father didn't support us. He was a very successful guy. But then, the family had very expensive tastes. My brothers went to private school in Switzerland. We traveled quite a bit. I went to Dalton High School in New York with all the other brothers. There were four of us, altogether. None of these things were cheap. Marlene was a big part of all that, making all that possible. She saw luxury as a necessity.

"My mother was her manager, and she earned money as well. It wasn't easy getting Marlene on stage after a few champagnes and whatever else, you know. My mother lives in Palm Springs now. She's eighty-seven, and she's a spitfire.

"My brother Michael was the firstborn of us children, and when he was born, Marlene became the world's most glamorous grandmother. This was a mixed bag for her. On one hand, it was terrible, because it aged her. She wasn't really vain about her age, but she was worried about people not hiring her because of her age. She wanted to work, and she needed to work. It wasn't vanity. She only acted badly and cared about age when she believed people didn't hire you because of your age. Personally she had no problem with it. It was the others who cared, not her. Then, they turned it into a publicity coup, and she posed in *Life* magazine with Michael, and all that other stuff.

"In a strange way, my eldest brother, Michael, ended up being more her son than anyone else's. That relationship existed pretty much through her whole life. I was the youngest, and I was the business guy. I ended up knowing a lot where business was concerned, and all those kind of things, but Michael was always the golden child. He was born blond, like Marlene and my mother. All the other children look like my father, including me, which is Italian dark hair. So, Marlene always had a special crush on my brother Michael, but she adored all the kids. Well, what can you do? Not everybody gets loved by everybody, you know.

"My brother Michael is thirteen years older than I am, my brother Peter, eleven. Paul and I are closer in age. We're four years apart. There was two sets of kids. The older set grew up in a time when Marlene was still working at full tilt, my mother was working in early television, and she won an Emmy for her work. She was nominated for two Emmys for her television work. My mother wasn't only an Emmy-winning actress in television, but she was working on stage. She was earning money, my father was earning money in business. He licensed toys. He was also a scenic designer for Broadway and for commercials. He did a lot of television commercials, and it was profitable.

"Everybody in the family was making money. Everyone was doing well, so my brothers grew up in a very different environment than I did. We came of age in, let's say, the late sixties, early seventies, and at that point, Marlene, pretty much from age seventy on, pulled back from everything. She was born in 1901, so when she hit seventy, she pretty much stopped. It wasn't a matter of her choice. From 1970 on, when *we* came of age, the whole picture changed dramatically, in terms of income. But a lot of the spending went on.

"It was necessary for my mom to work hard, in terms of working with her mom to try and earn as much money as possible for Marlene's lifestyle. It was a lot of work, because Marlene at that time, after she fell, became addicted to pain killers. She had always been a drinker, not on the level with Judy Garland, but you add a little alcohol to pain pills, and it can cause problems. Marlene died an addicted person.

"She was very smart, which means she knew everything about how to treat her body and do other things which she thought would maintain her liver so it wouldn't fail her. She also battled cancer at one point, and it went into remission. She respected doctors more than actors, but she didn't like to go to see them. She was very, very conscious about medical possibilities, and I think it's a reason she lived so long. She went to a doctor in Switzerland where the cancer was diagnosed, and he really helped her. She beat the cancer.

"I think she ended up having a really good send-off, and I think at the end of the day, she would have been very happy to be next to her mother's grave. Her mother was the one woman she really adored and who she missed when she was away. Well, I think she missed her sister, too, though she didn't talk about that.

"You know, I never met the sister. I'd like to have met her. However, when I made my movie about my grandmother, I met her son. I hadn't even known I had a cousin.

"Marlene had maintained for years that she didn't have a sister. Well, I have a picture of her. I thought, 'Who is this?' I asked her who the little girl in the picture was.

"'I don't know,' she said.

"So, it was an unanswered question for a long time. She told Maximilian Schell flat out, I don't have a sister.

"But Marlene definitely *did* have a sister, Liesel. My grandmother just didn't approve of her sister's husband and what they did during the war, so she didn't like to discuss it. So she just did what Marlene could do very well. She completely erased her sister from the world. And she did it very clearly, very easily. She didn't want to talk about her sister, so simply, she *had* no sister. I don't think she could have erased her sister from her own memory.

"I'm sure it wasn't easy inside for her, but from the outside she could literally wipe someone off the face of the earth and that's what she did with her sister. For me, it was a very interesting situation to meet a relative, and I'd never even known I *had* that relative. My grandmothers on both sides were only children, and my mother's an only child, and my father is the only surviving brother of three, so when I was growing up there were *no* relatives. I had no cousins to play with, there was nobody. So, finding a cousin in my thirties was pretty shocking. I found him in Germany, and it was a fascinating meeting. We sat down and we talked about it. It was the first time he'd ever talked about his family's situation, because it was a very painful situation for everybody.

"My cousin, who was Georg Will, sold advertising for movies. He was a movie advertising guy, retired now, living in this little town on this tiny island off the coast of Germany. He's living in a very isolated place. He doesn't tell people about his mother's famous sister. It was different talking with me. He hadn't liked for people to know about his famous aunt because he knew during the war about the estrangement between the sisters. I guess he knew there were a lot of people in Germany who didn't like what Marlene did during the war and thought she was a traitor.

"An important part of Marlene's denying she had a sister was to protect her sister and her sister's family during World War II and maybe after, too. After the war, there must have been plenty of Germans who didn't like Marlene Dietrich and what she had done.

"But at the end of the war, Marlene found her sister and her husband, and Georg [their son], who had been in the Hitler Youth. They were in the Russian sector. Marlene rushed there and she vouched for them, which allowed them to continue operating a movie cinema, which is what they did during the war. They didn't starve like the other Germans did. The only time she saw them again was in the late sixties when she was in Berlin, on the Russian side of Berlin. That was the first time in twenty-five years.

"Marlene lived at 12, Avenue Montaigne. Her Paris apartment faced the street, and she stayed there for twenty-some years. At the end, she never left the apartment.

"My grandmother had no problem living by herself. She was able to stay pretty much by herself. Not many could do that. She enjoyed her own company.

"The place wasn't really big enough for two, unless they were very together. Marlene wouldn't have wanted to or been able to adjust to anyone living there with her. She could only just about put up with a maid who only came by.

"Still, I don't think she would have chosen to live alone like that if she could have chosen to live with Rudi, my grandfather. That was a real love affair. But he was long gone, and she'd had to accept that, because you can't quarrel with death.

"She had six phone lines. She had one of those old-fashioned phones, the ones that have all the push buttons on the bottom. Those were the six different phone lines. She used to call people day and night.

"My mother went a lot from New York to see her. That was more of a caretaker's job than it was anything else."

PERFORMING IN WASHINGTON, D.C., in November of 1973, Marlene leaned over the stage apron and extended her hand to the conductor Stan Herman. To make it easier for her, Herman stood on a stool. As she reached for his hand, the stool collapsed under his weight, and she fell into the orchestra pit.

"As I fell," Marlene said, "the skin on half of my leg was torn away. I should have immediately gone to Walter Reed Hospital, but I didn't think of it.

"Against all advice, I continued touring with my bandaged leg, which didn't heal. When I reached Dallas, I called my friend Dr. Michael De Bakey. I told him I could go to Houston on my day off if he would see me on Sunday. He instantly agreed, and on that Sunday he was at his clinic, waiting for me. He did a skin graft, which was successful, but it required a few months of recuperation. If I'd had it treated right away, it wouldn't have been so serious, but I was lucky it wasn't worse."

A few years later, Marlene suffered an even more serious injury while performing on stage in Australia, one that virtually ended her career.

"Performing in Sydney in 1976, I had a terrible accident," she told me. "I tripped over a cable backstage, and I broke my thigh bone.

"If there is anything one doesn't think about, and that is a good thing, it's one's thigh bone. After that night, there probably wasn't a day, or especially a night, that I didn't think about mine. It never let me forget.

"In the beginning, the pain was *so* intense. Later, it was a combination of the memory of that terrible pain and the lesser pain that never completely went away.

"An accident. A few seconds of missteps that couldn't be undone, in the last week of my Australian tour.

"I refused to go to the hospital. They got me back to my hotel. It was a terrible night, but my optimism protected me. It had to be all right.

"The next morning at the hospital, I had an X-ray, and I learned that my left femur was broken. My leg was placed in a cast, and I was flown to the University of California in Los Angeles. I chose California because Rudi was there, but Rudi was in a coma. In my cast, I was taken from California to New York without seeing Rudi. If I had, I knew he would have known, and I would have known."

At the UCLA medical center, she called Dr. Michael De Bakey, and he recommended a doctor in New York. She entered the Columbia Presbyterian Hospital where she was placed in traction.

RUDOLF SIEBER DIED ON June 24, 1976.

"From the moment I learned my Rudi had died," Marlene told me, "the call I most wanted to make more than any other, more than *all* the others, was one last phone call to Rudi. It wasn't something I had to say to him. I'd already said everything I had to say to him, many times. I knew everything about Rudi and the extent of his love for me.

"Rudi and I could be apart, but I knew he was always there for me. I could depend on him wherever I was in the world.

"We had told each other all the gooey words in the early days after we met. We said them sufficiently to last a lifetime, and they did. They lasted beyond the lifetime of the two of us, and will last as long as I am alive.

"If I could have made it, I don't know what Rudi would have said. I don't even know what *I* would have said. I might have been speechless, though I'm never speechless. I wanted to know Rudi and I were in the same world together, even if a continent or an ocean apart. I wanted to hear him breathing into the phone the way he tended to do. I didn't want to talk about big things, whatever those are. It was the little things I could talk about with him. Nothing was too small. He never thought anything I said was foolish and never treated it as trivial.

"We had a lovely passionate, romantic life together in those early days. We had a child together we both wanted and loved, and who was a forever bond between us. But we also were like a brother and sister, almost even a twin.

"The greatest regret of my entire life was that I left the hospital in Los Angeles without seeing my Rudi one last time. I was in a cast. He was in a coma, so others thought it better to ship me off.

"I didn't like to, but I had no way of knowing that those would be the last moments I could ever have with Rudi.

"Not insisting I be with Rudi for the moments we might have, whether he knew I was there or not, I would have known and I think Rudi would have known.

"That was the most terrible mistake of my life.

"I couldn't believe that Rudi would die before me. I was certain I would precede him. I was depending on him to take care of all of the details, the way he always had. He never let me down except in this, and he couldn't help it.

"There was always a lot of speculation as to why I never divorced Rudi, my first and only husband. It should have been the other way. The question should have been the other way around. It should have been, Why would I want a divorce?

"I was married to my best friend. He had started my career and had always encouraged me. He had taken care of our child when I couldn't be with her, done everything to make it easy for me to pursue my career. In truth, he regarded it, and justly so, as *our* career.

"Why would I want to have a divorce from the father of our beloved daughter? He was Maria's father, and we could never be divorced from her.

"I did not want to marry someone else. I did not want to have someone else's child during those years when I could have done so.

"When I had an affair, I would write or tell Rudi about it, in detail. He would say, 'Do you love him?' He didn't mean that delirious state of momentary passion that might better be characterized as a state of madness. I never loved anyone else the way I loved Rudi. So Rudi didn't need to be jealous.

"I would never have deliberately hurt Rudi if I could possibly have helped it. He was part of me."

MARLENE'S PLAN HAD BEEN that she and Rudi would retire someday and be together when her age and appearance no longer were what she felt made it possible for her to go on with her career. They would go to France, well outside Paris. They would be Monsieur and Madame Rudi Sieber, and ideally no one would know that the public self of Marlene Dietrich was Madame Sieber. She considered even going back to using the name she was born with, Marie Magdalene. She would be Marie Magdalene Sieber. It was, after all, her name. She knew that this idea, going to France, pleased Rudi. They had talked about it, speculated on it, imagined it. They talked about their life in a simple home she would enjoy caring for. She would cook all their meals, or just about all their meals. Occasionally they could drive to one of the great restaurants of France or, more often, go out to a little bistro near their home.

Rudi wasn't much older than Marlene, but his health had not held up as well as hers. He had always loved Paris and France, and he spoke French almost perfectly. That was something he never achieved with English. He could get along in English, but his accent and limited vocabulary prevented him from working as he wanted to do in America.

"So much of being successful in Hollywood," Marlene said, "was based on social and friendship connections. Worse than the language problem, Rudi genuinely never felt comfortable with Americans. He was more comfortable with the British. Rudi was *so* European.

"We would live out the remainder of our lives together. We had our youth together. We would grow old together, as companions, and we could be buried side by side. I was certain I would go first. Then Rudi could take care of everything for me, as he always had, all the details. I told what I wished for to Rudi.

"Then Rudi died first, so it was all different.

"There are people you think you can't live without. Then you have to. And you don't die. You live on. But life isn't ever the same.

"I owe him everything. Above all, I owe him my baby.

"After they put Tami away, I would have always taken care of her, because of what she had meant to Rudi.

"I've thought about it, in these years I've had some time to think, and I wondered if things could have worked out for Rudi and me if, when I married him at twenty-one, we'd had the family we planned, a few children, if we had lived a conventional life.

"Rudi would never have asked me to give up my career as long as I wanted it, but if it stalled, I would eventually have been discouraged and not wanted it. I enjoyed motherhood with Maria. I might have continued to be satisfied in the role of being a mother if more babies had come. Then there was Rudi's career. It wasn't a very secure career either. When we were married, we were young, and security was only a word. We had perfect confidence that everything would work for us. I believed we would have a wonderful end to our lives together. But life cheated me. Rudi, my love, died first. Oh, too soon!"

ONE AFTERNOON AT HIS New York City Park Avenue apartment, Douglas Fairbanks, Jr., showed me a collection of small nude female figures he had sculpted. He enjoyed painting, drawing, and sculpting, and he was extremely talented, especially at drawing and sculpting. All of the figures appeared to be of the same woman, but it was impossible to know, because they were all headless.

"Do you know who this is?" he asked.

"I have no idea."

"Marlene," he said. "Marlene Dietrich. I did busts of her, and full body nudes and drawings. When the romance ended, but the friendship remained, I offered them to her. She said, 'You keep them to remember me by. I don't need them. I have myself.'

"We were together almost five years, and we liked to take our holidays together. She really enjoyed posing, and she could stay very still, though it wasn't necessary. My artwork, such as it was, were hobbies for my pleasure, so it didn't require a still model for an exact representation. Actually, it was Marlene's exuberance I wanted to capture, her wonderful physicality and playfulness. There was an arch, a curve in her body when she posed. She was totally uninhibited about her nudity, a wonderful thing to be, but easy to understand when you gazed upon that body. She was far more beautiful without her clothes.

"I would like to have been that uninhibited about my body. Actually I have a very good one. I've always been very athletic, and I've enjoyed tennis, swimming, and other sports. I had my fabulously athletic father as a role model, but still I felt some inhibition about stripping off my clothes with a woman when I got down to my shorts. I felt it wasn't very masculine to be shy, but Marlene sensed my second of hesitation, so she grabbed my shorts and assisted in getting them down to my ankles. By then, I was more than ready to go the rest of the way.

"'Oh, Douggie, you're beautiful,' she said. Well, I never needed any more reassurance than that, at least not with Marlene.

"And I knew she had seen a few before me and never averted her eyes. Men know it's not proper to look at each other in showers or at athletic events. I remember doing it once, and I embarrassed myself by doing so. It was once when Larry Olivier and I were changing, and I was curious. He was such an esteemed 'swordsman,' if you know what I mean. Well, in case you're wondering, he was impressive.

"Marlene loved sex, at least she did with me. At the time, I assumed it was that special only with me. I hope so. It was certainly that special for me.

"Do you know why I decapitated the figures? I'll tell you.

"I realized I was getting up in years, and I didn't want anyone to find the nude figures and identify them.

"Marlene may have been uninhibited, but when she posed for the figures, she was only doing it for me, and I have a responsibility to protect them and her and not let the figures fall into other hands and be identified. They were done during the years of our affair when we were in love."

IN 1977, WHEN MARLENE was seventy-six, she agreed to play a small but extremely significant part in a major West German film, *Schöner Gigolo, armer Gigolo*, known as *Just a Gigolo* in English. The film, financed in part by the Berlin Senate, was to have an international cast, which included Curd Jürgens, Kim Novak, and Maria Schell. The part that Marlene ultimately played was originally intended for Trevor Howard and was to be shot in Berlin. Casting Marlene in what was originally planned to be a man's part after she had been away from the screen for so many years was screenwriter Joshua Sinclair's idea. I talked with him in Beverly Hills in 2010. Sinclair, who lives in Vienna, was passing through Los Angeles for a few days, and he told me the plot.

### Just a Gigolo (1978)

Berlin of the 1920s. The map of post–World War I brings with it the realization that the fabled military might of Prussian Germany has been crushed for the first time in its history. This is an era of change, a time of upheaval, when the runaway inflation and poverty of the Weimar Republic are sowing the seeds of national socialism.

Paul Odski (David Bowie) is a young Prussian aristocrat whose upbringing has led him to expect heroism, but instead he finds deceit when he returns to a Berlin that is vanquished in body and spirit. Paul is a lost soul in a city that has lost its soul.

Having no skills other than those of commanding a military regiment, Paul drifts from job to job, failing in each and every relationship that comes his way, until he meets the Baroness von Semering (Marlene Dietrich). He discovers that there is one "military regimen" at which he can excel—as a gigolo at the Eden Bar. He hires himself out as a dancer to war widows who love to drown their sadness in champagne and rented companionship.

When this depraved drudgery leads him to contemplate suicide, Paul is accidentally killed in street fighting between Nazis and communists. Having had no political affiliations whatsoever, his death is as meaningless as his life has become, yet in death Paul unwittingly finds the heroism he had sought.

"If you're going to make motion pictures like it's a nine-to-five job," Sinclair told me, "if you're not going to think to do the impossible or dare to do the impossible, then I think you might as well do something else for a living. For me, being involved in films was a venture into the impossible."

An American, Sinclair had been a doctor specializing in tropical diseases who also had a doctorate in comparative theology so he could, he hoped, follow in the footsteps of Albert Schweitzer. Then he found out he couldn't function in the heat of India, and he decided he didn't want to be a missionary, "but I had to have a mission, so I went back to what I'd always done, writing."

Born into a family of writers, he said he started writing and acting in movies when he was growing up in Rome. "I was in *The Garden of the Finzi-Contini*, and I wrote some of my own dialogue. I worked with De Sica, and that same summer I worked with Joe Losey. What I loved about motion pictures was the adventure into the unknown. I decided I would take writing motion pictures seriously.

"I wrote some films while I was in college. One of them was *Lili Marleen*, a Fassbinder film which was successful. I had done a couple of westerns. I've never told this story before.

"When I was studying in Rome, my father's friend Rolf Thiele called me from Munich and said he had a script he wanted me to read and tell him what I thought. It was a script in Italian by Ennio de Concini, who had won an Academy Award for *Divorce, Italian Style*. Thiele was a producer in Munich who had been a noted German director. I was one of the few people he knew who could read Italian and knew something about writing. I read it.

"I said, 'It's a good script and it's written by Ennio de Concini, one of the greatest writers alive.' It was the adaptation of *Die Himmel hat viele Farben*, which is the story of Lale Andersen. She was a very famous singer during the Third Reich who was in love with a Jew. I said, 'It's a good story, but there are some things that I might suggest.' He flew me into Munich, and we had dinner together.

"I started to tell him how I would do it and ended up changing quite a lot of the movie. I figured that was the end of it. But Rolf was going through a bad period in his life. He'd just turned seventy and wasn't well. He'd married a woman who was only twenty-eight years old, and that's a good way for any man of his age to die of many heart attacks quickly. So I tried to tell him that maybe the film was not such a good idea.

"I became his confidant. He said, 'How do you think we should make this movie? Who do you think should be in it?'

"I said, 'I think the Lale Andersen character should be Diane Keaton.' The script was sent to Diane Keaton. This was 1977, and she liked it, but the funding of the film changed. It was funded entirely out of Berlin.

"I went back to the university. On the summer break, Rolf would call me every now and then on the house phones in the dorm, or write me a letter. He said, 'Can you meet me in London to look for the director of the film?' He thought an English director would be right.

"So, I said, 'Sure. If you pay the way, I'll meet you in London.'

"We met in London and stayed at the Grosvenor, and he had a terrible attack of kidney stones. We checked him into a hospital and I said, 'I'm going back.'

"He said, 'Oh, no, you're not. You're producing the movie.'

"I said, 'I wouldn't know how to produce a movie if my life depended on it.'

"'Well, first go out and look for a director.'

"I knew some people in London, and I ended up talking to David Hemmings, who was drinking beer in a pub. He liked the script. I went back to Rolf in the hospital and said David Hemmings will direct it. He said, 'Well, now let's get some more people on it.'

"'Who?'

"'I don't know. Go out and find some actors.'

"A friend knew Richard Johnson very well, so, I went to see Richard at the National. He had just turned down James Bond. I said, 'I have a script, and I'd like to give it to you for your opinion about who should be in it.' We didn't know about casting directors. After he read it, he said, 'You should give it to Kim.' Kim Novak was his wife. So we sent the script to Kim, and she said she would do it.

"Richard said, 'There's a role in here, the colonel of the Eden Bar, that would be very good for Trevor Howard.' In the movie, when the Prussian soldiers come back from World War I having lost the war, they have nothing more to live for. All these Prussian soldiers, and this really happened, turn into gigolos at the Eden Bar in Berlin. This was Berlin, the Weimar Republic, when everybody was starving in the twenties. Richard gave the script to Trevor, and he said, 'Yeah, I'd love to play the colonel.'

"We went back to Berlin, and for me that was the end of the movie. Rolf felt better, and I said, 'I'm glad I could help. I'm just the writer. Maybe someday you can give me some money for all the work I've done, and goodbye.'

"He said, 'You've got to help out on other things.'

"I was about to leave Berlin to go back to school. That evening, I talked to some people in Berlin, and I walked down the Kufürstendamm. The Wall was still up. I went past the Eden Bar and all these places, and I looked at them, and I felt just a little bit into the city.

"I wondered what the city was really like back in the twenties. I had *written* about it, but I hadn't really known it. I had seen a lot of photographs. But there I was, there in Berlin, and I walked the same streets that had such good and bad history.

"I went by the Eden Bar, and I saw a dancer there who reminded me of Dietrich, because she had the tuxedo on. Right out of *The Blue Angel*.

"I went back all excited with my inspiration. I said, 'The person to play the head of the Eden Bar who runs the gigolos is Marlene Dietrich!' She was living in Paris at the time on Avenue Montaigne.

"Rolf just looked at me as if I'd just said tomorrow morning there'll be three suns instead of one. 'That's impossible.'

"I said, 'No, we've got to try it.'

"He said, 'Look, you're asking Marlene Dietrich to come out of retirement, after seventeen years, to sing in a movie after twenty-five years of not doing it, to come and work on a German production, which she swore she would never do again, in Germany, which she swore she'd never visit again. Forget it.

"'She has just turned down Billy Wilder. I don't know if that registers with you. You're a kid. She's not going to do another movie. And she'll never do a movie that has to do with Germany.'

"'You can't even photograph the woman. She's disappeared from the face of the earth. She lives like a hermit on Avenue Montaigne. She'll never get in front of a camera again. She said that, and she means it. She's seventy-six.'

"I went up to my room, with my tail between my legs. Then I called him and said, 'Can I try? I've got another two weeks before I have to be back and start classes. Can you finance me if I try to get Dietrich?' He thought about it, and I knew he was thinking, 'The kid's crazy. But why not? As long as it doesn't cost me much.'

"I called up a friend of mine who was in London. That was the only contact I had in the film business. I asked him, 'Do you know somebody who knows somebody who knows somebody who knows Marlene Dietrich?' I think he laughed, maybe, twenty minutes.

"He said, 'Are you drunk? What do you need her for?'

"'I want her to do a movie.'

"It was so absurd that he said, 'I'll see what I can come up with.'

"He called me the next morning, in Berlin, and said, 'Look, Eddy Marouani in Paris handles all of her music, recordings, and everything else. So, Eddy Marouani may be the one you're looking for.'

"I called Eddy Marouani in Paris and said, 'I would like Marlene Dietrich to be in the movie we're doing in Berlin.' So, Eddy, with his beautiful French accent, said, 'Who are you?'

"'I'm a guy who wrote a script called *Just a Gigolo*, and we have David Hemmings directing, we've got Kim Novak attached, and other people.' At the time, we had Kim, we had Sydne Rome, and Curd Jürgens, who Rolf brought.

"He said, 'Can you come and visit me here? She lives in Paris.'

"Rolf said, 'Okay, *go* to Paris.'

"I went to Paris, stayed at L'Hôtel, because that's where Oscar

Wilde died. I figured as long as I'm committing suicide, I might as well stay where Oscar Wilde died.

"I went to see Eddy, near Champs-Elysées. He was a big record manager and publicist at the time, and he handled Marlene Dietrich.

"He sort of inspected me when I walked in, to see what kind of weirdo I was. He said, 'Do you have money for this movie?' which is of course what everybody asks right away.

"I said, 'We have the money coming from Berlin.' In those days, it was film fund money.

"He said, 'All I can do is ask Terry Miller, but he's retired. Terry Miller handled her movie career. Now she hasn't had a movie career in something like seventeen years. But you can ask him. I only handle her music.' Terry Miller lived in Lagos, Portugal.

"I went to Lisbon, then down to Lagos. Miller lived three miles down the road. I didn't have any money for cabs or anything else. It was pouring rain, and I walked through the rain, drenched, up to Terry Miller's house. I couldn't call him because he didn't have a telephone. I knocked on his door.

"He opens the door and sees this kid there, drenched, with drops running down his nose, and he says, 'What can I do for you?' He probably thought I was a homeless person.

"I said, 'Are you Terry Miller, who manages Marlene Dietrich?'

"'Yes, I *managed* Marlene Dietrich.'

"I said, 'I would like her to be in my next film.' And he laughed and laughed and laughed. I was still in the rain. He finally said, 'Come in, kid.'

"Fortunately, he had a wife who was more compassionate. She said, 'Look, you could spend the night here, but you have to leave tomorrow, because what you're asking is impossible.'

"I said, 'Fine.' I went to bed thinking, 'I should have listened to everybody who said this is impossible.'

"The next morning, it was a beautiful day. The beach, sea, wonderful. Everybody was happier that day. Terry, who was in his seventies, hated the film business, wanted to get as far away from it as possible after forty years in it. He said, 'Look, kid, as long as you've come all this way, give me the script and I'll send it to her, and the worst that can happen is she'll have a laugh, and that'll be the end of that. Or she'll throw it away or she'll use it for a doorstop.'

"I said, 'There's only one problem. I haven't written a role for her yet in the movie. I have the movie, but there's no role for her, because I never thought of Marlene Dietrich playing a part in it. I just had the idea. I know it's a problem, but I haven't written her part.'

"So he's looking at me again a little bit like the Cheshire Cat in *Alice in Wonderland*. He said, 'Well, you've come all this way in the rain. What am I gonna send her?'

"I said, 'Look, get me paper. Do you have something to write with? A pen?'

"'I have a typewriter,' and he produced a Remington that looked like it was used by Hemingway when he was just starting out.

"He put this Remington there, and I said, 'Do you have any paper?'

"He said, 'I'm *retired*. I don't *want* paper.'

"'Well, you must have *something* I could write on, because if you give me something, I'll write her whole role now.' I could say that, because it was in my head.

"'But the only thing I have is toilet paper.'

"I said, 'Okay.' So he gave me a roll of toilet paper. I put it on the front of the table, in the sun of Portugal, threaded the toilet paper inside this 1920 Remington, and started to type. Fortunately it was heavy, not like the soft American kind, but it was still weird. You could see it was toilet paper.

"Three or four hours later, the wife, who was compassionate, kept bringing me sandwiches and lemonade, feeling very sorry for this kid who was making a fool of himself on their terrace in Portugal.

"I finished it. We folded the toilet paper and put it inside the script, and Terry wrote a note to Eddy Marouani saying, 'Pass this on to Dietrich, but transcribe.' Terry expected Marouani in Paris to type it out and put it inside the screenplay on the pages indicated, and she would read that.

"I left there and went back to the United States. The script with the toilet paper in it went to Paris. Eddy, being a practical joker, didn't transcribe it, left the toilet paper in, and sent the script with the toilet paper inside it with the role of Dietrich on the roll of toilet paper to Dietrich herself, with a little note, 'They sent this. I think it's a joke, but it's my duty to pass it on to you.'

"Dietrich got the script, written on toilet paper. Thinking the business was all toilet paper anyway, she thought it was very funny. She had a great sense of humor. She thought it was very original. Everybody else had been sending her what only *looked* like scripts. Now somebody was finally admitting what they were *really* sending. So she actually read it.

"She read the script, including the stuff I typed on the toilet paper.

"Eddy Marouani called me in the United States. I was at the University of Virginia then. He said, 'There's interest from Madame Dietrich. She would like you to call her.' This was like a voice from an angel. Because, for me, all these people, Bette Davis, Mae West, Ingrid Bergman, the people you've written about, they're icons. They're the people who were so important in my life as a kid growing up, watching the old movies playing on television downstairs in the basement. I used to watch *Million Dollar Movie* when I was, like, three. I *love* these movies.

"In the meantime, by the way, Trevor Howard was waiting to find out if he should sign or not. Rolf Thiele kept saying, 'We've got Trevor Howard. We're gonna lose Trevor Howard just because you're crazy enough to think Dietrich's gonna do this movie. Let me sign the contract with him before it's too late, because we have to start shooting in three months.'

"I said, 'Give me more time.'

"When I got the call from Eddy Marouani saying she's interested, he gave me the phone number, and I started calling Paris from Virginia. I said, 'Rolf, you're gonna have to send me some money because I need a lot of quarters here.'

"So I called Avenue Montaigne and I kept getting this lady answering the phone in French, and I would say, 'Madame Dietrich, *par favore.*' And she would say, 'Non, Madame Dietrich is not here.'

"I said, This is a practical joke they're playing on me. She's probably not interested at all. They're just making fun of me.

"So I called back Eddy, and I said, 'Eddy, she is telling me there's nobody there. This maid keeps answering.'

"And he says, 'Marlene Dietrich doesn't have a maid! She lives alone.'

"I'm thinking: Was there something strange about this maid's accent? It's Dietrich. I'm talking to Dietrich who's telling me she's not home.

"So I called again, and I heard this same voice, and I didn't ask for Madame Dietrich. I said, 'Madame Dietrich.' This caught her off guard, and she said, *'Oui.'*

"'I'm Joshua Sinclair. I'm calling about the film *Just a Gigolo.*' Click. She hung up.

"It was like trying to cast a butterfly. It was impossible to reach her. She was there. Right before she hung up, I could hear the breathing, like she was thinking about it, and then she hung up.

"I heard nothing more from anybody. After about a month, it was Christmas vacation, and Rolf sent me a letter saying, 'We're signing Trevor Howard.' I said, 'Wait. Let me check with Eddy. I haven't heard from him in a month.'

"He says, 'We all know you're crazy. I'm signing Trevor Howard.'

"I said, 'Give me twenty-four hours.' He said okay.

"I called Eddy. I said, 'Eddy, we're signing Trevor Howard. I haven't been able to speak to her. The last time I *think* I spoke to her, I believe she realized that I knew it was her, but she hung up. What am I supposed to do?'

"Being a good music producer, Eddy said, 'How much money do you think they'd be willing to pay?'

"I said, 'I don't know. As much as Billy Wilder or anyone else would be willing to offer. This is a big film. Curd Jürgens is in it, Maria Schell.'

"He said, 'Let me talk to her.'

"I said, 'Okay.' I gave him the phone number in my dorm. He called me back that evening, my time, and he said, 'Try her again.'

"I called again, and this time I actually spoke to her. She said, 'Who else is in the film?'

"I said, 'Kim Novak.'

"'Kim Novak? Is she still alive?'

"I said, 'She's only forty. She's alive, and from what I understand—I haven't met her yet—from what I understand, she's still very beautiful,' and I immediately said, 'as are *you*.' Then I sensed something which I never will forget. I sensed the feminine. That is, I realized that no matter how old you are, no matter how long you've been away from the silver screen, no matter how long you've been away from the camera, as an actress and a woman you still have that in you, that need—that need to be feminine, that need to be beautiful, ravishing.

"She said, 'Can you come to Paris?'

"I said, 'No, I have exams now, but I'll come as soon as I can. We need to decide soon.'

"And she said, 'Tell Monsieur Marouani when you will be here. Perhaps we can meet.' She hung up.

"So I'm thinking, 'I'm going to meet Marlene Dietrich.' That would be enough, whether she does the movie or not!

"I called Rolf, and I said, 'Rolf, every day, send Marlene Dietrich a rose. And every Saturday, a bottle of champagne, with love from the film set. Every day a rose, and in two weeks I'll be there. I just spoke to Dietrich on the phone.'

"He said, 'Okay. What do we do with Trevor Howard?'

"'We're going to have Dietrich.' It was the first time *I* believed it!

"She got a rose every day. One day, Eddy called me, and he said, 'You've got her attention. She wants to know who the romantic is.' And I said, 'When you're casting someone as important, as divine as Marlene Dietrich, you have to remember above all that she's a woman, so it's as if you're courting her. You're not asking her to work for you, you're courting her. You're asking her really to go on a date with you. That's the relationship for the camera, especially for someone from that generation.'

"The flower a day, all of this was courtship. 'Come on a date with me.'

"She got the point. She was highly intelligent.

"So I went back to Berlin, Christmas. We had to start shooting. David was there. We had already started shooting some things with Curd Jürgens and Maria Schell, all in Berlin.

"I called Eddy and I said, 'I'm back. What do you want me to do?' Eddy and I became good friends in the middle of all this, because Terry probably said, 'Be kind to this poor guy. He really *believes* in this.' It was contagious. The belief was contagious. Suddenly, people started to believe in the impossible. Even in Berlin they were saying, 'Do we have Dietrich?'

"We had a German playing the role of the gigolo, and somebody mentioned David Bowie should be playing that role. I knew somebody in Rome who knew David Bowie through Sydne Rome. When I went back to Berlin, David Bowie had appeared with his entourage.

"The producer's office was an empty desk, because Rolf Thiele was always ill. It was an empty desk with empty drawers. I was sitting behind this desk making a phone call. Suddenly, the door opened, David Bowie comes in with his entourage, slams his hand on the table. He says, 'I want two hundred twenty thousand dollars and five percent of France.' I have no idea why he wanted five percent of France, but that's what he wanted. And I looked at David Bowie, and I said to myself, My God, I'm looking at David Bowie.

"He probably thought I was the producer. I said, 'Fine with me, David. You can *have* it!'

"He said, 'Good. Write up the contract.'

"When he walked out, I said to myself, What just happened here?

"I said, 'Rolf, while you were gone, David Bowie came in. He wants a two-twenty fee, and five percent of France.'

"He said, 'Well, I expected more.' So they signed up David Bowie.

"In the meantime, I called up Eddy, and I said, 'Eddy, we've got David Bowie here.' David Bowie lived at the time in Kreuzberg, in Berlin, the red-light district. Kreuzberg is where Dietrich used to sing. So I was thinking we can use this, because it's a link. He had just done a song called 'Kreuzberg.' 'Kreuzberg' for Dietrich, I learned later, was a very important song, because it brought back memories of what Berlin was like in the twenties, before she left.

"I called Eddy and I said we have David Bowie.

"He said, 'Let me talk to her for a while. I'll call you in a couple of days.' He called and said, 'She wants to speak to you again,' and I said okay. So I called her again.

"She said, 'I'm going to write you a letter.' She wanted me to call her so she could announce to me that she was going to write me a letter. She said, 'I'm going to write you a letter with some questions. I read the script, and I have questions.'

"Three days later, I got this letter. The letter said, 'I'm happy that

David Bowie is in the movie. It's interesting for me because he wrote the song "Kreuzberg."' She asked me questions about the dialogue I had written for her. 'Is this line supposed to be a rhetorical question or is it a real question?' And I suddenly realized I'm dealing with a professional here.

"She's not like so many of these starlets who just read the lines any old way. She wants to understand what's behind it.

"We exchanged two or three letters. In the meantime, they were already shooting part of it, and everybody on the set heard that I was actually writing to Dietrich, and had talked with her, so they were starting to think, 'Maybe this is possible!'

"Trevor Howard, who had heard that he might not be doing the role because Marlene Dietrich would, thought that we were all crazy, and he said, 'They're thinking of getting Dietrich instead of me.' I don't know if he thought that was an insult or he thought that we were mad. He said, 'All right. But if you don't get Dietrich, ha-ha-ha, I'm still willing to play the role. I've got four days, and I'll do it still, if you don't get her.' He hadn't signed the contract yet.

"Eddy called me again the next day, and he said, 'How long do you need Dietrich, and what are you willing to pay her?'

"I said, 'Well, I have to call.'

"I called Rolf, and he said, 'I have to check with David Hemmings.'

"'We don't have time.'

"'Well, we need her four days, because that's what we were thinking of for Trevor Howard.'

"'What were you going to pay Trevor Howard?'

"'A hundred thousand.'

"I went back to Eddy and said, 'Eddy, it's four days, a hundred thousand dollars.'

"He looked at me, and he said, 'Two days and two hundred fifty thousand dollars.'

"'Is this a negotiation? Because if it is, you've gotta call some-body else, because I don't know how to do this.'

"'It's not a negotiation. Two days. Two hundred fifty thousand dollars.'

"'Okay, I'll try to do that . . .'

"'And,' he said, 'she won't shoot in Berlin.'

"I thought, How can we do the movie if she won't shoot in Berlin?'

"He said, 'Whatever you need her for, she'll shoot here in Paris.'

"I called Rolf again, and I said, 'Two-fifty, two days, and she won't shoot in Berlin. She'll shoot the Eden Bar scene in Paris.'

"Rolf got nervous. 'That's a lot of money. We don't have it. I don't know if we can do it in two days. We'll have to rebuild the Eden Bar in Paris. That will cost a fortune.'

"'But this is Marlene Dietrich. It's a coup. Don't you understand? She's going to *sing* "Just a Gigolo" in a movie? After twenty-five years. And the words of "Just a Gigolo": "There will come a day youth will pass away / Then what will they say about me? / When the end comes, I know, / They'll say 'Just a gigolo,' / And life goes on without me." Sung by Dietrich, it has so much *meaning*.' In fact, when she did sing it in the movie, she cried. She was moved by the words.

"He said, 'I'll call you back.' He did. He said, 'Okay. Have them make the contract and sign it.'

"'What do you mean, "Sign it"? I can't sign a contract.'

"He said, 'You have to sign it, because nobody can come there now.' I found that he wanted me to sign it because if something went wrong, it would be my responsibility.

"So I went to Eddy and said, 'Two-fifty, two days, fine.'

"'Something else. She wants a dress made here in Paris for her.'

"I said, 'Yes, the dress she wears in the Eden Bar will be made in Paris. No problem.' A couple hundred dollars for a dress. It ended up costing five *thousand* dollars.

"He wrote out the contract. He typed it there. Three pages on blue stationery.

"We crossed the Champs-Elysées, went to the Plaza Athénée to get a bacon, lettuce, and tomato sandwich, which is what she liked to eat. One of the reasons that Marlene Dietrich did not always have much money is because she used to do things like call room service *across the street* to order a bacon, lettuce, and tomato sandwich from the Plaza Athénée. It's a bit extravagant, you know. It's much more economical to order it from somewhere else, if you can find a place that has it.

"Anyway, we got the bacon, lettuce, and tomato sandwich, and went upstairs, but Eddy said, 'Wait here.' I had to wait outside.

"He went in. He didn't actually close the door to her apartment. It was just ajar. I heard a discussion in French. I knew some French, so I understood that there was some tension. I didn't know what it was.

"Then I heard a piano. I knew there were only two people in there, and one of them suddenly was playing the piano. I heard her voice in the background, and I heard Eddy. Eddy was trying to convince her. Back and forth. Finally, twenty minutes, a half-hour later, I was outside, and he came out with a signed contract. And he said, 'Sign it.' I signed it, then he went back in.

"Five or ten minutes later he came out again. He gave me back the contract. He kept a copy, and he said, 'You have Dietrich.'

"And on the way down in the elevator, it suddenly dawned on me I had Dietrich.

"I still hadn't seen her. I'd heard her voice through a door that was slightly ajar.

"I went out on the Champs-Elysées feeling king of the world. I went to a pay phone and called Thiele collect, and I said, 'We have a contract. We signed.

"'You've got her two days, two-fifty. She wants a dress made in Paris, but please say nothing to the press at all, ever, till we get word from Dietrich that it's okay. That's in the contract. I gave my word.'

"He said, 'Yeah, yeah, don't worry.'

"I got on a plane and went back to Berlin the next morning. When I arrived, the newsstands were full of 'Dietrich to Shoot a Movie in Berlin.' He had told the press.

"I stormed into his office. He was sitting there, doing who-knows-what, because there was nothing in there. There wasn't even paper. He was staring at the wall.

"I said, 'You betrayed me! I gave this lady my word.'

"'I didn't do it.'

"'Then who did? You were the only one who knew.'

"He said, 'The telephones are tapped in Paris.'

"I said, 'Look—this is not World War II. They are not tapping phones in Paris. You told the press!'

"'Yes, but you signed the contract. It's your problem now.'

"I realized then that I was dealing with a man of very little honor.

"I called Eddy, and he said, 'Yes, I know. You had nothing to do with it.' Suddenly, it was a binding contract that Dietrich wanted. 'She'll show up for work, but she wants the two hundred and fifty thousand dollars now!'

"Over Christmas, Marlene wanted to start doing the dresses. Rolf said, 'You have to handle this. You have to go back there and tell them the story was a mistake.'

"So I went back. I still hadn't met Dietrich. I had only spoken to her one other time, to thank her, and there wasn't much in return. But suddenly there was more warmth. There was also the question of who was going to take the photographs of Dietrich, who the still photographer would be.

"The man who was to do the stills was Emilio Lari, a wonderful photographer in Rome. So, I went to Emilio, and I said to him that we had Dietrich and that he was going to do the stills. He was ecstatic. For a photographer to finally photograph Marlene Dietrich after all these years!

"I didn't know that something else was brewing in the background. Emilio came to me the next morning and said, 'David Hemmings and David Bowie have made a deal, without us, to do the photographs of Dietrich on the set. Since Bowie has the right in his contract, he has decided to close the set that is being built in Paris so his photographers can come in and photograph Dietrich.'

"Now, remember, I was doing all of this for nothing. I was getting expenses, and I think they gave me at the end ten thousand dollars. But this upset me. I had given her my word to control the press.

"I went to Rolf, and I said, 'Rolf, this can't happen.'

"'Well, there's no way we can avoid it, because he has it in his contract.'

"'There *is* a way. David has to do a big rock concert in Australia on the fourth of April. Why don't we move the Dietrich shoot to the fourth of April? That way, David can't be there, and if he can't be there, there's no way he can close the set.'

"'Do you think you can get away with it?'

"'Of course. You're the producer.'

"So he moved the date.

"Three, four o'clock in the morning, David Hemmings and David Bowie come storming into my hotel room in Berlin. They had been drinking and were very angry. I thought they had come to kill me. They said, 'What the fuck do you think you're doing?'

"I was half-asleep, and I said, 'I don't know what you're talking about.'

"'Who do you think you are?' Bowie said. 'You think you can just come and tell us when you shoot? You're gonna *force* the film to be shot on the fourth.'

"Hemmings said, 'Those scenes can be shot before the fourth, so David can do it.'

"Bowie said, 'You made a deal behind our backs.'

"They had a whole row there, in my room. I was nobody. Not that I'm anybody today, but I was *really* nobody. I'm talking to David Bowie, who is already a rock star, and David Hemmings, who *was* a movie star. He'd been in *Blow-Up*, the great Antonioni film, and others, and I'm trying to defend myself from these two guys who knew the film business, the rock business, the music business backwards and forwards.

"There was a big quarrel in the office the next day. David [Bowie] definitely did not want to do this scene without Dietrich. His point of view would be shot, without Dietrich, in Berlin, and then Dietrich would be shot separately in Paris. The two would never meet. And for Bowie, the big thing was to shoot with Dietrich.

"I said, 'All you had to do was allow the still photographer to do it, and you would have had this. The money's coming from Berlin, and they run it. They run the set. So you're going to have to break your contract with Australia, which will cost you millions of dollars or shoot those two days in Berlin without Dietrich.'

"I said to Hemmings: 'You may be upset now, but do you know what it means to you as a director, to have directed Dietrich? I mean, that puts you up there with a handful of the very best. That should be worth millions to you if you really love this business. This may well be her last movie.' I went back to school. Dietrich had to shoot the scene. I still hadn't met her. Strangely enough, the shooting came at spring break. So, I went back, to Berlin, and then to Paris. In the meantime, they had rebuilt the Eden Bar in Paris.

"I went alone to Avenue Montaigne in the limousine to pick her up. Eddy was waiting for me there. I waited downstairs while Eddy went up, brought her down, and I finally met her. She looked at me with a twinkle in her eye, like 'This is the guy who's sending me roses.' She was wonderful, absolutely wonderful.

"In the car, I sat in the back seat with her. Eddy didn't go with us. She looked like Marlene Dietrich, at seventy-six, who hadn't been in front of a camera for a long time and had sort of lost something, I don't know what, but you lose something when you're not in front of a camera for a while as an actor. She was still glamorous. She still had an incredible aura. She was still Marlene Dietrich.

"But we didn't know what to do. When we arrived, makeup came over. What to do with her? How to make her look like herself.

"She had a wig on, sort of a short, reddish blond wig. She was dressed in a two-piece suit, and she looked a little bit like a grand-mother. She wasn't *trying* to be glamorous. I think she was just try-ing to earn this two hundred fifty thousand and make this movie. I didn't know that inside Marlene Dietrich was the real film business. But let me insert a parenthesis here.

"Before I went back to school, I had to stop off in Paris because somebody had to oversee the dress of Dietrich. Everyone else was afraid. I didn't know much about dresses, so I wasn't afraid. I went to Paris to the address of Madame de Warren.

"I sat down next to this magnificent lady—very, very chic. A heavy guy with a pigtail came and sat down across from us. He had sketches, and he was sketching, left and right. He said, 'The dress must be like this.' Marlene Dietrich still had beautiful legs. There was a slit down the side of the dress, and it was wonderful. Five thousand dollars. It looked a little bit like a Chanel because Ma-dame de Warren also worked with Chanel. It was dark blue, which you can see in the movie. There was a hat with a veil over it, be-cause Marlene wanted a veil for her face.

"It was all fine, except for this German guy with a pigtail I was sitting across from. He kept telling me, 'This is the way it has to be. Madame Dietrich wants this and wants that.' Later, when I went back to Berlin, Rolf said, 'Oh, that was Karl Lagerfeld. He's Chanel now.'

"I was *so* ignorant about fashion, I didn't even know who Karl Lagerfeld was.

"Back to the day she shot her scene in Paris:

"We were in the backseat of the car. We didn't say a word. She looked at me every now and then like she was trying to figure out, 'How did I get myself into this?'

"We got to the S.E.P. Studios, which is in the Bois de Boulogne, went up in the elevator, Dietrich, myself, and Eddy. I walked into the studio, and she took my arm. I almost had a heart attack. She actually took my arm, and I walked her into the studio, and there was a crew there, David Hemmings in the corner and people there, and a grand piano. Of course, David Bowie was in Australia singing. It was the set which you see in the movie.

"Makeup came over. Anthony Tavelle, who had been Bowie's makeup guy, who worked for *Harper's* and *Cosmopolitan*, was one of the best. He came to me and said, 'Can I touch up Dietrich? Can I do her makeup?'

"They disappeared behind a screen. Forty-five minutes later, he reappeared with Dietrich, looking as she looks in the movie.

"With this hat on and this beautiful dress, she looks like a forty-year-old. There she was again, Marlene Dietrich, just like she'd been when she left the film business. What he had done was to take a photograph of Dietrich from the sixties and use surgical tape to pull her face back. He had given her a lift and put a wig on her head, a beautiful wig, and the hat over that and the dress. She came out looking beautiful. In fact, as I said, in the photographs she looks in her forties or maybe fifties. Totally different. Everybody was spellbound, because we were suddenly face-to-face with Marlene Dietrich, really! And then something happened.

"She saw herself in the mirror. She had seen herself in the mirror when they were doing makeup, but suddenly there was a full-length mirror, on the set, and she saw herself. She went back to Dietrich. Those twenty-five years melted. Those seventeen years of not being in front of a camera melted. As far as she was concerned, she went right back to that mood.

"In a way, she took over the set. And she did something very strange. She started to speak German. She realized, This is my scene. I'm gonna run it, because she always ran her part in her films. I guess she said to herself, If these people are speaking German, I have to be in control. Forget what I might have said. I'm going to speak German.

"This was the first time in decades she had worked with a German crew. She wasn't working in Germany, but she was working with a German crew. That meant everybody spoke German on that set.

"Remember what she sings in *The Blue Angel*, 'Ich bin von Kopf bis Fuss auf Liebe angestellt,' 'I am from my head to the bottom of my feet created for lovemaking.' That's what the song means. She translated it into 'Falling in love again' like she translated 'Lili Marleen.' She didn't sing in German.

"During World War II, on the North African front, there on one side was Rommel, and on the other side Montgomery. When the soldiers went to sleep at night, they would go to sleep on the German side listening to Lale Andersen singing 'Lili Marleen,' and on the English side listening to Marlene Dietrich singing 'Lili Marleen.' And the wonderful thing is the troops used to hear each other's songs. It was like stereo. The desert carries all that sound, and we used this in *Lili Marleen* later.

"So she started to speak to the crew in German. The crew, they were in tears. Everybody was in tears because it was impossible, incredible to see Marlene Dietrich there. David Hemmings was lost in German. He was looking at me. I'm thinking, 'You're the director. Go direct!'

"David didn't know German, so Dietrich was talking directly to the crew. She was talking directly to the gaffers, to the lighting technicians, saying, 'Back, a little bit lower.' She took over the set! We were all ornaments on her set. She was the director, really, for her part, although David did a good job.

"She realized that everybody was a bit lost because she was just too much. I guess she was used to being too much.

"So David sat her down. We did the whole scene. She recited everything perfectly. Then, at the end of the first take, she would look to me in back and to David Hemmings, who was right in front of her, and say, 'Okay. Let's do another one.'

"David, who was totally in her control, said, 'Yeah. Right,' like, 'It's your film, you know!'

"She did another scene. Then she said, 'Maybe you should do one more, just in case.' We did one more of that, and then it came the time for her to sing her song. She had asked for her own pianist to come.

"There was this beautiful piano, which you see in the movie. She started to sing the song for the first time. Then she said, 'Let me do it again,' and she did it a second time.

"The second time, she started to cry. Not really cry, but her eyes are moist, and you see it in the movie. And everybody on the set was crying.

"It was incredible. To hear her say those words with her voice. Dietrich sang, but she also recited while she was singing. It wasn't like a mezzo-soprano. She was someone who spoke the words to music, and it was magnificent. On stage, as you see in the movie, she was saying, 'There will come a day, youth will pass away, what will they say about me,' and started to realize in her own mind, 'What are they going to say about me? What was I? Who was Dietrich?' She knew this was going to be her last film.

"At the end of the song, she looked around, she said to David, 'Do you have it in the can?'

"And he said, 'I think so.'

"'Do you want to do it again?' She was pushing us.

"He said, 'I don't think we need to . . .'

"'Let's do it again.' She sang it again. Then she said, '*Now* we have it in the can.'

"Afterwards, she addressed the crew in German.

"'I've been accused of being a traitor,' she said, 'but I was never against Germany. It was the Nazis I hated.

"'Now you're all going home, but I can't go home because they took my country away from me and they took my language away from me. You can't understand how that feels if you haven't been through it, and I hope you never will.'

"From the beginning, nobody was supposed to know that the assistant who came and waited for her on the set was Maria Riva, her daughter. I don't know why, but we were supposed to refer to her as Mrs. Patterson. So, whenever there was anything, she would say, 'Mrs. Patterson!' and her daughter, Maria Riva, would come and help.

"Then, when it was finished, she got back into the car and went back to her house. She was paid the money, two hundred fifty thousand dollars. It was paid into a Swiss account. I thought that was the end of it.

"I didn't speak to her again after that. I mean, we didn't speak at all. She sort of looked at me as she was going away. She looked over her shoulder at me as she was being escorted by 'Mrs. Patterson,' off the set to her home, and that was the end of the shoot on the second day."


"THOUGH IT HAD BEEN a closed set, somehow a photographer had come in the night before the first day and slept on the catwalk, and we didn't know. He had taken some photographs, and sneaked them out. I didn't see him, but one of the gaffers, Axel, came over to me and said, 'Look up there.' I did, and there was a guy on the catwalk taking photographs. Two of the gaffers went up and got him, brought him down, and Axel says, 'What do we do?'

"I said, 'Strip him.'

"They stripped him and told him to leave the set. So this poor

French photographer left the set almost naked, without his camera, without anything. We wanted to make sure there was no film. But somehow, he had smuggled some film out.

"The next day, Emilio Lari, who was taking the photographs, said, 'We need some stills,' and she knew that, of course. This was the first time the still photographs had been taken, which is a whole different concept for an actor.

"He said, 'Do you mind?'

"She said no, and he started to click with his automatic camera. As he was clicking, clicking, clicking, she turned into a model. She came to life again. She posed in all these different ways. She said, 'Is this all right? This is my good side.' A woman who had hated photographers, who had bodyguards to keep these cameras away from her for so many years, suddenly came to life again, became a *Vogue* model. Those photographs are beautiful.

"I found out the next morning that those photographs that had been smuggled out were now in the hands of a press agency in Paris, and they were going to use them.

"I called up the press agency and said, 'Look, it was a closed set, and we can sue you for a billion dollars, which we will. There are penal charges here, breaking and entering. The proof is that you have these photographs. If you publish them, it means you are an accessory to breaking and entering, which according to French law is punishable by at least fifteen years in prison.' I said, 'I'm going to send you away for fifteen years.

"'But besides all of that, *do you really want to do this to Marlene Dietrich?* It's France, which gave her exile, which loved her. Is France going to do this to Dietrich in her last film?'

"He said, 'Yes, but the editor . . .'

"I said, 'Are *you* going to allow it? Because if you are, I'll know about it because it'll be in the newspapers tomorrow.'

"I waited. The next day, nothing in the papers. I called him back, and I said, 'Did you make the right decision?'

"He said, 'Of course. We couldn't do it.'"

"I said, 'Tell me: Were you worried about Dietrich or about the lawyers?'"

"He said, 'Actually, Dietrich.'"

"I said, 'Good. The French remain French.'"

"I went back to Berlin. I thought I would never hear about this again. I was going back to school.

"I was in Berlin two months later. I went back because I got attached to this film, and I went back whenever I could. I was in the editing room with David Hemmings. I got a phone call while we were editing the film. I said, 'Who's on the phone?'"

"'Marlene Dietrich.'"

"I picked up the phone and said, 'Hi, how are you?'"

"She said, 'What do you like to eat?'"

"'I don't know.' I hadn't spoken to her since that day on the set. I said, 'Just about anything. Why?'"

"'I'm inviting you to dinner, and I was thinking about what you'd like to eat. What would you like me to cook?'"

"'How about wiener schnitzel? I hear that you spent time in Vienna.'"

"'Fine. Wiener schnitzel it is.'"

"She said, 'Come Sunday.'"

"Again, I went to the producer, because I never had any money, and he finally paid me something—a year late.

"In Paris, I went to the Avenue Montaigne with a flower, a rose, and another bottle of champagne, and appeared at the door. The door opened, and I finally saw the apartment. I walked in, put the bottle and the rose down, and I saw her again, but as the grandmother, a beautiful grandmother. I still had in my mind the Dietrich that was in the film.

"At the entrance of the apartment itself, there was a long dining room table. Then, on the left, there was a living room with two grand pianos, back to back. On one wall, there was a photograph of

Hemingway. That was the only photograph. The rest of the room was full of books. She was a bookworm. Then, next to the entrance on the right was a kitchen. She went directly into the kitchen and started to cook wiener schnitzel.

"She said, 'Can you fix phones?'

"'I suppose so. I don't know.'

"'My phone is on the blink.' Suddenly I became her grandson. 'The phone's around the corner. You'll find it.' And she's just sitting, cooking, right?

"She had a regular kitchen and a stove. A little kitchen on the side. It must have been five feet by ten. Something like that. And she was cooking on the stove, with a window at the very end that looked on to Avenue Montaigne.

"I was on the floor with a telephone and a screwdriver. She had put a screwdriver next to the telephone, waiting for my arrival.

"I was wearing a white shirt. I didn't know how to dress. But how do you dress for dinner with Dietrich? So I just wore what I had.

"I was on the floor taking apart her telephone, fixing it, and she was talking about all the things that the people who said they were writing her biographies were saying about her. The terrible things that she supposedly did to Maria, and all this stuff, and she was very, very upset about it.

"'I don't know where they get those terrible things and ideas,' she said. 'I suppose they just make them up.'

"She had a book, just the cover, the paper jacket of a book. I don't remember which one it was, but there was a photograph of the biographer on the back of it, and she was sticking pins in it. She said, 'It's so terrible the things they say.'

"I said, 'Well, now you've done something and you've shown people that you're still as beautiful as you always were.'

"She said, 'How does it look in the movie?'

"I said, 'Fantastic,' and we talked about the movie. Then she brought the wiener schnitzel to this long table, which was really in front of the door. It was a small apartment.

"We were sitting down, and she said, 'Would you like champagne?'

"I don't drink, but I said, 'Of course.' I'm not going to say no to Dietrich. She made a motion for me to open it, and I opened this bottle of Dom Perignon, and I poured two glasses, and sat across from her.

"Behind her was a poster of *The Blue Angel*, and as I was eating I realized I was having dinner with the Blue Angel, the *real* Blue Angel! The wiener schnitzel was delicious, but I wasn't really thinking about the food.

"I guess when you're in shock, things don't hit you. It suddenly hit me what we had done. The movie, the last words that Dietrich had said on the screen, I wrote.

"I was so emotional at the time that she noticed it. And she looked at me, and she said, 'Do you have a girlfriend?'

"I said, 'Yes.' I did have a girlfriend who was driving me crazy.

"She said, 'Never trust women.'

"'Why?'

"'*Never trust women.*'

"'How am I supposed to live with that?'

"'You live with women, but you just don't trust them.'

"Then we went into the living room.

"'I never realized I was a sex symbol,'" she told me. "'Interviewers would say, "Tell us who all your love affairs were with and all the people you loved. Tell us about your love affair with Gary Cooper." I didn't *have* a love affair with Gary Cooper. How can you have a love affair with a guy whose vocabulary was, "Yup"? That was his vocabulary with me. I assumed he had more to say to others.'

"And then I saw Hemingway's photograph. She looked at me, and I had a sense from that—she didn't have to say it—but I had a sense that he was one of the great loves of her life, maybe not an affair, but someone she deeply cared about. Maybe it was because she was a bookworm and she loved his writing, but it was the only visible photograph, on the far end of the living room. It was signed, 'To Marlene, from Ernie.'

"Just before I left, she said, 'I have to have all of your phone numbers.' Remember, we're talking about one of the most important people, probably, in the history of motion pictures, one of the five most important, who lived alone, rather vulnerable. Not too many friends or people to talk to, because she was probably too famous or had probably tired of the entire human race, because of what she'd been through. So many people had taken advantage of her, of the publicity, and she was *way* too smart to not realize that they were taking advantage of her.

"So I realized she was alone and vulnerable, and she said, 'Give me your phone number, because I don't want to lose touch.' So, I gave her all the phone numbers I had. I had one in Rome, one at the university, one in Berlin.

"I was standing by one of those high radiators, like they have in Paris, right at the entrance. I told her I would call to let her know what was happening with the film, and we would have to do some publicity with the stills, and I would let her know how that was going and ask for her advice. She said, 'Fine, fine.' She was very, very accessible then.

"Right before I left, she hugged me, and this was probably one of the most important moments of my life. The realization: You are *hugging* Marlene Dietrich. You're not talking to Marlene Dietrich, you're *hugging* Marlene Dietrich. How many men throughout her life would have died to hug Marlene Dietrich, to hold that woman in their arms. And here I was, this idiot, this upstart, at the entrance with the door slightly open, with Marlene Dietrich in my arms.

"I had no thought of how old she was at the time. In fact, when I told Emilio Lari later, the still photographer, he said, 'You should see a psychiatrist. You have a grandmother complex.'

"I said, 'No. The age melted away. She was eternal, literally eternal.' He'd been joking, of course.

"I got a phone call from Maximilian Schell. He called me and said, 'How did you get Dietrich, because I would like to have her in my film.'

"I said, 'I don't know if she will *be* in your film.'

"He said, 'The producer will give you a hundred thousand dollars if you get her for us.' That was a lot of money for someone who's going to college.

"I said, 'Well, I don't know. Call me tomorrow or the next day.' He did.

"All the night, I was thinking I'll probably not be in the film business, because I'll do something else. I didn't know what I was going to do, but this is Marlene Dietrich's last movie, most likely, and the last words she ever will say may be the words I wrote. Now, isn't that worth more than a hundred thousand dollars for a romantic?

"So the next day, I said, 'I'm sorry. I can't do anything, not for any amount of money. The last words she says in a motion picture will probably be by me. That's enough for me.'

"I called Marlene a few times after that. In the meantime, David Bowie and David Hemmings had been to see her, and said, 'We'd like to do some photographs with you,' because Bowie, of course, being a big pop star, hadn't given up on anything. He wanted to have some stills taken with her, together, where he would dress up as he would in *Just a Gigolo*, just as if he had been there when we shot it.

"She said no. 'I did the movie. I think you're a great singer, but no.'

"I think David Bowie was at the height of his career, or close to it, but he couldn't get Marlene Dietrich to do some stills with him.

"There was always something very, very dignified about her, and professional. She also knew probably that there was something magical about that makeup, the set, the way she looks in the movie. She wouldn't look like that again, and she wouldn't disturb the magic."

When Marlene spoke with me about *Just a Gigolo*, she said, "I'll tell you the sensation I remember most clearly. It was when my feet first touched the sidewalk outside my apartment. It was strange. I hadn't walked on cement for a long time."

IN THE EARLY 1980S, Marlene Dietrich was in her Paris apartment watching more television than interested her. She only liked the news, and an occasional tennis match. What she especially didn't like were old movies, hers or anyone else's. She couldn't help noticing, however, that she was still being seen on television. Moreover, someone was earning money from her old films, and it wasn't she. "It's terrible," she said, "to confront your eighties without having money or knowing how to get it. It takes away your energy."

Then the idea of a Marlene Dietrich television special occurred to her. It could include clips from her films, with a host and commentator interviewing an unseen Marlene about them. The interviewer would be someone Marlene chose or of whom she approved. It would be made especially for the United States, but could be shown elsewhere.

Marlene's first choice of a director and interviewer was Orson Welles. No one disagreed with her that Welles was a genius, a fine director, a perfect voice, and an appropriate personality, one who would present the right contrast to her and with whom she already had great rapport. Welles, however, was not available.

Marlene said, "My heart was so set on Welles that almost anyone else would have been unwelcome and would face an undeserved hostility on my part." Maximilian Schell was suggested.

As well as being a celebrated actor, he was a director. He was fluent in German and English, and they already knew each other, if only casually, from *Judgment at Nuremberg*.

"I did not really know Max Schell during *Judgment at Nuremberg*," Marlene said. "He was not directing or producing, so I could only judge the way he looked and his acting on screen. He scored very high on both counts. A very handsome man. A fine actor."

While Marlene was dedicated to a total emphasis on her past career, Schell was interested in her life in the present. She did not want to be seen at all, so the audience was only to hear her voice, though Schell was hoping he could persuade her to be glimpsed occasionally.

The clips Marlene had intended using were available only at exorbitant rates. Even stills were costly. She hadn't expected these costs.

Marlene said her apartment was to be off limits to cameras. Only audio recording equipment was permitted. The modern audio equipment Schell brought with him looked rather amateurish to her, not worthy of a star of her magnitude.

Although Marlene would have preferred to do the film in English for American television, Schell's producers insisted on German. This was because the money was coming from German sources. Schell said he felt more secure in German. Marlene said it didn't make any difference, but sometimes she had to ask Schell for a German word she had forgotten and now knew only the English or French equivalent.

From the beginning, it was clear that Dietrich and Schell were on a collision course. Schell finally telephoned his producer in Munich to say that he was simply not the right man for this job. "Let her get Orson Welles," he said.

Then Schell got an idea worthy of Welles, and of Schell. If he wanted a contemporary portrait of Marlene Dietrich, as she really was in 1983, he had it, even to the extent of the portrait's subject not being willing to be portrayed. If she wouldn't let him photograph her apartment, even without her, then he would rebuild her apartment in Munich, just as the Eden Bar had been rebuilt in Paris for *Just a Gigolo.* Then he could show everything except Madame Dietrich, which was an accurate portrayal of the lady as she was at that point in her life.

The documentary that was made became *Marlene: A Feature,* which played in theaters, as Schell intended. It won as best documentary from the New York Film Critics, the National Society of Film Culture, and the National Board of Review. It was also nominated for a best feature documentary Oscar by the Academy of Motion Picture Arts and Sciences.

The film puts the audience in the position of a camera that gets to see everything in the apartment except what it's there for: Marlene Dietrich. She is overheard speaking with Schell, whose back the audience does see. Technicians, who were not in the Paris apartment, make comments that clarify the action and advance the "plot."

Marlene scorned sentimental nostalgia, calling it *"Quatsch,"* yet she was clearly moved when she heard some of her old Berlin songs. For this sequence, Schell contrasted the nostalgic music and her poignant comments with a long aerial view of bombed-out, demolished Berlin.

I spoke with him at his home in Austria. He said he hadn't enjoyed the experience of working with Marlene Dietrich, but she won his respect.

"Now that it's over, and a long time has passed, I can say honestly what at that time I never thought I would ever be able to say: I'm not ashamed of it. Better yet, I'm glad I did it. She was unforgettable."

ONE DAY IN THE late 1970s, I was having lunch with Douglas Fairbanks, Jr., at the George V hotel in Paris, only a few blocks from

Marlene's flat. He said, "Why don't we amble by and see if we can say hello to Marlene?"

I suggested that she would more likely want to see him alone, and that they would enjoy it more without me. I also thought she might like some notice in advance, so she could put on makeup and a dress for the occasion.

He didn't have her phone number with him, but he said he could call her from downstairs, and we could always walk in the park or go into the shops for an hour or two until she was ready. He said he would like to go into Dior and buy her a scarf. "Marlene always loved scarves," he remembered, and one of her favorite shops, Christian Dior, was right by her apartment.

He called from her lobby and said he was in Paris and asked if they could meet. The rest of the call lasted only seconds.

She had answered, saying she was Miss Dietrich's maid, that Miss Dietrich was out of town and she did not know when she would be returning. Then she hung up. He said that wasn't the first time that had happened.

Some years before, he had called when he was in Paris, and Marlene had said she would see him. His wife, Mary Lee, was with him and wanted to go with him because she was curious to meet Marlene. He called Marlene back and asked her if she minded if he brought his wife along.

"Apparently she minded," he told me. "She hung up.

"Then, she called me in Palm Beach as if nothing had happened—about a year later."

"I CAN'T SAY I ever thought about money," Marlene told me. "Only what it bought.

"I don't think I ever felt poor until I had to stop and think before I picked up my phone to call the Plaza Athénée hotel and ask them to send over my favorite sandwich—bacon, lettuce, and tomato on toast. Ummm. They make the toast perfectly from wonderful bread. The outside of the bread is toasted, but the inside still has its delicious bread taste. They use such delicious tomatoes, and the bacon is crisp, but never burnt.

"I don't order my sandwich by the label. Of course, I'm certain it's possible to find other places that will make a good bacon, lettuce, and tomato sandwich. I haven't looked into it. Why should I. I always felt if I found something perfect, why would I look for another place? Mayonnaise is a luxury for me. I only want a touch, homemade. The Plaza Athénée hotel makes the best.

"I never thought about the price because I always felt too rich to think about the price of a sandwich.

"I would give up eating my favorite treat before I would drop my standard for it. I would never lower my standard. I do not order from the Plaza Athénée to impress anyone. I do not do it even for my self-image. I do it because it's what I do. I enjoy it."


Tom Pierson, Carroll Righter's friend and associate, remembered his visit with Righter to Marlene's Avenue Montaigne apartment.

"I was in Paris with Carroll, and he called Marlene Dietrich, who was more than happy to hear from him and immediately invited him to have lunch with her at her apartment. He asked her if he could bring me along. Obviously she said yes, because he said to me, 'Please be there at twelve sharp.' I wasn't inclined to be late, and Carroll was very punctual. I made sure I got there early. Carroll was already there.

"At noon, Carroll had the concierge call up and announce him. We sat and waited. Ten minutes. That wasn't important. Twenty minutes. Nothing at all. Half an hour. I was glad I'd brought along a book.

"It was after one o'clock, more than an hour after Carroll had called, when Miss Dietrich called down and said we could come up.

"Her door was open, just a crack, and Marlene saw Carroll and opened it, and they embraced for it seemed like ten minutes. We went in and she said to Carroll, 'It's too bad you didn't come earlier. I'd have made you lunch.'

"I walked over to the window so they could talk freely and not be inhibited by me. The apartment was cluttered with a lot of stuff, but it was orderly and very clean.

"I had some papers I'd finished looking at, and I stepped into the kitchen and dropped them into the garbage pail. It didn't have anything in it except an empty bottle, vodka, I think.

"Marlene came into the kitchen, followed by Carroll. She asked me if I wanted something to eat. Carroll was standing behind Marlene, and he was shaking his head no.

"I said, 'No, thank you. I'll just have a glass of water.' Marlene indicated the sink.

"In 1980, Carroll accurately predicted his own death. A few months after Carroll died, the phone rang one night very late in California. I answered. It was Marlene Dietrich in Paris.

"She said, 'Karl? I want to speak with Karl.' She always called him Karl.

"I said, 'This is Tom, Miss Dietrich. Carroll is in heaven.'

"And she said, 'Tell him I called. Please ask him to call me back.'

"That was the last time I heard from her."


"WHAT I MISS IS having people around to recharge my batteries. Intellectually, I mean," Marlene told me. "Most of the people in my life who could have done that have disappeared from the world, not just from my world. They were usually older than I was, and now there are only a few left and I can't see them—because I don't want them to see me. They are all men, and men are allowed to age. I would have to have my guests blindfolded, or with bags over their heads. That does not seem polite.

"Shortly after I retired into seclusion, Douglas [Fairbanks] called me in person to say that he was in London and that he would like to take me out to dinner, or bring dinner to my home, or come for tea, anything I wanted. I was tempted. I hesitated because I was thinking of what was involved, my makeup person coming over, my hairdresser, choosing an outfit and making certain I was perfectly groomed, a day of getting myself ready, a week of sleepless nights, about meeting someone I hadn't seen, who hadn't seen me for a long time, not to mention fixing up my apartment. It was always clean, but I had so much in it, I would have to clear a place, so the person could sit.

"While I was hesitating, Douglas added, 'My wife is with me.' I wondered what *that* meant. Was he considering bringing her with him? Shocking. I didn't need to ask. For all I knew, she was standing at his side while he spoke with me. Could he have changed so much? I didn't need to know. I answered him about our meeting, 'Perhaps.'

"A few days later, Douglas called me. I pretended to be my maid, a maid I didn't have. I did my best French accent. I gave a good performance. I said, 'Madame Dietrich has been called away, and she did not leave word when she will be returning.'

"That was not far from the truth as far as our meeting again was concerned. We never met again. I think he suspected I was my maid answering the phone."

ONE OF THE LAST people to visit Marlene Dietrich after she had stopped seeing anyone besides her daughter and grandson David was John Springer's wife, June.

"In the late eighties, I was in Paris, walking on the Avenue Montaigne," June told me, "and I realized I was passing Marlene's apartment. I said to myself, 'I think I'll call up from downstairs and say hello.'"

Marlene answered and spoke the words she never spoke in those days. She said to June, "Come up."

"She mostly talked about me," June remembered. "That was strange. She asked me questions. She seemed to want to know all about me, about what I was doing in New York, what I was doing in Paris. She listened and she really seemed interested.

"It was funny. She talked to me more in that visit than in all the years before. She was seeing me because of John.

"What came through to me was she loved Paris *so* much. Even though she didn't go out, she knew very well that she was in Paris, and that made her happy."

THE LAST TIME I saw her, as I was preparing to leave, she asked me to hand her the mirror on the table. It was a magnifying mirror.

As I put on my jacket, she was struggling with her makeup pencil, drawing brown lines around her eyes. "Black lines show up too much against my pale white skin. I would look like a clown. I never use black."

She put down the mirror. "I give up. I can't see well enough anymore to draw on the Marlene Dietrich face. I think it's time to stay at home.

"I don't feel like a prisoner here, because my door is not locked from the outside. The choice to go out is mine. I can make that choice every day. I never have to say to myself, 'I am never going out again.' I can say to myself, 'Not today, but perhaps tomorrow . . .'

"But there is nothing I want to do outside that would be worth seeing ugly photographs of myself in the paper.

"I am asked where I want to be buried. Well, it seems obvious—where I have chosen to live is where I would want to be for eternity,

France. If I am going to be in close proximity with ghosts, I prefer French-speaking ghosts.

"Even though I am retired from public life, private life still holds pleasures—my telephone, my greatest extravagance, which keeps me in contact with those I hold dear and find interesting. I have time to read, and I love to listen to music, Debussy, Fauré. I hope to be around for awhile.

"My last trip to Germany showed me that I belong to a long-ago Germany. It made me feel like a tourist in the country where I was born. There were too many hostile people who felt I was a traitor. I understand how they feel, but I no longer am comfortable there. I don't live in the past, but I do treasure my memories of Berlin as it was, once upon a time, before the Nazis.

"In America, which was a welcoming home for me for so long, they don't let you hide there from your own celebrity. Even dead, I'd be afraid for my privacy. Someone might try to get a picture of me to sell to the tabloids. I owe everything to the United States—my life, my career.

"But I have chosen France. I would like a place, though, more pastoral than Paris. I can see it in my mind, a beautiful, quiet French village. I do not object to visitors, but I prefer that they have come specially to visit me, a bit out of their way, not just passers-by.

"The only requirement I have is, it should be near a three-star restaurant.

"I would like for people to go for a three-star meal, a wonderful lunch before or after they come to visit the place where I will be re-siding. It will be a sort of religious experience.

"Even before I had ever seen Paris, I fell in love with its lan-guage, and I wanted to be like Mlle Breguand, my French teacher from Paris. Since then, I have looked for her every day of my life, whenever I am in Paris. In the beginning, I ran up and hugged French ladies wearing white gloves. It was so embarrassing.

"Recently I had to admit to myself that I would never find her.

Too late. If we met on the street, I would not recognize her, and she certainly would not recognize the little girl with blond curls who became an old lady with a wig of straight hair.

"For the last part of my life, I have chosen to live in Paris. When the press would ask me why I chose this flat on the Avenue Montaigne to retire to, I felt like answering them flippantly, 'Because I wanted to be near Dior.'

"I think my mother would be proud of my commitment to what I feel is my duty to preserve Marlene Dietrich's image, to being Marlene Dietrich. I feel she would be especially proud of my dedication and my discipline. I would sacrifice a great deal to protect the Dietrich image. I shall always do so."

In her last years, Marlene Dietrich never left her flat in Paris, first by choice, and then by necessity, as she lost her ability to walk.

Marlene died May 6, 1992, in her Paris apartment. She was buried next to her mother in Berlin.

When I last saw her, Marlene said to me, "Later, I'm going to take a walk in Paris."

What she meant, she explained to me, was that she was going for a walk through the streets of Paris in her mind, replaying her memories of the Paris she knew and loved so well.

# Filmography

**Der kleine Napoleon** (*The Little Napoleon*) (Union-Film, 1923)
CAST: *Napoleon Bonaparte:* Egon von Hagen. *Jérômes Bonaparte:* Paul Heidemann. *Georg von Melsungen:* Harry Liedtke. *Jeremias von Katzenellenbogen:* Jacob Tiedtke. *Charlotte:* Antonia Dietrich. *Liselotte:* Loni Nest. *Annemarie:* Alice Hechy. *Florian Wunderlich:* Kurt Vespermann. *Marshal:* Paul Biensfeldt. *Director of the Royal Ballet:* Kurt Fuss. *Prima Ballerina:* Marquisette Bosky. *Kathrin:* Marlene Dietrich. *Valet:* Wilhelm Bendow.
PRODUCTION: *Director:* Georg Jacoby. *Script:* Robert Liebmann, Georg Jacoby.

**Tragödie der Liebe** (*Tragedy of Love*) (Joe May-Film, 1923)
CAST: *Ombrade:* Emil Jannings. *Musette:* Erika Glässner. *Countess Manon de Moreau:* Mia May. *The Judge:* Kurt Vespermann. *Lucy:* Marlene Dietrich.
PRODUCTION: *Director:* Joe May. *Script:* Leo Birinsky, Adolf Lantz. *Cameramen:* Sophus Wangöe, Karl Platen. *Sets:* Paul Leni. *Costumes:* Ali Hubert. *Production Assistant:* Rudolf Sieber.

**Der Mensch am Wege** (*The Man by the Wayside*) (Osmania-Film, 1923)
CAST: *Schuster:* Alexander Granach. *The Human Angel:* Wilhelm

Dieterle. *With:* Heinrich George, Wilhelm Völcker, Emilia Unda, Marlene Dietrich.

PRODUCTION: *Director and Script:* Wilhelm Dieterle. *Cameraman:* Willy Hameister. *Assistant Cameraman:* Willy Habantz. *Sets:* Herbert Richter-Luckian.


*Der Sprung ins Leben (The Leap into Life)* (Oskar Messter-Film, 1924)

CAST: *A circus acrobat:* Xenia Desni. *Her partner:* Walter Rilla. *A student:* Paul Heidemann. *His aunt:* Frida Richard. *The student's friend:* Käthe Haack. *The Ringmaster:* Leonhard Haskel. With Olga Engl, Marlene Dietrich, Hans Brausewetter.

PRODUCTION: *Director:* Johannes Guter. *Producer:* Oskar Messter. *Script:* Franz Schulz. *Photographer:* Fritz Arno Wagner. *Sets:* Rudi Feldt.


*Die freudlose Gasse (Joyless Street)* (Hirschal-Sofar-Film, 1925)

CAST: *Hofrat Rumfort:* Jaro Fürth. *Greta Rumfort:* Greta Garbo. *Rosa Rumfort:* Loni Nest. *Maria Lechner:* Asta Nielsen. *With:* Max Kohlhase, Sylvia Torf, Marlene Dietrich.

PRODUCTION: *Director:* G. W. Pabst. *Script:* Willy Haas. *Cameramen:* Guido Seeber, Curt Oertel, Walter Robert Lach. *Sets:* Hans Sohnle, Otto Erdmann. *Assistant Director:* Marc Sorkin. *Editor:* Anatol Litvak.


*Manon Lescaut* (UFA, 1926)

CAST: *Manon Lescaut:* Lya de Putti. *Des Grieux:* Vladimir Gajdarov. *Maréchal des Grieux:* Eduard Rothauser. *Marquis de Bli:* Fritz Greiner. *De Bli's son:* Hubert von Meyerinck. *Manon's aunts:* Frida Richard, Emilie Kurz. *Susanne:* Lydia Potechina. *Tiberge:* Theodor Loos. *Lescaut:* Sigfried Arno. *Claire:* Trude Hesterberg. *Micheline:* Marlene Dietrich.

PRODUCTION: *Director:* Arthur Robison. *Script:* Hans Kyser, Arthur

Robison. *Cameraman:* Theodor Sparkuhl. *Sets and Costumes:* Paul Leni.

### Eine Dubarry von Heute (*A Modern Dubarry*) (Felsom-Film, 1926)
CAST: *Toinette:* Maria Corda. *Sillon:* Alfred Abel. *Cornelius Corbett:* Friedrich Kayssler. *General Padilla:* Gyula Szöreghy. *King of Asturia:* Jean Bradin. *Kerbelian:* Hans Albers. *Count Rabbatz:* Alfred Gerasch. *Clairet:* Alfred Paulig. *Theater Director:* Hans Wassmann. *Servant:* Karl Platen. *Levasseur:* Eugen Burg. *A coquette:* Marlaine (sic) Dietrich.
PRODUCTION: *Director:* Alexander Korda. *Script:* Robert Liebmann, Alexander Korda, Paul Reboux. *Cameraman:* Fritz Arno Wagner. *Sets:* Oscar Friedrich Werndorff.

### Madame wünscht keine Kinder (*Madame Wishes No Children*) (Fox Europa-Film, 1926)
CAST: *Elyane Parizot:* María Corda. *Paul Le Barroy:* Harry Liedtke. *Louise Bonvin:* Maria Paudler. *Mother:* Trude Hesterberg.
PRODUCTION: *Director:* Alexander Korda. *Script:* Adolf Lantz, Bela Balázs. *Cameramen:* Theodor Sparkuhl, Robert Baberske. *Sets:* Oscar Friedrich Werndorff. *Producer:* Karl Freund. *Associate Producer:* Karl Hartl. *Production Assistant:* Rudolf Sieber.

### Kopf hoch, Charly! (*Head High, Charly*) (Ellen Richter-Film, 1927)
CAST: *Frank Ditmar:* Anton Pointner. *Charlotte Ditmar:* Ellen Richter. *John Jacob Bunjes:* Michael Bohnen. *Harry Moshenheim:* Max Gulsdorff. *Margie Quinn:* Margaret Quimby. *Rufus Quinn:* George de Carlton. *Marquis d'Ormesson:* Angelo Ferrari. *Duke Sanzedilla:* Robert Scholz. *Prince Platonoff:* Nikolai Malikoff. *Frau Zangenberg:* Toni Tetzlaff. *Edmée Marchand:* Marlene Dietrich. *A seamstress:* Blandine Ebinger.
PRODUCTION: *Director:* Willi Wolff. *Script:* Robert Liebmann, Willi Wolff. *Cameraman:* Axel Graatkjaer. *Sets:* Ernst Stern.

*Der Juxbaron (The Phony Baron)* (Ellen Richter-Film Production, 1927)
CAST: *The "Baron":* Reinhold Schünzel. *Hugo Windisch:* Henry Bender. *Zerline Windisch:* Julia Serda. *Sophie:* Marlene Dietrich. *Hans von Grabow:* Teddy Bill. *Hilde von Grabow:* Colette Brettel. *Baron von Kimmel:* Albert Paulig. *Fränze:* Trude Hesterberg.
PRODUCTION: *Director:* Willi Wolff. *Script:* Robert Liebmann, Willi Wolff. *Cameraman:* Axel Graatkjaer. *Sets:* Ernst Stern.

*Sein grösster Bluff (His Biggest Bluff)* (Nero-Film, 1927)
CAST: *Henry and Harry Devall:* Harry Piel. *Madame Andersson:* Toni Tetzlaff. *Tilly, her daughter:* Lotte Lorring. *Mimikry:* Albert Paulig. *Hennessy:* Fritz Greiner. *Count Koks:* Charly Berger. *Sherry:* Boris Michailow. *Yvette:* Marlene Dietrich. *Goliath, a dwarf:* Paul Walker. *The Maharaja of Johore:* Kurt Gerron.
PRODUCTION: *Directors:* Harry Piel, Henrik Galeen. *Script:* Henrik Galeen. *Cameramen:* Georg Muschner, Gotthardt Wolf. *Sets:* W. A. Herrmann.

*Wenn ein Weib den Weg verliert (If a Wife Loses Her Way)* U.S. title: *Café Electric* (Sascha-Film, Austria, 1927)
CAST: *Göttlinger:* Fritz Alberti. *Erni:* Marlene Dietrich. *A friend of Erni:* Anny Coty. *Fredl:* Willi Forst.
PRODUCTION: *Director:* Gustav Ucicky. *Script:* Jacques Bachrach. *Cameraman:* Hans Androschin. *Sets:* Artur Berger.

*Prinzessin Olala (Princess O-la-la, or The Art of Love)* (Super-Film, 1928)
CAST: *The Prince:* Hermann Böttcher. *Prince Boris:* Walter Rilla. *The Chamberlain:* Georg Alexander. *Princess Xenia:* Carmen Boni. *Hedy:* Illa Meery. *Chichotte de Gastoné:* Marlene Dietrich. *René:* Hans Albers.
PRODUCTION: *Director:* Robert Land. *Script:* Franz Schulz, Robert Land. *Cameraman:* Willy Goldberger. *Sets:* Robert Neppach.

*Ich küsse Ihre Hand, Madame* (*I Kiss Your Hand, Madame*) (Super-Film, 1929)

CAST: *Jacques:* Harry Liedtke. *Laurence Gerard:* Marlene Dietrich. *Adolphe Gerard:* Pierre de Guingand. *Talandier:* Karl Huszar-Puffy.

PRODUCTION: *Director:* Robert Land. *Assistant Director:* Friedel Buckow. *Cameramen:* Carl Drews, Gotthardt Wolf. *Assistant Cameramen:* Fritz Brunn, Fred Zinnemann. *Sets:* Robert Neppach. *Title Song:* Ralph Erwin (music) and Fritz Rotter (lyrics).

*Die Frau, nach der man sich sehnt* (*The Woman One Longs For*) (Terra-Film, 1929)

CAST: *Stascha:* Marlene Dietrich. *Dr. Karoff:* Fritz Kortner. *Mrs. Leblanc:* Frida Richard. *Charles Leblanc:* Oskar Sima. *Henry Leblanc:* Uno Henning.

PRODUCTION: *Director:* Kurt Bernhardt. *Script:* Ladislaus Vajda. *Cameraman:* Curt Courant. *Sets:* Robert Neppach.

*Das Schiff der verlorenen Menschen* (*The Ship of Lost Men*) (Max Glass-Wengeroff Film Production, 1929)

CAST: *Captain Fernando Vela:* Fritz Kortner. *Miss Ethel:* Marlene Dietrich. *Morain, escaped convict:* Gaston Modot. *T. W. Cheyne:* Robin Irvine.

PRODUCTION: *Director:* Maurice Tourneur. *Producer:* Max Glass. *Script:* Maurice Tourneur. *Cameraman:* Nicolas Farkas. *Sets:* Franz Schroedter. *Assistant Director:* Jacques Tourneur.

*Gefahren der Brautzeit* (*Dangers of the Engagement Period*) (Strauss-Film, 1929)

CAST: *Baron van Geldern:* Willi Forst. *Evelyne:* Marlene Dietrich. *Yvette:* Lotte Lorring. *Florence:* Elza Temary. *McClure:* Ernst Stahl-Nachbaur. *Miller:* Bruno Ziener.

PRODUCTION: *Director:* Fred Sauer. *Script:* Walter Wassermann, Walter Schlee. *Cameraman:* László Shäffer. *Sets:* Max Heilbronner.

**Der blaue Engel (*The Blue Angel*) (Erich Pommer Production-UFA, 1930)**

CAST: *Professor Immanuel Rath:* Emil Jannings. *Lola Lola Fröhlich:* Marlene Dietrich. *Kiepert:* Kurt Gerron. *Guste:* Rosa Valetti. *Mazeppa:* Hans Albers. *The Clown:* Reinhold Bernt. *Director of the school:* Eduard von Winterstein. *Beadle:* Hans Roth. *Students:* Rolf Müller (*Angst*), Rolant Varna (*Lohmann*), Karl Balhaus (*Ertzum*), and Robert Klein-Lörk (*Goldstaub*). *The Publican:* Karl Huszar-Puffy. *The Captain:* Wilhelm Diegelmann. *The Policeman:* Gerhard Bienert. *Rath's Housekeeper:* Ilse Fürstenberg.

PRODUCTION: *Director:* Josef von Sternberg. *Producer:* Erich Pommer. *Script:* Robert Liebmann, based on *Professor Unrath* by Heinrich Mann. *Adapted for screen by:* Carl Zuckmayer and Karl Vollmöller. *Cameramen:* Günther Rittau, Hans Schneeberger. *Sets:* Otto Hunte, Emil Hasler. *Editor:* Sam Winston. *Music:* Friedrich Holländer. *Sound:* Fritz Thiery. *Orchestra:* Weintraub's Syncopators. *Songs:* Friedrich Holländer and Robert Liebmann. *English lyrics:* Sam Lerner.

**Morocco (Paramount, 1930)**

CAST: *Tom Brown:* Gary Cooper. *Amy Jolly:* Marlene Dietrich. *Kensington:* Adolphe Menjou. *Adjutant Caesar:* Ullrich Haupt. *Anna Dolores:* Juliette Compton. *Corporal Tatoche:* Francis McDonald. *Colonel Quinnovieres:* Albert Conti. *Madame Caesar:* Eve Southern. *Barratière:* Michael Visaroff. *Lo Tinto:* Paul Porcasi.

PRODUCTION: *Director:* Josef von Sternberg. *Script:* Jules Furthman. *Photographer:* Lee Garmes. *Art Director:* Hans Dreier. *Costumes:* Travis Banton. *Editor:* Sam Winston. *Songs:* "Give Me the Man" by Leo Robin and Karl Hajos; "Quand l'Amour Meurt" by Cremieux.

**Dishonored (Paramount, 1931)**

CAST: *X27:* Marlene Dietrich. *Colonel Kranau:* Victor McLaglen. *Colonel Kovrin:* Lew Cody. *Head of Secret Service:* Gustav von Seyffertitz. *General von Hindau:* Warner Oland. *Youthful officer:*

Barry Norton. *Officer of court:* Davison Clark. *General Dymov:* Wilfred Lucas. *Manager:* Bill Powell.

PRODUCTION: *Director:* Josef von Sternberg. *Script:* Daniel N. Rubin. *Photographer:* Lee Garmes. *Music:* Karl Hajos. *Costumes:* Travis Banton.

### *Shanghai Express* (Paramount, 1932)

CAST: *Shanghai Lily:* Marlene Dietrich. *Captain Donald Harvey:* Clive Brook. *Hui Fei:* Anna May Wong. *Henry Chang:* Warner Oland. *Sam Salt:* Eugene Pallette. *Mr. Carmichael:* Lawrence Grant. *Mrs. Haggerty:* Louise Closser Hale. *Eric Baum:* Gustav von Seyffertitz. *Major Lenard:* Emile Chautard.

PRODUCTION: *Director:* Josef von Sternberg. *Script:* Jules Furthman. *Photographer:* Lee Garmes. *Art Director:* Hans Dreier. *Music:* W. Franke Harling. *Costumes:* Travis Banton.

### *Blonde Venus* (Paramount, 1932)

CAST: *Helen Faraday:* Marlene Dietrich. *Edward Faraday:* Herbert Marshall. *Nick Townsend:* Cary Grant. *Johnny Faraday:* Dickie Moore. *Ben Smith:* Gene Morgan. *"Taxi Belle" Hooper:* Rita La Roy. *Dan O'Connor:* Robert Emmett O'Connor. *Detective Wilson:* Sidney Toler. *Charlie Blaine:* Francis Sayles.

PRODUCTION: *Director:* Josef von Sternberg. *Script:* Jules Furthman and S. K. Lauren. *Photographer:* Bert Glennon. *Art Director:* Wiard Ihnen. *Music:* Oscar Potoker. *Costumes:* Travis Banton.

### *Song of Songs* (Paramount, 1933)

CAST: *Lily Czepanek:* Marlene Dietrich. *Waldow:* Brian Aherne. *Baron von Merzbach:* Lionel Atwill. *Frau Rasmussen:* Alison Skipworth. *Walter von Prell:* Hardie Albright. *Fräulein von Schwertfeger:* Helen Freeman.

PRODUCTION: *Director and Producer:* Rouben Mamoulian. *Script:* Leo Birinski, Samuel Hoffenstein. *Photographer:* Victor Milner. *Cos-*

*tumes:* Travis Banton. *Music:* Karl Hajos, Milan Roder. (*Song:* "Jonny," music by Frederick Hollander, English lyrics by Edward Heyman.)

### The Scarlet Empress (Paramount, 1934)

CAST: *Catherine the Great:* Marlene Dietrich. *Count Alexei:* John Lodge. *Grand Duke Peter:* Sam Jaffe. *Empress Elizabeth:* Louise Dresser. *Catherine as a child:* Maria Sieber. *Prince August:* C. Aubrey Smith.

PRODUCTION: *Director:* Josef von Sternberg. *Script:* Manuel Komroff. *Photographer:* Bert Glennon. *Art Directors:* Hans Dreier, Peter Ballbusch, Richard Kollorsz. *Costumes:* Travis Banton. *Special Effects:* Gordon Jennings.

### The Devil Is a Woman (Paramount, 1935)

CAST: *Concha Perez:* Marlene Dietrich. *Don Pasqual:* Lionel Atwill. *Antonio Galvan:* Cesar Romero. *Don Paquito:* Edward Everett Horton. *Señora Perez:* Alison Skipworth.

PRODUCTION: *Director and Photographer:* Josef von Sternberg. *Script:* John Dos Passos, S. K. Winston. *Assistant Photographer:* Lucien Ballard. *Art Director:* Hans Dreier. *Costumes:* Travis Banton. *Editor:* Sam Winston.

### Desire (Paramount, 1936)

CAST: *Madeleine de Beaupre:* Marlene Dietrich. *Tom Bradley:* Gary Cooper. *Carlos Margoli:* John Halliday. *Mr. Gibson:* William Frawley. *Aristide Duvalle:* Ernest Cossart. *Dr. Edouard Pauquet:* Alan Mowbray. *Police Officer:* Akim Tamiroff.

PRODUCTION: *Director:* Frank Borzage. *Producer:* Ernst Lubitsch. *Script:* Edwin Justus Mayer, Waldemar Young, Samuel Hoffenstein. *Photographer:* Charles Lang. *Art Director:* Travis Banton. *Song:* "Awake in a Dream," by Frederick Hollander and Leo Rubin.

*The Garden of Allah* (Selznick-International, released through United Artists, 1936)

CAST: *Domini Enfilden:* Marlene Dietrich. *Boris Androvsky:* Charles Boyer. *Count Anteoni:* Basil Rathbone. *Father Roubier:* C. Aubrey Smith. *Irena:* Tilly Losch. *Batouch:* Joseph Schildkraut. *Hadj:* Henry Brandon. *Sand Diviner:* John Carradine. *De Trevignac:* Alan Marshal.

PRODUCTION: *Director:* Richard Boleslawski. *Producer:* David O. Selznick. *Script:* W. P. Lipscomb, Lynn Riggs. *Photographer:* W. Howard Greene. *Photographic Adviser:* Harold Rosson. *Music:* Max Steiner. *Production Designer:* Lansing C. Holden. *Art Directors:* Sturges Carne, Lyle Wheeler, Edward Boyle. *Costumes:* Ernest Dryden. Editor: Hal C. Kern, Anson Stevenson. *Sound:* Earl A. Wolcott. *Special Effects:* Jack Cosgrove.

*Knight Without Armor* (Alexander Korda-London Films, released through United Artists, 1937)

CAST: *Alexandra:* Marlene Dietrich. *A. J. Fothergill:* Robert Donat. *Duchess:* Irene Vanbrugh. *Vladinoff:* Herbert Lomas. *Colonel Adraxine:* Austin Trevor. *Axelstein:* Basil Gill. *Maronin:* David Tree. *Poushkoff:* John Clements.

PRODUCTION: *Director:* Jacques Feyder. *Producer:* Alexander Korda. *Script:* Lajos Biró, Arthur Wimperis. *Adaptation:* Frances Marion. *Photographer:* Harry Stradling. *Camera Operator:* Jack Cardiff. *Sets:* Lazare Meerson. *Costumes:* Georges Benda. *Music:* Miklós Rósza. *Music Director:* Muir Matheson. *Special Effects:* Ned Mann. *Editor:* Francis Lyon. *Recording Director:* A. W. Watkins. *Technical Adviser:* Roman Goul.

*Angel* (Paramount, 1937)

CAST: *Maria Barker:* Marlene Dietrich. *Sir Frederick Barker:* Herbert Marshall. *Anthony Halton:* Melvyn Douglas. *Graham:* Edward Ever-

ett Horton. *Walton:* Ernest Cossart. *Grand Duchess Anna Dmitri-
evna:* Laura Hope Crews.
PRODUCTION: *Director:* Ernst Lubitsch. *Script:* Samson Raphaelson.
*Photographer:* Charles Lang. *Costumes:* Travis Banton. *Special Ef-
fects:* Farciot Edouart. *Music:* Frederick Hollander. *Art Directors:*
Hans Dreier, Robert Usher. *Editor:* William Shea. *Sound:* Harry
Mills, Louis Mesenkop. *Song:* "Angel," by Frederick Hollander and
Leo Robin.

### Destry Rides Again (Universal, 1939)
CAST: *Frenchy:* Marlene Dietrich. *Tom Destry:* James Stewart. *Wash
Dimsdale:* Charles Winninger. *Boris Callahan:* Mischa Auer. *Kent:*
Brian Donlevy. *Lily Belle Callahan:* Una Merkel.
PRODUCTION: *Director:* George Marshall. *Producer:* Joe Pasternak.
*Script:* Felix Jackson, Henry Myers, Gertrude Purcell. *Photographer:*
Hal Mohr. *Marlene Dietrich's Costumes:* Vera West. *Art Director:*
Jack Otterson. *Musical Director:* Charles Previn. *Music:* Frank Skin-
ner. *Editor:* Milton Carruth. *Sound:* Bernard B. Brown. *Assistant Di-
rector:* Vernon Keays. *Songs:* "Little Joe the Wrangler," "You've Got
That Look (That Leaves Me Weak)," "The Boys in the Back Room,"
by Frederick Hollander and Frank Loesser.

### Seven Sinners (Universal, 1940)
CAST: *Bijou Blanche:* Marlene Dietrich. *Bruce:* John Wayne. *Little
Ned:* Broderick Crawford. *Sasha:* Mischa Auer. *Dr. Martin:* Albert
Dekker. *Tony:* Billy Gilbert. *Antro:* Oscar Homolka. *Dorothy:*
Anna Lee.
PRODUCTION: *Director:* Tay Garnett. *Producer:* Joe Pasternak. *Script:*
John Meehan, Harry Tugend. *Photographer:* Rudolph Maté. *Art Di-
rector:* Jack Otterson. *Marlene Dietrich's Costumes:* Irene. *Costumes:*
Vera West. *Music:* Frank Skinner. *Musical Director:* Charles Previn.
*Sound:* Bernard B. Brown. *Songs:* "I've Been In Love Before," "I Fall

Overboard," and "The Man's in the Navy," by Frederick Hollander and Frank Loesser.

### The Flame of New Orleans (Universal, 1941)

CAST: *Claire Ledoux:* Marlene Dietrich. *Robert Latour:* Bruce Cabot. *Charles Giraud:* Roland Young. *Zolotov:* Mischa Auer. *First Sailor:* Andy Devine. *Second Sailor:* Frank Jenks. *Third Sailor:* Eddie Quillan. *Auntie:* Laura Hope Crews. *Bellows:* Franklin Pangborn.

PRODUCTION: *Director:* René Clair. *Producer:* Joe Pasternak. *Script:* Norman Krasna. *Photographer:* Rudolph Maté. *Music:* Frank Skinner. *Musical Director:* Charles Previn. *Art Directors:* Jack Otterson, Martin Obzina, Russell A. Gausman. *Costumes:* Rene Hubert. *Editor:* Frank Gross. *Sound:* Bernard B. Brown. Songs: "Sweet as the Blush of May," "Salt o' the Sea," "Oh, Joyous Day," by Charles Previn and Sam Lerner.

### Manpower (Warner Bros.–First National, 1941)

CAST: *Hank McHenry:* Edward G. Robinson. *Fay Duval:* Marlene Dietrich. *Johnny Marshall:* George Raft. *Jumbo Wells:* Alan Hale. *Omaha:* Frank McHugh. *Dolly:* Eve Arden. Policeman: William Gould.

PRODUCTION: *Director:* Raoul Walsh. *Producer:* Mark Hellinger. *Associate Executive Producer:* Hal B. Wallis. *Original Screenplay:* Richard Macaulay, Jerry Wald. *Photographer:* Ernest Haller. *Music:* Adolph Deutsch. *Art Director:* Max Parker. *Costumes:* Milo Anderson. *Musical Director:* Leo F. Forbstein. *Editor:* Ralph Dawson. *Sound:* Dolph Thomas. *Special Effects:* Byron Haskin, H. F. Koenekamp. *Makeup:* Perc Westmore. *Songs:* "I'm in No Mood for Music Tonight," "He Lied and I Listened," by Frederick Hollander and Frank Loesser.

### The Lady Is Willing (Columbia, 1942)

CAST: *Elizabeth Madden:* Marlene Dietrich. *Dr. Corey McBain:* Fred MacMurray. *Buddy:* Aline MacMahon. *Kenneth Hanline:* Stanley Ridges. *Frances:* Arline Judge.

PRODUCTION: *Director and Producer:* Mitchell Leisen. *Script:* James Edward Grant, Albert McCleery. *Photographer:* Ted Tetzlaff. *Music:* W. Franke Harling. *Supervising Art Director:* Lionel Banks. *Art Director:* Rudolph Sternad. *Editor:* Eda Warren. *Sound:* Lodge Cunningham. *Dance Director:* Douglas Dean. *Musical Director:* Morris Stoloff. Song: "Strange Thing (And I Find You)," by Jack King and Gordon Clifford.

### The Spoilers (Universal, 1942)

CAST: *Cherry Malotte:* Marlene Dietrich. *Alex McNamara:* Randolph Scott. *Roy Glennister:* John Wayne. *Helen Chester:* Margaret Lindsay. *Dextry:* Harry Carey. *Bronco Kid:* Richard Barthelmess. *Marshal:* William Gould.

PRODUCTION: *Director:* Ray Enright. *Producer:* Frank Lloyd. *Script:* Lawrence Hazard, Tom Reed. *Photographer:* Milton Krasner. *Editor:* Clarence Kolster. *Music:* Hans J. Salter. *Musical Director:* Charles Previn. *Costumes:* Vera West. *Art Directors:* Jack Otterson, John B. Goodman. *Sets:* Russell A. Gausman, Edward R. Robinson. *Sound:* Bernard B. Brown.

### Pittsburgh (Universal, 1942)

CAST: *Josie Winters:* Marlene Dietrich. *Cash Evans:* Randolph Scott. *Pittsburgh Markham:* John Wayne. *Doc Powers:* Frank Craven. *Shannon Prentiss:* Louise Allbritton. *Shorty:* Shemp Howard. *Joe Malneck:* Thomas Gomez. *Dr. Grazlich:* Ludwig Stössel. *Morgan Prentiss:* Samuel S. Hinds. *Mine operator:* Paul Fix. *Johnny:* William Haade. *Mort Brawley:* Douglas Fowley.

PRODUCTION: *Director:* Lewis Seiler. *Producer:* Charles K. Feldman. *Script:* Kenneth Gamet, Tom Reed. *Additional Dialogue:* John Twist.

*Photographer:* Robert De Grasse. *Music:* Frank Skinner, Hans J. Salter. *Costumes:* Vera West. *Art Director:* John B. Goodman. *Musical Director:* Charles Previn. *Editor:* Paul Landres. *Special Effects:* John P. Fulton.

### Follow the Boys (Universal, 1944)

CAST: *Tony West:* George Raft. *Gloria Vance:* Vera Zorina. *Kitty West:* Grace McDonald. *Nick West:* Charley Grapewin. *Louie Fairweather:* Charles Butterworth. *Laura:* Ramsay Ames. *Annie:* Elizabeth Patterson. *Dr. Henderson:* Regis Toomey. *Walter Bruce:* George Macready. *Chick Doyle:* Frank Jenks.

*As themselves:* Jeanette MacDonald, Orson Welles's Mercury Wonder Show, Marlene Dietrich, Dinah Shore, Donald O'Connor, Peggy Ryan, W. C. Fields, the Andrews Sisters, Artur Rubinstein, Sophie Tucker, the Delta Rhythm Boys, Maria Montez, Lon Chaney, Jr., Andy Devine, Turhan Bey, Gloria Jean, Nigel Bruce, Thomas Gomez, Gale Sondergaard, Louise Beavers, Evelyn Ankers, Noah Beery, Jr., Clarence Muse.

PRODUCTION: *Director:* Eddie Sutherland. *Producer:* Charles K. Feldman. *Photographer:* David Abel. *Dance:* George Hale. *Art Directors:* John B. Goodman, Harold H. MacArthur. *Musical Director:* Leigh Harline. *Editor:* Fred R. Reitshaus, Jr. *Costumes:* Vera West. *Sound:* Bernard B. Brown. *Original Screenplay:* Lou Breslow, Gertrude Purcell.

### Kismet (MGM, 1944)

CAST: *Hafiz:* Ronald Colman. *Jamilla:* Marlene Dietrich. *Caliph:* James Craig. *Mansur, the Grand Vizier:* Edward Arnold. *Feisal:* Hugh Herbert. *Marsinah:* Joy Ann Page. *Karsha:* Florence Bates. *Agha:* Harry Davenport. *Moolah:* Hobart Cavanaugh. *Alfife:* Robert Warwick. *Court dancers:* Beatrice and Evelyne Kraft. *Amu:* Barry Macollum. *Jehan:* Victor Kilian. *The Miser:* Charles Middleton. *The Gardener:* Harry Humphrey. *Captain of Police:* Nestor Paiva. *The*

*Café Girl:* Eve Whitney. *Retainer:* Minerva Urecal. *Herald:* Cy Kendall. *Fat Turk:* Dan Seymour. *Assassin:* Dale Van Sickel. *Meuzin:* Pedro de Córdoba.

PRODUCTION: *Director:* William Dieterle. *Producer:* Everett Riskin. *Script:* John Meehan. *Photographer:* Charles Rosher. *Music:* Herbert Stothart. *Art Directors:* Cedric Gibbons, Daniel B. Cathcart. *Sound:* Douglas Shearer. *Editor:* Ben Lewis. *Costumes:* Irene, executed by Karinska. *Special Effects:* A. Arnold Gillespie, Warren Newcombe. *Songs:* "Willow in the Wind," "Tell Me, Tell Me, Evening Star," by Harold Arlen and E. Y. Harburg.

### Martin Roumagnac (*The Room Upstairs*) (Alcina, 1946)

CAST: *Blanche Ferrand:* Marlene Dietrich. *Martin Roumagnac:* Jean Gabin. *Martin's sister:* Margo Lion. *The consul:* Marcel Herrand. *Blanche's uncle:* Jean D'Yd. *The Lover:* Daniel Gélin. *The Lawyer:* Jean Darcante.

PRODUCTION: *Director:* Georges Lacombe. *Producer:* Marc Le Pelletier. *Screenplay:* Pierre Very. *Photographer:* Roger Hubert. *Art Director:* Georges Wakhevitch. *Music:* Marcel Mirouze.

### Golden Earrings (Paramount, 1947)

CAST: *Colonel Ralph Denistoun:* Ray Milland. *Lydia:* Marlene Dietrich. *Zoltan:* Murvyn Vye. *Byrd:* Bruce Lester. *Hoff:* Dennis Hoey. *Himself:* Quentin Reynolds. *Professor Krosigk:* Reinhold Schünzel.

PRODUCTION: *Director:* Mitchell Leisen. *Producer:* Harry Tugend. *Script:* Abraham Polonsky, Frank Butler, Helen Deutsch. *Photographer:* Daniel L. Fapp. *Art Directors:* Hans Dreier, John Meehan. *Special Effects:* Gordon Jennings. *Set Decorators:* Sam Comer, Grace Gregory. *Music:* Victor Young. *Editor:* Alma Macrorie. *Costumes:* Mary Kay Dodson. *Dance:* Billy Daniels. *Makeup:* Wally Westmore. *Sound:* Don McKay, Walter Oberst. *Song:* "Golden Earrings" by Victor Young, Jay Livingstone, and Ray Evans.

## A Foreign Affair (Paramount, 1948)

CAST: *Phoebe Frost:* Jean Arthur. *Erika von Schluetow:* Marlene Dietrich. *Captain John Pringle:* John Lund. *Colonel Rufus J. Plummer:* Millard Mitchell. *Hans Otto Birgel:* Peter Van Zerneck. *Pianist:* Frederick Hollander.

PRODUCTION: *Director:* Billy Wilder. *Producer:* Charles Brackett. *Script:* Charles Brackett, Billy Wilder, Richard L. Breen. *Adaptation:* Robert Harari. *Photographer:* Charles B. Lang, Jr. *Special Effects:* Gordon Jennings. *Editor:* Doane Harrison. *Music:* Frederick Hollander. *Costumes:* Edith Head. *Songs:* "Black Market," "Illusions," "Ruins of Berlin," by Frederick Hollander.

## Jigsaw (Tower Pictures, released through United Artists, 1949)

CAST: *Howard Malloy:* Franchot Tone. *Barbara Whitfield:* Jean Wallace. *Nightclub Patrons:* Marlene Dietrich, Fletcher Markle. *Nightclub waiter:* Henry Fonda. *Street loiterer:* John Garfield. *Secretary:* Marsha Hunt. *Columnist:* Leonard Lyons. *Barman:* Burgess Meredith.

PRODUCTION: *Director:* Fletcher Markle. *Producers:* Edward J. Danziger, Harry Lee Danziger. *Script:* Fletcher Markle, Vincent McConnor. *Photographer:* Don Malkames. *Music:* Robert W. Stringer. *Editor:* Robert Matthews. *Special Effects:* William L. Nemeth. *Sound:* David M. Polak. *Makeup:* Fred Ryle.

## Stage Fright (Warner Bros.–First National, 1950)

CAST: *Eve Gill:* Jane Wyman. *Charlotte Inwood:* Marlene Dietrich. *Smith:* Michael Wilding. *Jonathan Cooper:* Richard Todd. *Commodore Gill:* Alistair (Alastair) Sim. *Nellie:* Kay Walsh. *Mrs. Gill:* Sybil Thorndike.

PRODUCTION: *Director and Producer:* Alfred Hitchcock. *Script:* Whitfield Cook. *Adaptation:* Alma Reville. *Additional Dialogue:* James Bridie. *Photographer:* Wilkie Cooper. *Editor:* Edward Jarvis. *Art Director:* Terence Verity. *Music:* Leighton Lucas. *Jane Wyman's*

*Costumes:* Milo Anderson. *Marlene Dietrich's Costumes:* Christian Dior. *Sound:* Harold King.

### No Highway in the Sky (20th Century-Fox, 1951)

CAST: *Mr. Honry:* James Stewart. *Monica Teasdale:* Marlene Dietrich. *Marjorie Corder:* Glynis Johns. *Dennis Scott:* Jack Hawkins. *Sir John:* Ronald Squire. *Elspeth Honey:* Janette Scott.

PRODUCTION: *Director:* Henry Koster. *Producer:* Louis D. Lighton. *Script:* R. C. Sherriff, Oscar Millard, Alec Coppel. *Photographer:* Georges Perinal. *Editor:* Manuel del Campo. *Art Director:* C. P. Norman. *Sound:* Buster Ambler. *Marlene Dietrich's Costumes:* Christian Dior.

### Rancho Notorious (Fidelity Pictures, distributed by RKO-Radio Pictures, 1952)

CAST: *Altar Keane:* Marlene Dietrich. *Vern Haskell:* Arthur Kennedy. *Frenchy Fairmont:* Mel Ferrer. *Kinch:* Lloyd Gough. *Beth:* Gloria Henry. *Baldy Gunder:* William Frawley. *Maxine:* Lisa Ferraday. *Geary:* Jack Elam.

PRODUCTION: *Director:* Fritz Lang. *Producer:* Howard Welsch. *Script:* Daniel Taradash. *Photographer:* Hal Mohr. *Editor:* Otto Ludwig. *Production Designer:* Wiard Ihnen. *Set Decorator:* Robert Priestley. *Marlene Dietrich's Costumes:* Don Loper. *Costumes:* Joe King. *Music:* Emil Newman. *Sound:* Hugh McDowell, Mac Dalgleish. *Makeup:* Frank Westmore.

### Around the World in 80 Days (Michael Todd Company, Inc., released through United Artists, 1956)

CAST: *Phileas Fogg:* David Niven. *Passepartout:* Cantinflas. *Mr. Fix:* Robert Newton. *Aouda:* Shirley MacLaine. *With:* Charles Boyer, Joe E. Brown, Martine Carol, John Carradine, Charles Coburn, Ronald Colman, Melville Cooper, Noel Coward, Finlay Currie, Reginald Denny, Andy Devine, Marlene Dietrich, Luis Miguel Dominguin,

Fernandel, John Gielgud, Hermione Gingold, José Greco, Cedric Hardwicke, Trevor Howard, Glynis Johns, Buster Keaton, Evelyn Keyes, Beatrice Lillie, Peter Lorre, Edmund Lowe, Victor McLaglen, Colonel Tim McCoy, A. E. Matthews, Mike Mazurki, John Mills, Alan Mowbray, Robert Morley, Edward R. Murrow, Jack Oakie, George Raft, Gilbert Roland, Cesar Romero, Frank Sinatra, Red Skelton, Ronald Squire, Basil Sydney, Richard Wattis, Harcourt Williams.

PRODUCTION: *Director:* Michael Anderson. *Producer:* Michael Todd. *Associate Producer:* William Cameron Menzies. *Script:* S. J. Perelman, James Poe, John Farrow. *Music:* Victor Young. *Costumes:* Miles White. *Photographer:* Lionel Lindon. *Editors:* Gene Ruggiero, Paul Weatherwax. *Art Directors:* James Sullivan, Ken Adam.

### The Monte Carlo Story (Titanus Production, released through United Artists, 1957)

CAST: *Marquise Maria de Crevecoeur:* Marlene Dietrich. *Count Dino della Fiaba:* Vittorio de Sica. *Mr. Hinkley:* Arthur O'Connell. *Jane Hinkley:* Natalie Trundy.

PRODUCTION: *Director:* Samuel A. Taylor. *Producer:* Marcello Girosi. *Script:* Samuel A. Taylor. *Photographer:* Giuseppe Rotunno. *Production Manager:* Nino Misiano. *Art Director:* Gastone Medin. *Sound:* Kurt Dobrawsky. *Costumes:* Elio Costanzi.

### Witness for the Prosecution (Edward Small-Arthur Hornblow Production, released through United Artists, 1957)

CAST: *Leonard Vole:* Tyrone Power. *Christine Vole:* Marlene Dietrich. *Sir Wilfrid Roberts:* Charles Laughton. *Miss Plimsoll:* Elsa Lanchester. *Brogan-Moore:* John Williams. *Mayhew:* Henry Daniell.

PRODUCTION: *Director:* Billy Wilder. *Producer:* Arthur Hornblow, Jr. *Script:* Billy Wilder, Harry Kurnitz. *Adaptation:* Larry Marcus. *Photographer:* Russell Harlan. *Marlene Dietrich's Costumes:* Edith Head. *Costumes:* Joseph King. *Makeup:* Ray Sebastian, Harry Ray, Gustaf

Norin. *Editor:* Daniel Mandell. *Sets:* Howard Bristol. *Art Director:* Alexandre Trauner. *Music:* Matty Malneck. *Sound:* Fred Lau.

### Touch of Evil (Universal-International, 1958)
CAST: *Ramon Miguel Vargas:* Charlton Heston. *Susan Vargas:* Janet Leigh. *Hank Quinlan:* Orson Welles. *Peter Menzies:* Joseph Calleia. *"Uncle" Joe Grandi:* Akim Tamiroff. *With:* Marlene Dietrich, Zsa Zsa Gabor, Mercedes McCambridge, Joseph Cotten.
PRODUCTION: *Director:* Orson Welles. *Producer:* Albert Zugsmith. *Script:* Orson Welles. *Costumes:* Bill Thomas. *Music:* Henry Mancini. *Assistant Director:* Phil Bowies. *Photographer:* Russell Metty.

### Judgment at Nuremberg (Roxlom Production, released through United Artists, 1961)
CAST: *Judge Dan Haywood:* Spencer Tracy. *Ernst Janning:* Burt Lancaster. *Colonel Tad Lawson:* Richard Widmark. *Mme Bertholt:* Marlene Dietrich. *Hans Rolfe:* Maximilian Schell. *Irene Hoffman:* Judy Garland. *Rudolf Petersen:* Montgomery Clift. *Captain Byers:* William Shatner. *Senator Burkette:* Edward Binns. *Judge Kenneth Norris:* Kenneth MacKenna. *Emil Hahn:* Werner Klemperer. *General Merrin:* Alan Baxter.
PRODUCTION: *Director and Producer:* Stanley Kramer. *Associate Producer:* Philip Langner. *Script:* Abby Mann. *Photographer:* Ernest Laszlo. *Editor:* Fred Knudtson. *Music:* Ernest Gold. *Production Designer and Art Director:* Rudolph Sternad. *Costumes:* Jean Louis, Joseph King. *Sets:* George Milo.

### The Black Fox (Arthur Steloff-Image Production, released by Heritage Films, 1962)
PRODUCTION: *Director and Producer:* Louis Clyde Stoumen. *Executive Producer:* Jack Levin. *Script:* Louis Clyde Stoumen. *Narrator:* Marlene Dietrich. *Animation Supervision:* Al Stahl. *Editors:* Kenn Collins, Mark Wortreich. *Music:* Ezra Laderman.

## Paris When It Sizzles (Paramount, 1964)

CAST: *Richard Benson:* William Holden. *Gabrielle Simpson:* Audrey Hepburn. *Police Inspector:* Grégoire Aslan. *Alexander Meyerheim:* Noel Coward. *With:* Marlene Dietrich, Tony Curtis, Mel Ferrer, and the voices of Fred Astaire and Frank Sinatra.

PRODUCTION: *Director:* Richard Quine. *Producers:* Richard Quine, George Axelrod. *Script:* George Axelrod. *Photographer:* Charles Lang, Jr. *Music:* Nelson Riddle. *Sets:* Jean d'Eauboune. *Audrey Hepburn's Costumes:* Hubert de Givenchy. *Marlene Dietrich's Costumes:* Christian Dior. *Editor:* Archie Marshek.

## Just a Gigolo (Leguan, 1978)

CAST: *Paul von Przydodski:* David Bowie. *Cilly:* Sydne Rome. *Helga:* Kim Novak. *Captain Hermann Kraft:* David Hemmings. *Mutti:* Maria Schell. *Prince:* Curd Jürgens. *Baroness von Semering:* Marlene Dietrich.

PRODUCTION: *Director:* David Hemmings. *Producer:* Rolf Thiele. *Script:* Ennio de Concini, Joshua Sinclair. *Photographer:* Charly Steinberger. *Editor:* Alfred Srp. *Production Designer:* Peter Rothe. *Music:* Günther Fischer. *Costumes:* Mago, Ingrid Zoré. *Choreographer:* Herbert F. Schubert. *Sound:* Gunther Kortwich. *Songs:* "Revolutionary Song," by David Bowie and Jack Fishman; "Jonny," by Frederick Hollander and Jack Fishman; "I Kiss Your Hand, Madame," by Ralph Erwin, Fritz Rotter, and Sam Lewis; "Just a Gigolo," by L. Casucci and Irving Caesar; "Don't Let It Be Too Long," by Günther Fischer and David Hemmings.

# Index